STUDIES IN HYSTERIA

Nervous and Mental Disease Monograph Series No. 61

STUDIES
IN
HYSTERIA

BY

DR. JOSEPH BREUER AND DR. SIGMUND FREUD

AUTHORIZED TRANSLATION WITH AN
INTRODUCTION

BY

A. A. BRILL, Ph.B., M.D.

1950

NERVOUS AND MENTAL DISEASE MONOGRAPHS

NEW YORK

Fourth Printing, 1950

The price of this book is $4.00

Printed in the United States of America
COOLIDGE FOUNDATION, PUBLISHERS
NEW YORK

CONTENTS

PREFACE

In 1893 we published our experiences concerning a new method of investigation and treatment of hysterical phenomena,[1] and added to it in the briefest way possible the theoretical views at which we arrived. This "preliminary communication" is herewith reprinted as an illustrative and demonstrative thesis.

We are also adding here a series of case histories, the selection of which was unfortunately not determined merely by scientific considerations. Our experience was obtained in private practice from an educated and well read social class, and its contents repeatedly touch upon the most intimate life and destiny of our patients. It would be a serious breach of confidence to publish such information, and a danger lest the patients be recognized and the facts, which were confided solely to the physician, spread in their circle. We have, therefore, been constrained to dispense with some of the most instructive and most convincing observations. This naturally concerned in the first place those cases in which sexual and marital relations were of etiological significance. It is for this reason that we can adduce only very incomplete evidence for our view that sexuality plays the principal rôle in the pathogenesis of hysteria as a source of psychic traumas, and as a motive of "defense" of the repression of ideas from consciousness. We just had to refrain from publishing those observations which savored strongly of sex.

The case histories are followed by a series of theoretical explanations, and in the last chapter on therapy, the technique of the "cathartic method" is discussed as it has developed in the hands of the neurologist.

If different or even contradictory views are occasionally represented, let this not be considered as a vacillation of the conception. It arises from the natural and justified differences of opinion of two observers, who agree concerning the facts and principal views, but whose interpretations and assumptions do not always coincide.

J. BREUER.
S. FREUD.

April, 1895.

[1] Ueber den psychischen Mechanismus hysterischer Phänomene. Neurol.-Centralblatt, 1893, Nos. 1 and 2.

INTRODUCTION

In 1907 when I became Freud's translator, the present volume was the standard work for those who aspired to become specialists in the virgin field of psychoanalysis. The cases and theories in the *Studien über Hysterie* were read, studied and discussed in the psychoanalytic circle of Zurich, where I first saw the crepuscular light of psychoanalysis. But, at that time Freud was no longer collaborating with Breuer, his former teacher and friend, to whom he pays so much homage and gives so much credit whenever he speaks about the early period of the psychoanalytic movement.

When I discussed with Professor Freud the material to be included in the first book that I was to translate into English, I found that the first chapter (13 pages) which we wished to include in " The Selected Papers on Hysteria and Other Psychoneuroses," [1] formed part of the *Studien über Hysterie*. Unlike the other chapters written separately by each author, this was the only chapter of this book which was written conjointly by both Breuer and Freud. It was, therefore, necessary to obtain Dr. Breuer's permission for this translation, and as Professor Freud could not personally introduce me to his former friend and teacher, I felt somewhat uneasy when I called upon Dr. Breuer. I was naturally very anxious to translate the first book on psychoanalysis into English and feared lest Dr. Breuer would place some obstacle in the way of my ambitious project. But when I met this venerable gentleman, he received me very graciously, listened attentively to my rather nervous recital, and although he did not seem very enthusiastic about my undertaking, he readily granted my request and wished me luck in this new venture. The whole interview was quite pleasant; yet, when I left him, my feeling of relief was tinged with considerable tension. In my anxiety to gain my end, I seemingly forgot to tell him that I only needed his permission for the translation of the first chapter of the *Studien*. I felt that I was not specific enough in detailing my request; indeed, I was somewhat uncertain about what I had said to him. But I had his written permission, and, therefore, dismissed these vague thoughts.

[1] Monograph Series No. 2.

Yet, as I prepared the translation, and even after "The Selected Papers" had been published, I was again and again annoyed by the visits of this ghost, which always made me feel somewhat guilty. I was wont to allay my pangs of conscience by saying to myself that not all of Freud's own contributions to the *Studien über Hysterie* were incorporated into "The Selected Papers." As a matter of fact, only 122 pages of the *Studien über Hysterie* were put into English. The rest of Freud's cases and Breuer's clinical and theoretical material, especially his classical case of Anna O., *had never been translated into English.*[1]

There is no need of entering into what happened after the "Selected Papers" appeared in English in 1909. I then devoted all my leisure time to the translation of Freud's other works,[2] and perforce played an active part in the development of the psychoanalytic movement. But the old ghost refused to remain buried. Now and then, it came to life and annoyed me with the thought that I had deliberately kept from Breuer the fact that I did not intend to translate any of his works. Moreover, for many years physicians, psychologists and laymen read the *Studien über Hysterie,* and when they discovered that the greater part of this work had never been translated, they either wrote to Professor Freud, to the publishers, or to me and expressed the wish to translate it. As a matter of fact, this volume is most valuable not only to all students of psychoanalysis, but to all those who are interested in the development of psychopathology in general. To the psychoanalyst it is the *fons et*

---

[1] The need for stressing this statement seems justified by the fact that even serious students of psychoanalysis are under the erroneous impression that this work has already been translated into English. The reader may refer here to the footnote on page 10 of the translation of Dr. Fenichel's *Clinical Psychoanalysis.*

[2] Three Contributions to the Theory of Sex—1910. New edition. Nervous and Mental Disease Pub. Co., 1936.

The Interpretation of Dreams—1912. New translation, 3rd edition, George Allen and Unwin, Ltd., London, and the Macmillan Co., New York, 1933.

The Psychopathology of Everyday Life. Macmillan Co., New York, and Fisher, Unwin, London, 1914.

Wit and Its Relation to the Unconscious. Moffat, Yard, New York, 1916.

Leonardo da Vinci, Moffat, Yard, New York, 1916. New translation with introduction, Dodd, Mead and Co., New York, 1932.

The History of the Psychoanalytic Movement. Monograph Series, Nervous and Mental Disease Pub. Co., 1916.

Totem and Taboo. Moffat, Yard Co., New York, 1917.

Reflections on War and Death (with Alfred Kuttner). Moffat, Yard, New York, 1918.

Psychoanalysis: Exploring the Hidden Mysteries of the Mind. Encyclopedia Britannica, 1924.

origo of everything that was later formulated, while to the psychopathologist it gives a comprehensive view of the theories and clinical concepts of the neuroses in the beginning of the 20th century. For in developing their new technique and theories the authors have thoroughly discussed and evaluated the views of their predecessors and contemporaries. The present generation of psychopathologists will surely be interested in the valuable contributions of such pioneers as Benedikt, Binet, Cabanis, Janet, Moebius, Oppenheim and others.

In addition, this book contains Freud's *first* contributions to analysis. The cases he gives here seem at first sight simple in comparison to his later works, but one must not forget that it is from this material that he constructed his whole system of psychoanalysis. Indeed, it is fascinating and instructive to see the patience and acumen displayed by the master in the very beginning of his psychoanalytic career. I am sure that the younger generation of psychoanalysts, many of whom are steeped in theoretical speculations, will greatly benefit by the clinical material and the theoretical principles soberly presented here by the master.

Last, but not least, in paying my debt to the shade of Dr. Joseph Breuer, I am not just easing my conscience, but I am presenting to the reader of today a pioneer, who not only introduced the greatest movement in the history of psychopathology, but whose views are as refreshing and instructive today as they were revolutionary and novel at the end of the 19th century.

A. A. Brill.

STUDIES IN HYSTERIA

CHAPTER I

THE PSYCHIC MECHANISM OF HYSTERICAL PHENOMENA

(PRELIMINARY COMMUNICATION)

By Dr. Joseph Breuer and Dr. Sigmund Freud

Actuated by a number of accidental observations, we have investigated over a period of years the different forms and symptoms of hysteria for the purpose of discovering the cause and the process which first provoked the phenomena in question, and which in a great many of our cases frequently appeared years before. In the great majority of cases we did not succeed in elucidating this starting point from the mere history, no matter how detailed it might have been, partly because we had to deal with experiences about which discussion was disagreeable to the patients, but mainly because they really could not recall anything. Often they had no inkling of the causal connection between the causative process and the pathological phenomenon. It was generally necessary to hypnotize the patients and reawaken the memory of the time in which the symptom first appeared, but we thus succeeded in exposing that connection in a most precise and convincing manner.

This method of examination in a great number of cases has furnished us with results which seem to be of theoretical as well as of practical value.

It is of *theoretical value* because it has shown us that in the determination of the pathology of hysteria the accidental factor plays a much greater part than is generally known and recognized. It is quite evident that in *"traumatic"* hysteria it is the accident which evokes the syndrome. Moreover, in hysterical crises, if the patients state that in each attack they hallucinate the same process which evoked the first attack, here, too, the causal connection seems quite clear. But the situation is more obscure in the other phenomena.

Our experiences have shown us *that the most varied symptoms which pass as spontaneous, or, as it were, as idiopathic attainments of hysteria, stand in just as stringent connection with the causal*

1

trauma as the transparent phenomena mentioned. To such causal factors we are able to refer neuralgias as well as the different kind of anesthesias, often of years' duration, contractures and paralyses, hysterical attacks and epileptiform convulsions, which every observer has taken for real epilepsy, *petit mal* and tic-like affections, persistent vomiting and anorexia, even up to the refusal of nourishment, all kinds of visual disturbances, constantly recurring visual hallucinations, and similar affections. The disproportion between the hysterical symptom of years' duration and the former cause is the same as the one we are regularly accustomed to see in the traumatic neuroses. Very often they are experiences of childhood which have established more or less intensive morbid phenomena for all succeeding years.

The connection is often so clear that it is perfectly manifest how the causal event produced just this and no other phenomenon. It is quite clearly determined by the cause. Thus, let us take the most banal example: if a painful affect originates while eating, and is repressed, it may produce nausea and vomiting, and then continue for months as an hysterical symptom. The following examples will illustrate what we mean:

A very distressed young girl, while anxiously watching at a sick bed, fell into a dreamy state, had terrifying hallucinations, and her right arm, which was at the time hanging over the back of the chair, became numb. This resulted in a paralysis, contracture, and anesthesia of that arm. She wanted to pray, but could find no words, but finally succeeded in uttering an English children's prayer. Later, on developing a very grave and most complicated hysteria, she spoke, wrote, and understood only English, whereas her native tongue was incomprehensible to her for a year and a half.

A very sick child finally fell asleep. The mother exerted all her will power to make no noise to awaken it, but because she resolved to do so, she emitted a clicking sound with her tongue ("hysterical counter-will"). This was later repeated on another occasion when she wished to be absolutely quiet, and developed into a tic, which in the form of tongue clicking accompanied every excitement for years.

A very intelligent man was present while his brother was anesthetized and his ankylosed hip stretched. At the moment when the joint yielded and crackled, he perceived severe pain in his own hip, which continued for almost a year.

In other cases the connection is not so simple, there being only, as it were, a symbolic relation between the cause and the pathological phenomenon, just as in the normal dream. Thus, psychic pain may result in neuralgia, or the affect of moral disgust may cause vomiting. We have studied patients, who were wont to make the most prolific use of such symbolization. In still other cases such a determination is at first sight incomprehensible, yet in this group we find the typical hysterical symptoms, such as hemianesthesia, contraction of the visual field, epileptiform convulsions, and similar symptoms. The explanation of our views concerning this group must be deferred for a more detailed discussion of the subject.

Such observations seem to demonstrate the pathogenic analogy between simple hysteria and traumatic neurosis, and justify a broader conception of "traumatic hysteria." The active etiological factor in traumatic neurosis is really not the insignificant bodily injury, but the affect of the fright; that is, the *psychic trauma*. In an analogous manner our investigations show that the causes of many, if not of all, cases of hysteria can be designated as psychic traumas. Every experience which produces the painful affect of fear, anxiety, shame, or of psychic pain may act as a trauma. Whether an experience becomes of traumatic importance naturally depends on the person affected, as well as on the condition which will be mentioned later. In ordinary hysterias we frequently find, instead of one large trauma, many partial traumas, grouped causes which can be of traumatic significance only when summarized, and which belong together insofar as they form small fragments of the sorrowful tale. In still other cases a connection with a real efficacious event or with a period of time of special excitability raises seemingly indifferent situations to traumatic dignity, which they would not have attained otherwise, but which they retain ever after.

But the causal connection of the causative psychic trauma with the hysterical phenomena does not mean that the trauma, as an *agent provocateur* would release the symptom which would then become independent and continue as such. On the contrary, we must maintain that the psychic trauma or the memory of the same acts like a foreign body which even long after its penetration must be considered as an agent of the present, the proof of which we see in a most remarkable phenomenon, which at the same time adds to our discoveries a distinctly practical interest.

We found, at first to our greatest surprise, that the *individual hysterical symptoms immediately disappeared without returning if we succeeded in thoroughly awakening the memories of the causal process with its accompanying affect, and if the patient circumstantially discussed the process in the most detailed manner and gave verbal expression to the affect.* Recollections without affects are almost utterly useless. The psychic process, which originally elapsed, must be reproduced as vividly as possible so as to bring it back into the *statum nascendi,* and then thoroughly "talked out." If it concerns such irritating manifestations as convulsions, neuralgias, and hallucinations, they are once more brought to the surface with their full intensity, and they then vanish forever. Functional attacks like paralyses and anesthesias likewise disappear, but naturally without any appreciable distinctness of their momentary aggravation.[1]

It would be quite reasonable to suspect that one deals here with an unintentional suggestion. The patient expects to be relieved of his suffering and it is this expectation and not the discussion that is the effectual factor. But this is not so. The first observation of this kind, in which a most complicated case of hysteria was analyzed and the individual causal symptoms separately abrogated, occurred in the year 1881, that is, in a "pre-suggestive" period. It was brought about through a spontaneous auto-hypnosis of the patient and caused the examiner the greatest surprise.

In reversing the sentence: *cessante causa cessat effectus,* we may conclude from this observation, that the causal process continues to act in some way even after years, not indirectly by means of a chain of causal links, but directly as a provoking cause, just perhaps as in the wakeful consciousness where the memory of a psychic pain may later call forth tears. In other words: *The hysteric suffers mostly from reminiscences.*[2]

---

[1] The possibility of such a therapy was clearly recognized by Delboeuf and Binet, as is shown by the accompanying quotations: Delboeuf, *Le magnétisme animal,* Paris, 1889: "On s'expliquerait des lors comment le magnétiseur aide à la guerison. Il remet le sujet dans l'état où le mal s'est manifesté et combat par la parole le même mal, mais *renaissant.*" (Binet, *Les altérations de la personnalité,* 1892, p. 243): ". . . peut-être verra-t-on qu'en reportant le malade par un artifice mental, au moment même où le symptome a apparu pour la première fois, on rend ce malade plus docile à une suggestion curative." In the interesting book of Janet, *L'Automatisme Psychologique,* Paris, 1889, we find the description of a cure brought about in a hysterical girl by a process similar to our method.

[2] We are unable to distinguish in this preliminary contribution what there is new in this content, and what can be found in such other authors as Moebius and Strümpell, who present similar views on hysteria. The greatest similarity to our theoretic and therapeutic accomplishments we accidentally found in some published observations of Benedict, which we shall discuss later on.

II

It would seem at first rather strange that long-forgotten experiences should exert so intensive an influence, and that their recollections should not be subject to the decay into which all our memories sink. We will perhaps gain some understanding of these facts by the following examinations.

The blurring or loss of an affect of memory depends on a great many factors. In the first place, it is of great consequence whether there was an energetic reaction to the affectful experience or not. By reaction we here understand a whole series of voluntary or involuntary reflexes, ranging from crying to an act of revenge, through which according to experience affects are discharged. If the success of this reaction is of sufficient strength, it results in the disappearance of a great part of the affect. Language attests to this fact of daily observation, in such expressions as " to give vent to one's feeling," to be "relieved by weeping," etc. If the reaction is suppressed, the affect remains united with the memory. An insult retaliated, be it only in words, is differently recalled than one that had to be taken in silence. Language also recognizes this distinction between the psychic and physical results, and designates most characteristically the silently endured suffering as " grievance." The reaction of an injured person to a trauma has really only then a perfect " cathartic " effect if it is expressed in an adequate reaction like revenge. But man finds a substitute for this action in speech through which help the affect can well-nigh be ab-reacted [3] *(abreagirt)*. In other cases talking in the form of deploring and giving vent to the torments of the secret (confession) is in itself an adequate reflex. If such reaction does not result through deeds, words, or in the most elementary case through weeping, the memory of the occurrence retains above all an affective accentuation.

The " ab-reaction," however, is not the only form of discharge at the disposal of the normal psychic mechanism of the healthy person who has experienced a psychic trauma. The memory of the trauma, even where it has not been ab-reacted, enters into the great complex of the associations. It joins the other experiences which are perhaps

[3] The German *abreagiren* has no exact English equivalent. It will, therefore, be rendered throughout the text by " ab-react "; the literal meaning is to react away or to react off. It is the act of giving vent in speech and action to repressed experiences, and thereby disburdening one's self of their unconscious influences. It has different shades of meaning, from defense reaction to emotional catharsis, which can be discerned from the context.

antagonistic to it, and thus undergoes correction through other ideas. For example, after an accident the memory of the danger and (dimmed) repetition of the fright is accompanied by the recollection of the further course, the rescue, and the consciousness of present security. The memory of a grievance may be corrected by a rectification of the state of affairs by reflecting upon one's own dignity and similar things. A normal person is in this way capable of dissipating the accompanying affect by means of association.

In addition, there appears that general blurring of impressions, that fading of memories which we call "forgetting," and which above all wears out the affective ideas no longer active.

It follows from our observations that those memories which become the causes of hysterical phenomena have been preserved for a long time with wonderful freshness and with their perfect emotional tone. As a further striking and a later realizable fact, we have to mention that the patients do not perhaps have the same control of these as of their other memories of life. On the contrary, *these experiences are either completely lacking from the memory of the patients in their usual psychic state, or at most exist in greatly abridged form.* Only after the patients are questioned in the hypnotic state do these memories appear with the undiminished vividness of fresh occurrences.

Thus, one of our patients in a hypnotic state reproduced with hallucinatory vividness throughout half a year everything that excited her during an acute hysteria on the same days of the preceding year. Her mother's diary, which was unknown to the patient, proved the faultless accuracy of the reproductions. Partly in hypnosis and partly in spontaneous attacks, another patient lived through with hallucinatory distinctness all experiences of a hysterical psychosis which she went through ten years before, and for the greatest part of which she had been amnesic until its reappearance. Also, some individual memories of etiological importance showed surprising integrity and sentient force of fifteen to twenty-five years' duration, and on their return exerted the full affective force of new experiences.

The reason for this we can seek only in the fact that these memories occupy an exceptional position in all the above mentioned relations, as far as vividness is concerned. For it *was really shown that these memories correspond to traumas which were not sufficiently 'ab-reacted,'* and on closer investigation of the reasons for this hindrance, we can find at least two series of determinants through which the reaction to the trauma was omitted.

To the first group we add those cases in which the patient had not reacted to psychic traumas because the nature of the trauma precluded a reaction, or because social relations made the reaction impossible, or because it concerned things which the patient wished to forget and which he, therefore, intentionally inhibited and repressed from his conscious memory. It is just such painful things which are found in the hypnotic state as the basis of hysterical phenomena (hysterical delirium of saints, nuns, abstinent women, and well-bred children).

The second series of determinants is not conditioned by the content of the memories, but by the psychic states with which the corresponding experiences in the patient have united. As a cause of hysterical symptoms, one finds in hypnosis even ideas which are insignificant in themselves, but which owe their preservation to the fact that they originated during a severe palayzing affect like fright, or directly in abnormal psychic conditions, as in the semi-hypnotic twilight states of day-dreaming, in auto-hypnosis, and similar states. Here, it is the nature of these conditions which makes a reaction to the incident impossible.

To be sure, both determinants can naturally unite, and as a matter of fact, they often do. This is the case when a trauma, in itself effectual, occurs in a state of a severely paralyzing affect, or from a transformed consciousness. But it may also happen that the psychic trauma evokes in many persons one of these abnormal states, which in turn makes the reaction impossible.

What is common to both groups of determinants is the fact that those psychic traumas which are not adjusted by reaction are also prevented from adjustment by associative elaboration. In the first group it is the resolution of the patient which strives to forget the painful experiences and in this way, if possible, to exclude them from association; in the second group the associative elaboration does not succeed because between the normal and pathological state of consciousness, in which these ideas originated, there is no productive associative relationship. We shall soon have occasion to discuss more fully these relationships.

Hence, we can say, *that the reason why the pathogenically formed ideas retain their freshness and affective force is because they are not subject to the normal fading through abreaction and through reproduction in states of uninhibited association.*

III

When we discussed the conditions which, according to our experience, are decisive in the development of hysterical phenomena from psychic traumas, we were forced to speak of abnormal states of consciousness in which such pathogenic ideas originate, and we had to emphasize the fact that the recollection of the effectual psychic trauma is not to be found in the normal memory of the patient, but in the hypnotized memory. The more we occupied ourselves with these phenomena the more certain became our convictions *that the splitting of consciousness, so striking in the familiar classical cases of double consciousness, exists rudimentarily in every hysteria, and that the tendency to this dissociation, and with it the appearance of abnormal states of consciousness which we comprise as "hypnoid," is the basic phenomenon of this neurosis.* In this view we agree with Binet and Janet, though we have had no experience with their remarkable findings in anesthetic patients.

Hence, to the often cited axiom, " Hypnosis is artificial hysteria," we should like to add another: " The existence of hypnoid states is the basis and determination of hysteria." These hypnoid states agree in all their diversities among themselves and with hypnosis in the one point, namely that the ideas arising in them are very intensive, but are excluded from associative relations with the rest of the content of consciousness. These hypnoid states are associable among themselves, and their ideation may thus attain various high degrees of psychic organization. In other respects the nature of these states and the degree of their exclusiveness differ from the rest of the conscious processes, as do the various states of hypnosis, which range from light somnolence to somnambulism, and from perfect memory to absolute amnesia.

If such hypnoid states have already existed before the manifest disease, they prepare the soil upon which the affect establishes the pathogenic memories with their resulting somatic manifestations. This behavior corresponds to hysteria, based on a predisposition. But our observations show that a severe trauma (like a traumatic neurosis) or a severe suppression (perhaps of a sexual affect) may bring about a splitting of ideas even in persons without predispositions. This represents the mechanism of the psychically acquired hysteria. Between these two extremes we have a series, in which the facility of dissociation in a particular individual and the magnitude of the affective trauma vary inversely.

We are unable to say anything new as to the determination of the predisposed hypnoid states. We presume that they often develop from " reveries," which are so frequent even in normal persons, for which, for example, the feminine handwork offers so much opportunity. The questions why " the pathological associations " formed in such states are so firm, and why they exert a stronger influence on the somatic processes than other ideas, are all indissolubly linked with the problem of the effectiveness of hypnotic suggestions in general. Our experiences in this matter do not show us anything new; but they rather throw light on the contradiction between the statement, " Hysteria is a psychosis," and the fact that among hysterics one may meet persons of the clearest intellects, the strongest wills, greatest principles, and of the subtlest minds. In these cases such characteristics hold true only in the person's waking thought; in his hypnotic state he is alienated just as we all are in our dreams. Yet, whereas our dream psychoses do not influence our waking state, the products of hypnotic states are projected into the waking state, as hysterical phenomena.

IV

Almost the same assertions that we have advanced about hysterical symptoms we may also repeat concerning hysterical attacks. As is known, we have *Charcot's* schematic description of the " major " hysterical attack, which in complete form shows four phases: (1) The epileptoid, (2) the major movements, (3) the *attitudes passionelles* (hallucinatory phase), and (4) the concluding delirium. By shortening or prolonging the attack and by isolating the individual phases, Charcot obtained all those forms of the hysterical attack, which are really observed more frequently than the complete *grande attaque*.

Our tentative explanation refers to the third phase, the *attitudes passionelles*. Wherever it is prominent, it contains the hallucinatory reproduction of a memory which was significant for the hysterical onset. It is the memory of a major trauma, the κατ ἐξοχὴν of the so-called traumatic hysteria, or of a series of partial traumas belonging together as they are found at the basis of the ordinary hysteria. Or, finally the attack may bring back those occurrences which, because of their encounter with a factor of a special predisposition, have become raised to traumas.

But there are also other attacks which ostensibly consist only of motor phenomena and lack the *passionelle* phase. If it is possible during such an attack of general twitching, cataleptic rigidity or an *attaque de sommeil,* to put one's self *en rapport* with the patient, or still better, if one succeeds in evoking the attack in a hypnotic state, it will then be found that here, too, the root of it is the memory of a psychic trauma, or of a series of traumas which make themselves otherwise prominent in an hallucinatory phase. Thus, a little girl had suffered for years from attacks of general convulsions, which could be, and were, taken for epilepsy. For differential diagnostic reasons she was hypnotized and she immediately lapsed into one of her attacks. On being asked what she saw, she said, " The dog, the dog is coming," and it actually turned out that the first attack of this kind appeared after she was pursued by a mad dog. The success of the therapy then verified our diagnostic decision.

An official, who became hysterical as a result of ill treatment by his employer, suffered from attacks during which he fell to the floor raging furiously without uttering a word or displaying any hallucinations. The attack was provoked in a state of hypnosis and he then stated that he lived through the scene during which his employer insulted him in the street and struck him with his cane. A few days later he came to me complaining that he had the same attack, but it was shown in the hypnosis this time that he went through the scene which was really connected with the onset of his disease; it was the scene in the court room, when he was unable to get satisfaction for the ill treatment which he received, etc.

The memories, which appear in hysterical attacks or which can be awakened in them, correspond in all other respects to the causes which we have found as the basis of continuous hysterical symptoms. Like these, they refer to psychic traumas which were prevented from adjustment through abreaction or through associative elaboration; like these, they were absent entirely or in their essential components in the total memory of normal consciousness, and showed themselves as parts of the ideation content of hypnoid states of consciousness with restricted associations. Finally they were also amenable to the therapeutic test. Our observations have often taught us that a memory which has hitherto provoked attacks becomes incapable of it when it is brought to reaction and associative correction in a hypnotic state.

The motor phenomena of the hysterical attack can in part be interpreted as the memory of general forms of reaction of the accompanying affect (like the fidgeting of the whole body to which the infant already resorts), in part as a direct motor expression of this memory, and in other parts they, like the hysterical stigmata in the permanent symptoms, elude this explanation.

A special estimation of the hysterical attack is obtained if one also takes into account the fact that in hysteria there are groups of ideas which originated in hypnoid states, which are excluded from associative activity with the rest, but are associable among themselves, and thus represent a more or less highly organized rudimentary second consciousness, a *condition seconde*. A persistent hysterical symptom, therefore, corresponds to an impingement of this second state upon a bodily innervation otherwise controlled by the normal consciousness. But an hysterical attack gives evidence of a higher organization of this second state, and if of recent origin, signifies a moment in which this hypnoid consciousness has gained control of the whole existence, that is, we have an acute hysteria; but if it is a recurrent attack containing a memory, we simply have a repetition of the same. Charcot has already given utterance to the thought that the hysterical attack must be the rudiment of a *condition seconde*. During the attack, the control of the whole bodily innervation passes over to the hypnoid consciousness. As familiar experiences show, the normal consciousness is not always entirely repressed by it; it may even perceive the motor phenomenon of the attack while the psychic processes of the same escape all knowledge of it.

The typical course of a grave hysteria, as is well known, is as follows: At first an ideation is formed in the hypnoid state, which, after sufficient growth, gains control in a period of " acute hysteria " of the bodily innervation and the existence of the patient, and creates permanent symptoms and attacks, and with the exception of some residuum then ends in recovery. If the normal personality can regain the upper hand, all that has survived the hypnoid ideation content then returns in hysterical attacks, and now and then it brings the person back into similar states which are again amenable to influences and eligible for traumas. Frequently a sort of equilibrium is then established between the psychic groups which are united in the same person; attack and normal life go hand in hand without influencing each other. The attack then comes spontaneously just as memories are wont to come, but just like memories it can also be provoked by the laws of association. The provocation of the attack results either through stimulating a hysterogenic zone or through a new experience which by similarity recalls the pathogenic experience. We hope to be able to show that there is no essential difference between the apparently two diverse determinants, and that in both cases a hyperesthetic memory is touched. In other cases this equilibrium shows a marked lability, the attack appears as a manifestation of the hypnoidal remnant of consciousness, as often as the normal person becomes exhausted and functionally incapacitated. We cannot disregard the fact that in such cases the attack becomes stripped of its original significance and may return as a contentless motor reaction.

It remains a task for future investigation to discover what conditions are decisive in determining whether an hysterical individuality should manifest itself in attacks, in persistent symptoms, or in a mingling of both.

V

We can now understand in what manner the psychotherapeutic method propounded by us exerts its curative effect. *It abrogates the efficacy of the original non-abreacted ideas by affording an outlet to their strangulated affects through speech. It brings them to associative correction by drawing them into normal consciousness (in mild hypnosis) or by eliminating them through medical suggestion in the same way as in somnambulism with amnesia.*

We maintain that the therapeutic gain obtained by applying this process is quite significant. To be sure, we do not cure the hysteria insofar as it represents a predisposition, for we really do not block the way for the recurrence of hypnoid states. Nor is our procedure capable of preventing the replacement of the laboriously abrogated phenomena by new ones. But once this acute stage has run its course and its remnants continue as permanent hysterical symptoms and attacks, our radical method can frequently remove them forever, and herein it seems to surpass the efficacy of direct suggestion, as practised at present by psychotherapists.

If by disclosing the psychic mechanisms of hysterical phenomena we have taken a step forward on the path so successfully started by Charcot with his explanation and experimental imitation of hysterotraumatic paralysis, we are well aware that in so doing we have only advanced our knowledge in the mechanisms of hysterical symptoms and not in the subjective causes of hysteria. We have grazed only the etiology of hysteria, and can only throw light on the causes of the acquired forms, *i.e.*, on the significance of the accidental factors of the neurosis.

CHAPTER II

CASE HISTORIES

OBSERVATION I. MISS ANNA O. (BREUER)

Miss Anna O. was twenty-one years old when she became ill in 1880. She was considerably burdened by her heredity; there were some psychoses in her large family. Her parents were nervous, but healthy. Up to the onset of the disease, the patient showed no sign of nervousness, not even during pubescence. She had a keen, intuitive intellect, a craving for psychic fodder, which she did not, however, receive after she left school. She was endowed with a sensitiveness for poetry and fantasy, which was, however, controlled by a very strong and critical mind. The latter made her also completely unsuggestible. Only arguments, no assertions had any influence upon her. Her will was energetic, impenetrable and persevering, sometimes mounting to selfishness; it relinquished its aim only out of kindness and for the sake of others.

To the essential features of her character may be added sympathetic kindness. The care and provision for some poor or sick person furnished her an excellent outlet even during her own illness, for she was gratifying a strong impulse. Her moods always showed a slight tendency to an excess of merriment or sadness, which made her more or less temperamental. The sexual element in her make-up was astonishingly undeveloped. The patient, whose life became as transparent to me as seldom happens in the case of one person to another, never experienced any love, and in the whole mass of hallucinations, which characterized her disease, this element of the psychic life never appeared.

With her puritanically-minded family, this girl of overflowing mental vitality led a most monotonous existence, although she probably exaggerated it to an excessive degree for her illness. She systematically nurtured day-dreaming, which she called her "private theater." While she was seemingly in touch with the persons of her environment, she in reality lived in the realm of fairyland; but when she was addressed, she always responded so that no one had any inkling of it. This psychic activity was carried on contemporaneously with her household duties, which she accomplished faultlessly. Later I shall show how readily this habitual dreaminess of her healthy state merged into the pathological.

The course of the disease may be divided into the following vaguely defined phases:

(A) The latent incubation, which lasted from the middle of July until the tenth of December, 1880. This phase, which in most cases escapes us, afforded us here such perfect insight that for that very reason I do not wish to underestimate its pathological interest. I will discuss later this part of the history.

(B) The manifest disease showed the following peculiar symptoms: Paraphasia, convergent strabismus, definite disturbances of hearing, paralyses and contractures which were complete in the right upper and in the two lower extremities, and incomplete in the left upper extremity and paralysis of the muscles of the neck. The contracture of the right-sided extremities gradually disappeared. During this period the patient began to show signs of improvement, which suddenly stopped in April through a severe psychic trauma, the death of her father, which was followed by:

(C) A period of continuous somnambulism alternating with normal states, a series of symptoms which continued until December, 1880.

(D) A gradual disappearance of these states and phenomena, which continued until June, 1882.

In July, 1880, the patient's father, whom she loved passionately, developed a peripleuritic abscess, which did not yield to treatment, and ended in his death in April, 1881. I was, therefore, not surprised that she gradually became reduced in health. No one, perhaps not even the patient, herself, knew what was taking place in her. Her condition gradually grew worse, she became very weak, anemic, and evinced a disgust for nourishment, so that despite her marked reluctance, it was found necessary to take her away from the sick man. The main reason for this step was a very intensive cough about which I was first consulted. I found that she had a typical nervous cough. Soon, there also developed a striking need for rest, distinctly noticeable in the afternoon hours, which merged in the evening into a sleep-like state, followed by strong excitement.

In the beginning of December she developed convergent strabismus. An ophthalmologist diagnosed this (mistakenly) as a paresis of the abducent muscles. From the eleventh of December until the first of April the patient remained bedridden.

In rapid succession there seemingly developed a series of new and severe disturbances.

Left-sided occipital pain; convergent strabismus (diplopia), which was markedly aggravated through excitement. She complained that the wall was falling over (obliquus affection). Profound analyzable visual disturbances, paresis of the anterior muscles of the throat, to the extent that the head could finally be moved only if the patient pressed it backward between her raised shoulders and then moved her whole back. Contractures and anesthesia of the right upper extremity, and somewhat later of the right lower extremity. These, too, were entirely extended, adducted, and rotated inwardly. Later, the same affection appeared in the left lower extremity, and lastly in the left arm, in which, however, the fingers remained slightly movable. Both shoulder joints, too, were not altogether rigid. The maximum contracture concerned the muscles of the upper arm, and even later when the anesthesia could be more precisely tested, the elbow region proved to be most anesthetic. In the beginning of the disease the anesthesia test was not properly given because the patient developed anxiety and refused her coöperation.

It was in this condition that I took the patient under treatment, and I soon became convinced that we were confronted with a severe psychic alteration. There were two entirely separate states of consciousness, which alternated very frequently and spontaneously, moving further apart during the course of the disease. In one of them she knew her environment, was sad and anxious, but relatively normal; in the other, she hallucinated, was "naughty"—i.e., she scolded, threw the pillows at people whenever and to what extent her contractures enabled her to, and tore with her movable fingers the buttons from the covers and underwear, etc. If anything had been changed in the room during this phase, if someone entered, or went out, she then complained that she was lacking in time, and observed the gap in the lapse of her conscious ideas. As this was disputed wherever possible, or when an effort was made to calm her when she complained that she was going crazy, there followed after each pillow throwing and similar behavior, the additional complaints of all the things that were done to her, and of the disorder in which she was left, etc.

These absences had already been noticed when she was still out of bed. She suddenly stopped in the middle of a sentence, repeated the last words, and after a brief period she went on. Little by little this took on the described dimensions and at the peak of the disease, when the contractures had also affected the left side, she was only half way normal for a very short period during the day. But even the moments of relatively clear consciousness were encroached upon by the disturbance. The most rapid changes of her mood went to extremes, from very transitory cheerfulness to deep feelings of anxiety, obstinate opposition to all therapeutic measures, and anxious hallucinations of black snakes for which she mistook her hair and laces, etc. At the same time she kept exhorting herself not to be so stupid, that this was only her hair, etc. In very clear moments she complained of the deep darkness in her head, that she could not think, that she was going blind and deaf, and that she had two egos, her real and an evil one, which forced her to evil things, etc.

During the afternoons she remained in a state of somnolence, which continued until about an hour after sunset. She then awoke and complained that something was tormenting her, or rather she always repeated the infinitive, "to torment, to torment."

For simultaneously with the development of the contractures there appeared a deep, functional disorganization of her speech. At first, it was noticed that she missed words; gradually, when this increased her language was devoid of all grammar, all syntax, to the extent that the whole conjugation of verbs was wrong. Most of the time she utilized an infinitive formed out of a weak past participle, and she never used any articles. In the further course of this development she missed words almost continuously, and searched for them laboriously in four or five languages, so that one could hardly understand her. In her effort to write she used in the beginning the same jargon until she was altogether prevented from writing by her contractures. There then followed two weeks of complete mutism. Continuous effort to speak elicited no sound. Here, the psychic mechanism of the disturbance became clarified for the first time. I felt that she was very annoyed over something and decided not to talk about it. When I guessed this and forced her to talk about it, the inhibition, which formerly made every expression impossible, disappeared.

This occurred contemporaneously with the return of motion in the left-sided extremities. In March, 1881, the paraphasia disappeared, but she now spoke only English, seemingly without knowing it, and quarreled with her nurse, who naturally did not understand her. And not until a few months later could I convince her that she spoke English. Yet, she herself understood her German-speaking environment. In periods of great anxiety she stopped speaking altogether, or she mixed together many idioms. During her best and most lucid hours she spoke either French or Italian. Between those periods and those during which she spoke English, there was a complete amnesia. The strabismus then diminished and finally appeared only during violent excitement. She was also able to carry her head normally. On the first of April she left her bed for the first time.

Her father, whom she idolized and whom she saw only rarely during her illness, died on April 5th. This was the most severe psychic trauma which could have happened to her. She then showed violent excitement, which was followed by a deep stupor, lasting for about two days, from which she awoke in a very alienated state. At first she was very much quieter, and her feeling of anxiety was essentially diminished. The contractures of both arms continued, likewise the not very deep anesthesia of the limbs. She also showed a high degree of narrowing of the visual field. From a bouquet which gave her much pleasure she could see only one flower. She also complained that she could not recognize people. Formerly, she could recognize faces without willful effort, now she had to repeat at this very troublesome "recognizing work" that "The nose is this way," or "The hair is that way; hence it must be so and so." All human beings appeared to her like wax figures without any relationships to herself. The presence of some of her relatives was very painful to her, and this "negativistic instinct" grew progressively. If anyone, whom she otherwise liked, entered the room, she recognized him, but after a short time she sank back into her brooding and the person in question no longer existed for her. She always recognized me, whenever I entered her room; she always felt my presence and remained cheerful as long as I talked to her, until the sudden encroachments of the hallucinatory "absences."

She spoke only English and understood nothing that was told her in German. The people about her were forced to speak English, and even the nurse managed in some way to make herself understood. She read only French or Italian and if she happened to read aloud to somebody, she translated it by sight into excellent English with surprising fluency.

She then began to write again, but in a peculiar manner. She wrote with her left hand, or she used printed, antique lettering, which she had collected into an alphabet from her Shakespeare.

If she took the smallest amount of nourishment, she later refused food altogether, but she allowed herself to be fed by me, so that her nutrition rapidly improved. But bread she always refused to eat. After being fed, she never omitted washing her mouth, and did this also if for some reason she did not eat. This indicated how absent-minded this act was.

The afternoon somnolence and the deep stupor around sunset continued. During these periods if she expressed herself at all, she was lucid, calm, and cheerful. I shall have to take this up again later with greater detail.

This relatively tolerable state did not last long. About ten days after her father died, a consultant was called in whom she ignored as completely as all strangers, while I demonstrated to him her peculiarities. When I requested her to read aloud in English from a French book, she said laughingly, " This is like an examination." The strange physician interjected some remarks and made efforts to make himself noticeable, but in vain. It was a real " negative hallucination," which has so often been reproduced experimentally since then. He finally succeeded in attracting her attention by blowing smoke into her face. She then suddenly saw a stranger, rushed to the door, grabbed the key, but fell to the floor unconscious. This was followed by a short outburst of anger, and then by a severe attack of anxiety, which I could calm only with a great deal of effort. Unfortunately, I had to leave the city the same evening, and when I returned after many days, I found that the patient's condition was markedly aggravated. Throughout the whole time she was entirely absentminded and full of anxiety. Her hallucinatory absences were filled with terrifying images of skulls and skeletons. As she lived through these things and dramatized them partially in speech, the people around her could understand most of the content of her hallucinations. In the afternoon she remained somnolent, and at sunset in a deep hypnosis, for which she coined in English the name of " clouds." If she was then able to relate the hallucinations of the day, she awoke lucidly, feeling calm and cheerful and soon got busy with drawing or writing, which continued throughout the night in a perfectly rational manner. She went to sleep at four o'clock, and the next morning the scene of the previous day was repeated. The contrast between the irresponsible girl, harassed by hallucinations during the day, and the perfectly clear girl at night, was most remarkable.

Despite the nocturnal euphoria, the psychic state became more and more aggravated. She showed intense suicidal impulses, which were quite dangerous because she lived on the third floor. It was for this reason that contrary to her will, the patient was removed to the country, to a suburb of Vienna, on June 7, 1881. I never threatened to take her away from home, but somehow she expected and feared it. This occasion, too, showed how the affect of anxiety dominated the psychic disturbance. Just as she merged into a period of calmness after the death of her father, now, too, she quieted down after the feared expectation had taken place. To be sure, this did not take place until after a disturbance of three days and three nights, which followed immediately her removal to the country. During this period she remained sleepless, took no nourishment, and was full of suicidal ideas (not so dangerous in the garden). She also broke windows, etc., and evinced hallucinations without absences, which she differentiated well from the others. Finally, however, she became quiet, took nourishment from the nurses, and was even willing to take chloral in the evening.

Before I proceed with the description of the further course, I will have to return and describe a peculiarity of the case, which I have thus far only cursorily indicated.

We had already noticed that hitherto the course of the disease was characterized by the fact that every afternoon the patient lapsed into a somnolent state, which changed to a deeper sleep about sunset (clouds). (This periodicity can be explained quite plausibly through the nursing situation, to which she had been subjected for many months. During the night she held vigils at her sick father's bedside or remained in her bed listening, full of anxiety, until the morning. In the afternoons she lay down for a short rest, as is the case with most nurses. It was this type of nocturnal vigilance and afternoon napping that was probably misplaced into her own disease and continued after her sleep had long ago changed into a hypnotic state.) The stupor lasted about an hour, when she became restless and tossed around in bed and repeated the words, " to torment, to torment," always with her eyes closed. On the other hand, it was noticed that in her day absences she seemingly developed some situation or story, the nature of which was detected through some words which she murmured. But it so happened, first accidentally, later intentionally, that someone near her uttered such a catch-word while the patient complained of torments. She immediately took it up and began to depict a situation, or relate a story. In the beginning haltingly, in her paraphasic jargon, but the further she went, the more fluent she became until in the end she spoke a clear German. (During the first period, before she completely adopted English speech.) The stories which were always sad were in part very pretty; they were in the style of Andersen's " Picture Book without Pictures," and were probably modeled on them. The beginning and the central point of the situation mostly dealt with a girl sitting, full of anxiety, near a patient. But quite different motives were also dilated upon. A few moments after finishing the story, she woke up and was apparently calm, or as she called it, " comfy " (comfortable). During the night she again became restless, and in the morning after a two hours' sleep she was apparently again in the midst of another set of ideas. If she sometimes could not tell me the story in the nocturnal hypnosis, there was no nocturnal restfulness; to bring this about, she had to tell me two stories on the following day.

The essential elements of the described manifestations, the accumulation and fusion of her 'absences' into nocturnal autohypnosis, the effectiveness of the fantastic products as a psychic stimulus, as well as the alleviation and removal of the tense state through talking in the hypnosis—all these remained constant throughout the whole year and a half of observation.

Following the death of her father, the stories naturally became more tragic, but only with the aggravation of her psychic state, which followed the above related violent breaking through of her somnambulism, did the nocturnal recitals lose the character of more or less free, poetic creations, and change into a series of frightful and terrifying hallucinations, which one could already infer during the day from the patient's behavior. But I have already described how completely her psyche was freed after, having been tortured by anxiety and terror, she reproduced the experiences of these terrifying pictures.

In the country, where I could not see the patient daily, the situation developed in the following manner: I came in the evening when I knew that she was in a state of hypnosis, and I took away from her the whole supply of fantasms which she had collected since my last visit. In order to obtain good results this had to be accomplished very thoroughly. Following this, she was quite tranquil and the next day she was very pleasant, docile, industrious and cheerful. The following day she was always more moody, peevish, and unpleasant; all of which became more marked on the third day. In this state of mind it was not always easy even in hypnosis to induce her to express herself, for which procedure she invented the good and serious name of "talking-cure," and humorously referred to it as "chimney-sweeping." She knew that after expressing herself, she would lose all her peevishness and "energy," yet whenever (after a long pause) she was in an angry mood she refused to talk, so that I had to extort it from her through urging and begging, as well as through some tricks, such as reciting to her a stereotyped introductory formula of her stories. But she never spoke until after she had carefully touched my hands and had become convinced of my identity. During the nights when rest could not be obtained through expression, one had to make use of chloral. I tried this a number of times before, but I had to give her 5 grams per dose, and sleep was preceded by a sort of intoxication, which lasted an hour. In my presence she was cheerful, but when I was away, there appeared a most uncomfortable, anxious state of excitement (incidentally, the deep intoxication just mentioned made no change in the contractures). I could have omitted the narcotic because the talking, if it did not bring sleep, at least produced calm. In the country, however, the nights were so intolerable between the hypnotic alleviations, that we had to resort to chloral. Gradually, however, she did not need so much of it.

The persistent somnambulism remained away, but in its place there continued an alternation of two states of consciousness. In the middle of her talk, she hallucinated, ran away, attempted to climb a tree, and similar actions. If one held her firmly, she continued the conversation after the shortest period in fragmentary sentences, without noticing what happened between. But in the hypnosis all these hallucinations appeared later in her recital.

On the whole her condition improved, her nourishment was good, she permitted herself to be fed by the nurse through the mouth, but she asked only for bread, which she, however, refused as soon as it touched her lips. The contracture paresis of the limbs diminished perceptibly. She also displayed proper judgment and marked attachment for the consultant, my friend, Dr. B., who paid her regular visits. A Newfoundland dog, which she received as a present, and to which she became passionately attached, was of great help to her. When this pet once attacked a cat, it was wonderful to see how this weak girl grabbed a whip in her left hand and forcefully belabored the animal with it in order to rescue the victim. Later, she took care of some poor, sick people, which was also very beneficial to her.

The clearest demonstration that the ideational complexes produced in the "absences" of the "condition seconde" leave a pathogenic and exciting effect, and that they can be resolved through talking in a state of hypnosis, I received on my return from a vacation of many weeks. During this period no "talking cures" had taken place, for it was not possible to persuade the patient to tell her stories to anyone else, not even to Dr. B. with whom she now entertained a cordial relationship. I found her in a sad moral state, she was indolent, disobedient, moody, and even irritable. During the evening recitations it came to light that her fantastic poetic vein was apparently becoming exhausted. She reproduced more and more stories about her hallucinations and something of what had angered her during the past days. She developed everything fantastically, but more in the form of fantastic formulas than constructed poems. But no tolerable state occurred until after I made her come to the city for a week, and wrested from her every evening from three to five stories. When this was finished, everything which had accumulated during the weeks of my absence was worked up. And only then was the former rhythm of her psychic behavior reëstablished, so that on the first day following such an expression she was loving and cheerful, on the second day more irritable and disagreeable, and on the third day distinctly antagonistic. Her moral state represented a function of the time passed since her last recital, because every spontaneous product of her fantasy and every occurence perceived by the morbid part of her psyche continued as a psychic stimulus until it was reported in the hypnosis, and its effect thereby abrogated.

When the patient returned to the city in the fall (to a different residence than the one in which she became ill) her condition was tolerable both physically and mentally, inasmuch as only very few events, actually only important ones, were elaborated into psychic stimuli. I hoped for a continuous and progressive improvement if the permanent burdening of her psyche through new stimuli could be prevented by a regular therapeutic expression. At first, I was disappointed. In December her psychic condition became markedly worse. She was again excited, sadly depressed, irritable, and rarely had " a whole good day," even if nothing demonstrable " stuck " in her. Towards the end of December during the Christmas holidays she was particularly restless. Throughout the whole week she talked every evening, but told nothing new except fantasms which she elaborated day after day, during the holidays of 1880, while under the spell of strong anxiety affects. After the completion of this series there was a great alleviation.

It was now a year since she had lost her father and had become bedridden. From now on the condition became crystallized and systematized in a very peculiar manner. The two states of consciousness, which always alternated so that from morning until night the absences increased in frequency and finally developed into the *condition seconde,* which alone continued during the night—these two states differed not just as formerly through the fact that in the one (first) she was normal, and in the second alienated, but she lived in the one (first) just like in the winter of 1880–1881, and everything that happened later was fully forgotten therein. Only the awareness of her father's death still seemed to persist most of the time. The reliving of the past year occurred so intensively that she hallucinated her former room in her present home. When she wanted to go to the door, she ran to the oven, which now stood at the window, but in the old residence it was near the door. This change from one state into the other succeeded spontaneously, but it could, however, be called forth with the greatest ease by some sensory impression, which vividly recalled the former year. It was sufficient to show her an orange (the principal nourishment during the first period of her illness) to throw her back from the year 1882 to the year 1881. This reliving of the past year did not proceed in a general and indefinite manner, but she relived day by day the past winter. I could not have surmised this if she had not talked out daily in the evening hypnosis what had excited her in 1881 on the same day, and if the underlying facts had not been corroborated with unimpeachable correctness through her mother's secret diary from the year 1881. This reliving of the past year continued until the definite termination of the disease in July, 1882.

At the same time, it was very interesting also to see how these revived psychic stimuli, exerted their more normal effect from the second into the first state. Thus, it happened that the patient told me laughingly in the morning that she did not know why she was angry at me. Thanks to the diary, I knew what the whole thing was about, and it was also confirmed in the evening hypnosis. In the year 1881 on the same evening I had annoyed the patient very much. She said that something was wrong with her eyes, that she saw the wrong colors, that although she knew her dress was brown, she saw it blue. It was soon shown that she could distinguish all colors correctly on the test paper, but that the disturbance showed itself only on the material of her dress. The reason for this was that in the year 1881 on the same day she was very much occupied with a night-gown for her father, which was made of the same material, but dyed blue. At the same time there was also a very distinct anticipatory effect of these emerging stories, inasmuch as the disturbance of the normal state had already appeared before, whereas the memory itself gradually came up in the *condition seconde*.

The evening hypnosis was also richly burdened thereby, as she had to relate not only the fantasms of fresh productions, but also the expressions of "vexations" of 1881. (The fantasms of 1881 I had fortunately already removed at that time.) Thus, the amount of work to be accomplished between the patient and the physician increased enormously through a third series of individual disturbances, which also had to be accomplished in this manner. *The psychic events of the incubation period of the disease,* from July until December, 1880, which produced the sum total of hysterical phenomena, had to be "talked out," and with it the *symptoms disappeared.*

It was a great surprise to me, when for the first time, and accidentally, a disturbance, which had existed for a long time, disappeared in the evening hypnosis through an unprovoked conversation. In that summer there was a period of intensive heat, and the patient suffered very much of thirst, for without any apparent reason, she suddenly found it impossible to drink. She took the longed for glass of water in her hand, but as it touched her lips, she pushed it away like a hydrophobic. At the same time she was apparently, for a few seconds in an "absent" state. To alleviate this torturing thirst she lived exclusively on fruits, melons, and similar things. After this had continued for about six weeks, she spoke about her English governess, whom she did not like, and then related with all signs of disgust how she once entered her room and saw her little dog, that disgusting animal, drink out of a glass. She said nothing because she wanted to be polite. After she gave energetic expression to her strangulated anger, she asked for a drink, and without any inhibition drank a great deal of water, awaking from the hypnosis with the glass at her lips. With this the disturbance disappeared forever. In the same way many peculiar and persistent habits disappeared after their causative experiences were related. However, it was a great step forward when the first persistent contracture of the right leg, though now slightly diminished, disappeared in the same way. It was these experiences, namely, that the hysterical phenomena disappeared in the hypnosis, as soon as she reproduced the events which caused the symptom that gave origin to a therapeutic technical procedure which in logical sequence and systematic procedure left nothing to be desired. Every single symptom of this complicated, morbid picture was separately taken up, and the various occasions during which it appeared were related in reverse order, beginning with the days before the patient became bedridden, and backward to the time of its first appearance. When this was related, the symptom was thereby permanently removed.

In this manner she "related away" the contractures, the paralyses, the anesthesias, the various disturbances of sight and hearing, the neuralgias, coughs, trembling, and other symptoms, and finally also the disturbances of speech. Thus, in the disturbances of vision the following symptoms were separately removed: convergent strabismus with diplopia, the deviation of the two eyes to the right so that the extended hand always grasped the object towards the left, the narrowing of the field of vision, central amblyopia, makropsia, the sight of a skull in place of her father's head, and the inability to read. Only a few phenomena, which developed during the patient's invalidism, as the extension of the contracture paralysis to the left side, which probably had no psychic causation, were inaccessible to analysis.

To abbreviate the situation, by seeking to evoke directly in her memory the first occasion of a symptom, turned out to be quite impractical. She could not find it and became confused, and such attempts proceeded even more slowly than when she was allowed to "wind off" backwards the thread of the memory, slowly but surely. But as the evening hypnosis proceeded rather slowly, because the patient became fatigued and distracted from the "talking out" of the other two series, and also because the recollections required time to develop their full vividness, the following procedure developed: I visited her in the morning and hypnotized her (we followed empirically very simple hypnotic procedures), and asked her to tell me under mental concentration her thoughts concerning the symptom just reacted, in order to find out the causes which gave origin to it. The patient then described in rapid succession, in short phrases, these external causes, which I wrote down. In the evening hypnosis, she then related in considerable detail all the events which I had noted of the series. An example will show, with what exhaustive thoroughness, in every sense of the word, this was actually done. It always happened that the patient did not hear when I talked to her. This transient "not hearing" was differentiated in the following manner:

(a) Not hearing, that someone entered while in a state of distraction. She gave 108 detailed cases of it, mentioning persons and circumstances, and often also dates. The first person whom she did not hear entering was her father.

(b) Not understanding when many persons spoke. This occurred 27 times. The first time it was again her father and an acquaintance.

(c) Not hearing, when alone, when she was directly addressed; 50 times. The origin of it: when her father in vain asked her for wine.

(d) Becoming deaf from being shaken (as, for example, in a vehicle, etc.), 15 times. The origin: when her younger brother shook her in anger, when he caught her at night listening at the door of the sickroom.

(e) Becoming deaf from fright of a noise, 37 times. The origin of it was when her father had a choking attack from swallowing the wrong way.

(f) Becoming deaf in deep 'absences,' 12 times.

(g) Becoming deaf through long listening, so that when she was then addressed she could not hear, 54 times.

To be sure, all of these processes are for the most part identical, insofar that they can be traced to distraction, "absences," or to an affect of fright. But in the memory of the patient they were so distinctly separated that if she ever made a mistake in the order of their appearance, they had to be corrected and put in the right order, otherwise, she got stuck in her recital. The interest and significance which she imparted to the communicated events and the precision of her recitals left no room for inventions. Many of these events were of a purely subjective nature and could, therefore, not be controlled, the accompanying circumstances of the others could very well be recalled by persons of her environment.

Here, too, everything proceeded as was regularly observed when a symptom was "talked away"; the latter appeared with heightened intensity while it was related. Thus, during the analysis of the "not hearing," the patient was so deaf that now and then we could only understand each other through writing. The first cause was regularly some sort of fright, which she experienced while nursing her father, some neglect on her part, or something similar.

The recollections did not always run smoothly. Sometimes the patient had to exert enormous effort. Once the whole process was stopped for a time because a memory could not come to the surface. It concerned an hallucination, which was very terrifying to the patient. She saw a skull on her father while she was nursing him. She and some of the people about her recalled that once while she was still seemingly healthy, she paid a visit to one of her relatives and when she opened the door, she fell unconscious. In order to overcome this impediment, she now paid them another visit, and again fell unconscious on entering the room. In the evening hypnosis the impediment was overcome, it turned out that as she entered the room, she noticed a pale face in a mirror hanging across the door, but it was not her face, but that of her father with a skull—we have often observed that the fear of a memory, as in this case, inhibited its emergence, and it had to be forced out by the patient, or by the physician.

The following show among other things how strong the inner logic of the states was. As already noted, during this period, that is during the year 1881, the patient was always at night in her *condition seconde*. Once she awoke in the night and insisted that she had again been taken away from home, and got into a very bad state of excitement, which alarmed the whole household. The reason for this was simple. The previous night her visual disturbances were made to disappear through her "talking cure," and to be sure, also in the *condition seconde*. When she awoke at night, she found herself in a room unfamiliar to her, for the family had changed their residence since the spring of 1881. These very disagreeable incidents were prevented at her request, when I closed her eyes in the evening with the suggestion that she would not be able to open them until I would myself open them in the morning. Only once more was this disturbance repeated, when the patient wept in her dream and awakened with her eyes open.

As these tedious analyses of the symptoms referred to the summer months of 1880, during which her illness developed, I gained a full understanding into the *incubation and the pathogenesis* of this hysteria, which I will now briefly discuss.

In July, 1880, the patient's father was very sick while in the country, suffering from a sub-pleural abscess. Anna shared the nursing with her mother. She awoke once in the night with great anxiety about her very feverish patient; she was full of tension because a surgeon was expected from Vienna to operate on him. The mother was away for a short time, and Anna sat near the sickbed holding her *right arm* over the back of the chair. She sank into a state of day-dreaming, and saw how a black snake came out of the wall towards the patient, as if to bite him. (It is quite probable that on the lawn near the house there were some snakes, which at some previous time frightened this girl, and gave the memory for the hallucinations.) She wanted to drive away the reptile, but felt as if paralyzed. The right arm, which was hanging over the back of the chair, was " asleep " and was anesthetic and paralyzed, and as she looked at it, the fingers changed into small snakes with skulls (nails). It is probable that she made an effort to ward off the snake with her paralyzed arm, and thereby established the association of an anesthesia and paralysis with the snake hallucination. When the latter disappeared, she wished to pray in her anxiety, but the words refused to come. She could not talk at all until she finally remembered an *English* nursery rhyme, and only in this language could she continue to think and pray.

The blast of the locomotive, which announced the expected physician, interrupted this spookiness. But the following day as she wished to take a hoop out of the bush, into which it was thrown during play, a bent twig again evoked the snake hallucination. But this, as well as the contractures, appeared only in the short " absences " which, beginning with that night, became more frequent. (The contractures did not, however, become stabilized before December, when the patient had a thorough breakdown and could no longer leave her bed.) On an occasion which I have not noted and which I cannot recall, a contracture of the arm joined that of the right leg.

The tendency to autohypnotic absences was not established. On the day following that night, while waiting for the surgeon, she sank into such a deep absentmindedness, that the latter finally stood in her room and she never heard him enter. The constant feeling of anxiety prevented her from eating and gradually produced an intense disgust. With this exception all her individual, hysterical symptoms originated during an affect. It is not quite clear whether a complete momentary " absence " always appeared with it, but it is probable because the patient knew nothing of this whole connection while awake.

However, some symptoms did not seem to have originated during an " absence," but in an affect during the waking state; but they repeated themselves in the same manner. Thus, the various visual disturbances were traced to more or less individual, clearly determined causes, *e.g.,* while sitting at the sickbed with tears in her eyes, she was suddenly asked by her father what time it was. She saw indistinctly and had to exert herself to direct the watch near her eyes, so that the face of the watch appeared to her very large (makropsia and convergent strabismus), or she exerted a great deal of effort to suppress the tears, in order that her sick father should not see them.

A quarrel, in which she suppressed the answer caused a contracture of the glottis, which repeated itself on every similar occasion.

Speech was impeded (a) by anxiety, since the first nocturnal hallucination, (b) since she again had to suppress utterances (active inhibition), (c) since she was once unjustly scolded, and (d) in all analogous situations (aggravations).

The cough appeared for the first time while the patient kept a vigil at her father's bed and heard dance music coming from a neighboring house. She conceived a wish to be there, which was immediately followed by self-reproaches. Since that time she had reacted with a nervous cough throughout her whole illness, whenever she heard very rhythmic music.

I do not regret very much that the incompleteness of my notes makes it impossible to trace back here all hysterical symptoms to their causes. The patient did this in all of them with the one exception mentioned, and every symptom, as was stated, disappeared after the first cause was related.

In this way the whole hysteria came to an end. The patient, however, made a firm resolution that everything must be finished on the anniversary of her transfer to the country. In the beginning of June, she, therefore, exercised the "talking cure" with zealous energy. On the last day, with the additional help of arranging the room like her father's nursing room, she reproduced the above-related hallucinations, which were at the root of her whole disease, and in which she could think and pray only in English. Immediately thereafter she spoke German, and was then free from all the numberless individual disturbances which she formerly presented. She then left Vienna for a vacation, but it took considerable time before her psychic equilibrium was restored. She has since then enjoyed perfect health.

As much as I have suppressed of the interesting material of Anna A.'s case history, it, nevertheless, became more voluminous than a, not in itself unusual, hysterical disease seems to merit. But the description of this case was impossible without entering into its details, and the peculiarities of the same seem to me of such great importance that one might excuse the detailed history. For the eggs of the echinodermata are not important to embryology just because the sea urchin is such an interesting animal, but because their protoplasm is transparent, and, therefore, warrants the conclusion that what can be seen in them also takes place in eggs with opaque protoplasm.

It seems to me that the interest of this case lies above all in its far-reaching transparency and the explicableness of its pathogenesis.

As a predisposition for the hysterical disease, we find in this still perfectly healthy girl two psychic pictures:

(1) The monotonous family existence without a corresponding psychic labor for the unused excess of psychic activity and energy, which disburdened itself through continuous work of her phantasy and

(2) The habitual day-dreaming ("private theater") shows what laid the foundation for the dissociation of the psychic personality. At all events, even this is still within normal limits. Dreaming, as well as meditation during a more or less mechanical occupation, does not in itself condition a pathological splitting of consciousness, because every disturbance therein, as for example, every call, reëstablishes its normal unity, nor is it followed by any amnesia. Yet, in Anna O this day-dreaming created the soil upon which the anxiety and the affective expectation established themselves in the manner described, after it had transformed the habitual dreaming into an hallucinatory "absence." It is remarkable that the main features which continued almost constantly throughout two years were already perfect during the first manifestations of the onset of the disease. Thus, it already shows the existence of two states of consciousness, which at first appeared as a transitory "absence" and later became organized into a "double conscience," the speech inhibition, which was conditioned by the affect of anxiety, plus the accidental disburdening from the English nursery rhyme; later the paraphasia, the loss of the mother tongue, which was replaced by an excellent English, and finally, the accidental pressure paralysis of the right arm, which later developed into a right-sided contracture paralysis and anesthesia. The mechanism of the origin of this last affection corresponds perfectly to *Charcot's* theory of traumatic hysteria; that is, the existence of a hypnotic state, in which there occurs a slight trauma.

But, whereas in the patients in whom Charcot produced experimentally the hysterical paralysis, this soon became stabilized, and in those carriers of traumatic neuroses who are shocked by a severe fright-trauma the neurosis appears immediately, the nervous system of our young girl offered successful resistance throughout four months. The contracture, as well as the other disturbances which gradually joined it, appeared only during the momentary " absences," in the *condition seconde,* and left the patient during the normal state in full possession of her body and her senses, to the extent that neither she herself knew anything about it, nor did those about her see anything, especially as they were distracted by centering their attention on their very sick father.

But, inasmuch as since that first hallucinatory auto-hypnosis the " absences " with complete amnesia and accompanying hysterical phenomena kept on accumulating, the occasions for the formation of such new symptoms increased and fortified those already formed through more frequent repetitions. It was due to this that gradually every painful and sudden affect behaved exactly as the " absences " (when it did not perhaps always produce momentary absences). Accidental coincidents formed pathological associations in the form of sensory or motor disturbances, which thereafter appeared simultaneously with the affect. But they were always only momentary and transitory. Before the patient became bedridden, she had already developed a very large collection of hysterical phenomena, and nobody knew anything about it. But only after the patient broke down completely as a result of extreme weakness, inanition, insomnia, and the steady anxiety-affect, to the extent that she remained longer in the *condition seconde* than in the normal state—only then did the hysterical phenomena encroach also upon the latter and change from attack-like manifestations into chronic symptoms.

The question must now be asked, to what extent the statements of the patient were reliable, and whether the phenomena were really determined by the mode of origin and causation described by her. As far as the more important and more fundamental processes are concerned, the trustworthiness of the report, as far as I am concerned, is beyond question. I do not refer here to the question of the disappearance of the symptoms after they were " related away," they could quite readily be explained by suggestion. However, I always found the patient perfectly truthful and trustworthy. The subjects related were intimately connected with those things that were most sacred to her, and whatever was accessible to control through others was perfectly corroborated. Even the most talented girl would not be in any position to build up a system of statements, which would contain such a perfect inner logic, as given in the description of the history of the development of her illness. But one cannot, however, deny that in her logical conclusion she might have (to the best of her belief) attributed a causation to some symptoms which did not really exist. But I do not even think that this assumption is correct. The lack of significance of so many causes, the irrationality of so many connections speak directly for their reality. Thus, the patient could not understand how dance music could have ever made her cough. As an intentional fabrication this would be senseless. To be sure, I could imagine that a conscience scruple could cause a contraction of the glottis, and the motor impulse, which this girl, so fond of dancing, experienced, could have changed the contraction of the glottis into a nervous cough. I, therefore, consider the patient's statements as perfectly trustworthy and truthful.

To what extent are we justified in the assumption, that this hysteria is analogous also to the development of hysteria in other patients, or that something similar appears also where there is no such clearly split organization as a *"condition seconde"* ? In this respect I would like to point out that the whole history of the onset of the disease would have remained totally unknown to our patient, as well as to the physicians, if she had not possessed the above described peculiarity of recalling in hypnosis and of relating what she recalled. During the waking state she knew nothing of all this. What the state of affairs is in other cases cannot, therefore, be surmised from the examinations of wakeful persons, for with the best of intentions they can give no information. And how little the people around her observed all these processes I have already described. What the state of affairs is in other patients could, therefore, only be recognized through a procedure similar to the one furnished by hypnosis in Anna O. Above all, the only assumption that appears justified is that *similar* processes may occur more frequently than our lack of knowledge of the pathogenic mechanisms leads us to assume.

When the patient had become bedriddden and her consciousness constantly oscillated between the normal and the "second" state, the army of hysterical symptoms, which originated singly and were latent until they manifested themselves as chronic symptoms, was joined by a new group of symptoms which seemed to have had a different origin. I refer to the contracture paralysis of the left-sided extremities and the paralysis of the muscles of the head. I separate them from other phenomena because once they had disappeared, they never reappeared either in any form of attack, or in any sort of intimation during the conclusion of the phase of recovery when all the other symptoms usually became revived, even after they had been dormant for a long time. This also tallies with the fact that they never appeared in the hypnotic analysis, and were never brought back through affective or fantastic causes. I, therefore, would believe that they did not owe their existence to the same psychic processes as the other symptoms, but to the secondary extension of that unknown state, which forms the somatic foundation of hysterical phenomena.

During the whole course of the disease, the two states of consciousness existed side by side, the first, in which the patient was psychically normal, and the second, which we can readily compare with the dream, as far as it concerns the richness in fantasies, hallucinations, large gaps of memory, lack of inhibitions, and lack of control of encroaching thoughts. In this second state the patient seemed alienated. It appears to me that I have obtained a good insight into the nature of at least one kind of hysterical psychosis, and that is, that the psychic state of the patient was thoroughly dependent on the diffusion of this second state into the normal one. Every evening hypnosis furnished proof, that the patient was perfectly clear, organized, and normal in her feelings and volition, if no product of the second state acted as a stimulus in her "unconscious." The flourishing psychosis during every larger pause of this disburdening procedure, proved directly in what measure these products influenced the psychic process of the normal state. It is hard to avoid the expression that the patient was separated into two personalities, of which one was psychically normal and the other psychotic. I believe that the sharp distinction of the two states in our patient only clarifies a behavior which is an enigma in many other hysterical causes. In Anna O. it was very striking how the products of the "evil ego," as the patient, herself, called it, influenced her moral habits. If they had not been continuously removed, she would have been an hysteric of the malicious type, obstinate, lazy, hateful, and irritable, whereas after the removal of these stimuli, her true character always came to the surface, which was exactly the reverse of the one just described.

But no matter how distinctly the two states were separated, the "second state" not only mixed with the first, but as the patient expressed it, that at least frequently even during her worst states "there sat a keen and quiet observer somewhere in a little corner of the brain, who watched this crazy stuff." This continuous existence of clear thinking during the predominance of the psychosis produced a very remarkable expression. When after the end of the hysterical phenomena, the patient merged into a transitory depression, she alleged among other childish fears and self-reproaches, that she was not sick and that everything was only simulated. Similar things had apparently occurred many times.

After the disease has run its course and the two states of consciousness have fused together, the patients then regard themselves on retrospection, as uncured personalities, who have known all this nonsense. And they believe that they could have prevented everything if they had wanted to, that is, that they have intentionally produced this nuisance. This persistence of normal thinking during the second state might have fluctuated very much quantitatively, or might not have existed most of the time.

The surprising fact that from the beginning to the end of the disease all stimuli originating from the second state, as well as their results, had been removed through talking in the hypnotic state I have already described. I have nothing to add except the assurance that it was not a discovery of mine, which I have suggested to the patient, but that I was most surprised by it, and only after a series of spontaneous adjustments took place, there developed from it a therapeutic technique.

A few words should also be said about the final recovery from the hysteria. It proceeded in the manner described, under considerable disturbance of the patient and with an aggravation of her psychic state. One had the distinct impression that a large number of products of the second state, hitherto dormant, now forced themselves into consciousness, that they were recalled even though at first again in the *condition seconde,* but that they burdened and disturbed the normal state. One will have to take into consideration the question whether a psychosis with which a chronic hysteria ends up has not the same origin also in other cases.

Observation II. Mrs. Emmy von N. (Freud)

On the first of May, 1889, I became physician to a woman of about forty years of age, whose suffering, as well as her personality, inspired me with so much interest that I devoted to her a large part of my time and made it my task to cure her. She was hysterical, and as I discovered that she could very easily be put into a somnambulic state, I decided to treat her by that method of investigation in a state of hypnosis which I had learned from Breuer's history of his first patient. It was my first effort in the management of this therapeutic method. I was still far from mastering it, and, as a matter of fact, I have had neither enough practice in the analysis of morbid symptoms nor have I pursued them sufficiently and schematically. I will perhaps succeed best in illustrating the state of the patient as well as the medical procedure, if I reproduce the notes which I made every evening during the first three weeks of the treatment. Any better understanding subsequently acquired will be appended in notes and additional remarks.

May 1, 1889. I found a still youthful looking woman with fine, characteristically delineated features lying on a divan, a leather pillow under her neck; her face betrayed a tense, painful expression, her eyes were deep-set, her look downcast; her forehead was deeply wrinkled, and her naso-labial folds deeply grooved. She spoke with effort in a low voice, sometimes interrupted by a spastic speech impediment, which almost approached stuttering. At the same time her entwined fingers showed an incessant athetoid fidgetiness. She also frequently showed tic-like twitches in her face and in the muscles of her neck, whereby single muscles, especially the right sterno-cleido-mastoid, plastically stood out. Besides that, she frequently interrupted herself while speaking to produce a peculiar smacking, which I cannot imitate.[1]

What she said was entirely coherent and seemingly showed an unusual education and intelligence. It was, therefore, the more strange that every few minutes she suddenly stopped and contorted her face into expressions of fear and disgust, pointing her hand with the extended and curved fingers at me, and at the same time calling out with an anxious voice the words: " Keep quiet,—don't speak—don't touch me ! " She was probably under the impression of a stereotyped terrifying hallucination and warded off the interference of the stranger with this formula.[2]

This intercalation stopped as abruptly as it started, and the patient continued with her conversation, without spinning out the presently existing excitement and without excusing or explaining her behavior, probably she herself did not notice the interruption.[3]

Concerning her family history, I found the following: Her family came from mid-Germany, but had lived for two generations in the

---

[1] This smacking consisted of many sound measures. Some colleagues who were versed in hunting compared these sounds to the courting call of the woodcock.

[2] The words really corresponded to a protective formula, which will be explained later. I have observed such protective formulae since then in a patient suffering from melancholia, who tried to control her painful thoughts (wishes that something wrong might befall her husband, her mother, or blasphemings, etc.) in this manner.

[3] It was a case of hysterical delirium, which alternated with the normal state of consciousness, similar to an intercalation of a real tic into a voluntary motion, without disturbing it or fusing with it.

Russian Baltic Provinces, where they had a large estate. There were 14 children, of whom the patient was the thirteenth, but only four were living. She was carefully, but very compulsively brought up by an extremely over-active and strict mother. At the age of twenty-three, she married a highly endowed, capable man, who won for himself a prominent position as an industrialist, but who was much older than she. Shortly after the marriage, he died suddenly of heart failure. This event, as well as the rearing of her two girls, now 16 and 14 years old, who were sickly most of the time, having suffered from nervous disturbances, she gave as the cause of her disease. Since the death of her husband 14 years ago, she has been continuously ill in varying degrees of fluctuating intensity. Four years ago massage and electric baths afforded her transitory alleviation; otherwise, all her efforts to regain her health were in vain. She had traveled much and had numerous active interests in life. At the present time she lived on an estate in the Baltic near a large city. Having again suffered severely for months, during which she had been depressed, sleepless, and tortured by pain, she sought in vain alleviation in Abbazia. For the last six weeks she had been in Vienna under the treatment of a prominent physician.

Without a word of objection she followed my suggestion to separate from her two girls, who had a governess, and enter a sanitarium where I could see her daily.

On the evening of May 2d, I visited her in the sanitarium. It struck me that whenever the door was unexpectedly opened, she always became severely frightened. I, therefore, ordered that visiting physicians, as well as nurses, should knock on the door, and not enter until they heard: "Come in!" In spite of that, she made grimaces and trembled whenever anybody entered.

Her chief complaint referred today to a cold sensation and pains in the right leg, which emanated from the back, above the crest of the ilium. I prescribed warm baths and massage twice daily. She was an excellent subject for hypnosis. I held my finger before her and called out, "Sleep!" and she sank down with an expression of stupefaction and confusion. I suggested sound sleep and an improvement of all the symptoms, etc. She listened with closed eyes, but with unmistakably tense attention, but her features gradually became smoother and assumed a friendly expression. After the first hypnosis, there remained a vague memory of my words, and after the second, there already appeared a perfect somnambulism (and amnesia). I announced to her that I would hypnotize her and she assented without any resistance. She had never been hypnotized before, but I assumed that she must have read about it, although I did not know what impressions she had concerning the hypnotic state.[4]

[4] On awakening from hypnosis, she always looked around as if confused, and then turned her eyes to me; she seemed to have regained consciousness, put on glasses which she had taken off before she fell asleep, and again became cheerful and herself. In the course of the treatment which was given during

This treatment—warm baths twice daily, massage and hypnotic suggestions—was continued during the following days. She slept well and visibly recuperated, and spent the greater part of the day quietly in bed. She was not prohibited from seeing her children, reading, or taking care of her correspondence.

During the morning of May 8th, she entertained me in an apparently normal manner by telling me harrowing animal stories. She read in the paper, which lay in front of her on the table, that an apprentice tied up a boy and stuck a white mouse into his mouth, and that the resulting fright killed the boy. Dr. K. told her that he sent a box full of white rats to Tiflis. At the same time she showed the most plastic signs of horror. She clenched her hands and said: " Keep quiet, don't talk, don't touch me!—if such an animal should be in bed (horrified) just think if that were uncovered! There is a dead rat among them, one that was chew-ed! "

In the hypnosis I made an effort to drive away these animal hallucinations. While she slept, I picked up the newspaper; I actually found a story of an abuse by an apprentice, but there was nothing about mice or rats. She evidently added these deliriously while she was reading. In the evening I told her about our conversation concerning the white mice. She knew nothing about it, was very surprised, and laughed heartily.[5]

In the afternoon she had a so-called " neck-cramp," [6] but " it was short, lasting only two hours."

On the evening of May 8th, I requested her to talk of hypnosis, which she succeeded in doing after some effort. She spoke quietly and thought for a moment every time before she answered. The change in her features corresponded to the content of her story—they became calm as soon as my suggestions put an end to the impression of the story. I put the question why she became frightened so easily. She answered: " Those are memories from my early youth." " When? " " The first one at the age of five when my brothers and sisters threw dead animals at me. I then had my first fainting attack with convulsions, but my aunt said that this was disgusting, that one must not have such attacks,

---

this year over a period of seven weeks, and the next year for eight weeks, although we talked about everything possible, and I put her to sleep twice almost daily, she, nevertheless, put no question or observation concerning hypnosis, and in her waking state she seemed to ignore the fact that she was being hypnotized.

[5] Such a sudden intercalation of a delirium in the waking state was nothing unusual in her case, it often repeated itself during my observation. She used to complain in conversation that she often gave the most distorted answers, so that people could not understand her. During the first interview, at the question of how old she was, she answered quite seriously: " I am a woman of the past century." Weeks later, she explained that she thought at that time, in her delirium of a beautiful old cabinet which she acquired while traveling, as she was a collector of antique furniture. Being questioned about her age stimulated the idea of time. Her answer really referred to the age of this cabinet.

[6] A sort of migraine.

and they then stopped. Then at the age of seven, when I unexpectedly saw my sister in her coffin; then at the age of eight, when my brother so often frightened me by wrapping himself in white sheets and pretending he was a spook, then at the age of nine, when I saw my aunt in her coffin, and—suddenly—her lower jaw fell."

The series of traumatic events which she gave me in answer to my question, why she was so terrified, seemingly were already in her memory. In the short moment between my question and her answer she would not have been able to formulate so quickly the occasions from chronologically different periods of her life. At the end of every section of her story, she showed general twitchings, and her features expressed fear and horror; after the last one she gasped for breath. The words which described the terrifying content of her experiences were brought forth with effort and gasping. After that her features became calm.

In reply to my question, she asserted that during her recital of the scenes she visualized them plastically in their natural colors. She thought of these experiences quite frequently, thought of them again only in the last few days, but whenever she thinks of them, she always sees them in front of her with all the vividness of reality.[7] I now understand why she so frequently entertained me with animal scenes and images of dead bodies. My therapy consisted of wiping away these images so that she should no longer have them before her eyes. To fortify the suggestion, I stroked her a number of times over the eyes.

May 9th. Without any suggestion she slept well, but in the morning complained of stomach aches. She had felt them yesterday, in the garden when she had spent too much time with her children. She was satisfied when I restricted the visit of her children to two and a half hours. A few days before she had reproached herself for neglecting the children. I found her today somewhat irritable, she wrinkled her forehead, kept on smacking her lips, and showed impediments in her speech. During the massage she related to us that the governess of her children had brought an atlas on the history of civilization, and that she was severely frightened by some of its pictures, which represented Indians dressed as animals. " Just think, if they were living! " (Horrified.)

In the hypnosis I asked her why those pictures frightened her so much when she no longer was afraid of animals? The pictures reminded her of visions she had had during the death of her brother (at 19 years of age). I left this recollection for a later discussion. I then asked her whether she always talked in this stuttering manner, and how long she had had the tic or the peculiar smacking.[8] The stuttering was a pathological manifestation, and the tic she had had for five years since she once sat at the sickbed of her very sick daughter and wanted to

---

[7] We also obtained recollections in vivid visual images from other hysterical patients, and they were especially accentuated in pathogenic memories.

[8] In the waking state she replied to my question about the origin of the tic, that she did not know, but that she had had it for a long time.

remain very *quiet*. I attempted to weaken the significance of this memory by saying, that after all, nothing had happened to her daughter. She added that these disturbances repeat themselves whenever she is anxious or frightened. I told her not to be afraid of the Indian pictures, but rather to laugh heartily over them and show them to me. This actually took place after she awakened; she looked for the book and asked me whether I had already seen it, opened the page and laughed heartily at the grotesque pictures. There was not the least anxiety or tenseness in her features. Dr. Breuer called unexpectedly and was accompanied by the family physician. She became frightened and began to smack her lips so that both soon left. She explained her excitement by saying that whenever anyone appeared with the family physician she experienced a feeling of discomfort.

I also removed the stomach aches through hypnosis, by stroking and saying that she will probably expect the return of the aches after eating, but that they will not come.

Evening. For the first time she was cheerful and talkative and showed a sense of humor which I would not have expected in this serious-minded woman, and with a full assurance of her improvement she made merry, among other things, over the treatment of my medical predecessor. For some time she had the intention of giving up this treatment, but could not find any excuse for it, until a casual observation of Dr. Breuer, who once visited her, gave her this axcuse. As I expressed surprise at this information, she became frightened and reproached herself violently for having committed an indiscretion. However, I was seemingly able to calm her. There were no pains in the stomach despite her expectation of them.

In the hypnosis I asked about other experiences, which subsequently frightened her. She then reproduced a second series from her later youth just as promptly as the first, and again assured me that she visualized all these scenes frequently and vividly with all their colors. When she saw her cousin taken to an insane asylum (at the age of 15) she wanted to call out for help, but could not. She lost her speech until that evening. As she frequently spoke so much about insane asylums in her waking state, I interrupted her and asked if she recalled other occasions in which insane people were concerned. She then related that her own mother was at one time in an insane asylum, and then they had once a servant whose wife spent a long time in an insane asylum, and who used to tell her terrible stories of how patients were bound to their chairs, were punished, and similar experiences. While talking, she clenched her hands with horror and saw all these things right before her eyes. I made an effort to correct her ideas about mental hospitals without associating them with herself. Her features were relaxed.

She continued to relate her frightful memories: How she found her mother who had had a stroke, lying on the floor (at the age of 15), she lived four years longer, and then at the age of 19 she came home one day and found her mother dead with a distorted face. It was naturally more difficult to obliterate these memories. After a lengthy discussion I assured her that this picture, too, she would only see again blurred and dimmed. She then recounted how at 19, on lifting up a stone, she found a toad, and as a result, she lost her speech for hours.[9]

I became convinced during this hypnosis that she knew everything that had taken place during the previous hypnoses, but that she knew nothing about it in her waking state.

May 10th, morning. Today, for the first time she took a bran bath instead of a warm one. I found her with a peevish wrinkled face, her hands wrapped in a shawl, complaining of cold and pain. On being asked what happened, she stated that it was uncomfortable to sit in this short bathtub, she got pains from it. During the massage she repeated that she still felt badly about yesterday's betrayal of Dr. Breuer. I calmed her with the pious lie that I knew all about it from the beginning, and thus, I removed her excitement (her smacking and facial contortions). My influence was always already noticeable during the massage, when she became quieter and clearer, and even without hypnosis she always could give reasons for her moodiness. Nor was the conversation which we had during the massage as unintentional as it seemed. On the contrary it contained almost a complete reproduction of the memories and the new impressions which had influenced her since the last conversation, and frequently it went quite unexpectedly to pathogenic reminiscences which she related without being requested to do so. It seemed as if she had mastered my technique and had utilized the apparently unforced and casually conducted conversations to supplement the hypnosis. Thus, for example, she began to talk today about her family, and through all sorts of by-paths she came to the history of her cousin, who was a narrow-minded eccentric and whose parents caused him to have a number of his teeth pulled at the same time. This story was accompanied by gestures of fright, and by many repetitions of her protective formula: "Keep quiet—don't talk—don't touch me!" Following this, her features relaxed, and she looked cheerful. Thus, her conscious behavior was directed by her experiences of the somnambulic state, concerning which she knew nothing in the waking state.

In the hypnosis I repeated the question of what made her moody, and received the same answer, but in the reverse order. First, her blabbering of yesterday, and second, the pains from her uncomfortable posture in the bathtub. I also asked her today for the meaning of the formula: "Keep quiet . . . etc." She explained that whenever she had thoughts of anxiety, she was afraid of being interrupted in the stream of thought because everything would then become confused or still worse. The expression, "Keep quiet . . ." referred to the fact that the animal images, which appeared to her in her bad periods, assumed motion in front of her. Finally, the admonition, "Don't touch me"

---

[9] The toad was in all probability connected with a definite symbolism, which regretfully I made no attempt to investigate.

originated from the following experience: As her brother was so sick from too much morphine, and had such terrible attacks (at the age of 19) he frequently seized her. Furthermore, an acquaintance once went insane in her house and grabbed her by the arm (a third similar case which she could not precisely recall), and finally when her little girl was so sick (at the age of 28) she grabbed her so vehemently in her delirium that she almost choked her. Despite the marked differences in time she related these four cases in one sentence and in quick succession, as if she wished to construct one single event into four acts. All her information of such grouped traumas began with the word, " as," and the individual partial traumas were connected by " and." When I became aware that the protective formula constituted a defense against the return of similar experiences, I removed her fear by suggestion, and I actually never again heard the formula from her.

In the *evening,* I found her very cheerful. She laughingly related that she got frightened in the garden by a little dog, who barked at her. Her face was still slightly drawn, and there was an inner excitement which disappeared only after she asked me if I took amiss a remark she made during the morning's massage and I answered in the negative. The menses reappeared today after scarcely a two weeks' pause. I promised to regulate it through hypnotic suggestion, and suggested in the hypnosis an interval of twenty-eight days, which actually occurred.

In the hypnosis I also asked her whether she remembered what she told me last; in doing this I had in mind a task which still remained from last evening. She, however, began more correctly with the " Don't touch me " of the forenoon hypnosis. I consequently led her back to yesterday's theme. I asked her how this stuttering originated and she answered: " I do not know." [10] I, therefore, requested her to recall it for today's hypnosis. Today, she answered without any further reflection, but with great excitement and in a spastically difficult language: The horses once bolted with the carriage which held her children, and on another occasion while she was driving with her children in a storm, a tree was struck by lightning in front of the horses, the horses shied and the thought flashed through her mind, " Now, you must keep very quiet; otherwise, you will frighten the horses still more through your crying and then the coachman will not be able to control them." It was at this time that the stuttering appeared. This recital had unusually excited her. I also discovered from her that the stuttering appeared immediately after the first of these two events, but disappeared after a short time, only to reëstablish itself permanently after the second similar event. I wiped out the plastic memory of these scenes, but requested her to bring them to consciousness once more. She seemed

[10] The answer: " I don't know " may be correct, but it may also signify the displeasure of talking of these causes. In other cases I have later had the experience, that the more difficult it was for patients to recall things in hypnosis the more effort they had to use to force the event in question into their consciousness.

to make an effort, but remained calm, and henceforth, she spoke in the hypnosis without the slightest spastic impediment.[11]

As she felt disposed to give information, I questioned her further as to what events in her life frightened her to such an extent as to leave in her a plastic memory of the same. She answered with a collection of such experiences. A year after the death of her mother she was at the home of a friendly French woman who sent her with another girl into the next room for an encyclopedia, and there she saw a person rise from the bed, who looked exactly like the woman she had just left. She remained rigid, as if rooted to the spot. Later, she heard that it was just a doll. I explained this apparition as an hallucination, and appealed to her to explain it further, and her face relaxed.

She then related how she nursed her sick brother, who, as a result of morphine addiction, lapsed into frightful attacks during which he frightened her by grabbing her. I noticed that she had already related this experience this morning, and to test her, I asked when this " grabbing " took place. To my pleasant surprise she now reflected for quite a while, and finally asked haltingly: " The little one? " About the two other aforementioned events she could not remember anything. My command to wipe out the memories had, therefore, had its effect. She continued telling how she nursed her brother, and suddenly her aunt appeared and stretched her pale head over a transom; she had come to convert him to the Catholic faith. I noticed that I, thereby, came upon the root of her constant fear of surprises, and I asked when other such experiences took place. She went on: How she had a friend in her home who liked to sneak very quietly into the room and suddenly there he stood: How after the death of her mother she was so sick that she went to a spa, and there an insane woman mistakenly came to her room at night, on many occasions right to her bed, and finally, how on her journey here from Abbazia a strange man four times suddenly opened the door of her compartment and always stared at her very rigidly. This frightened her so much that she called the conductor.

I wiped out all these memories, and I then awakened her and assured her that tonight she would sleep well, after I had omitted giving her this very suggestion in the hypnosis. A sign of general improvement was shown in the remark that she had read nothing today, that she was living in a happy dream, she, who always had to do something on account of her inner restlessness.

May 11th, Morning. Today we had an appointment with a gynecologist, Dr. N., who was to examine her oldest daughter on account of menstrual difficulties. I found Mrs. Emmy quite restless, but it now showed itself in lighter physical signs than before. From time to time,

---

[11] As was found, the patient's tic-like smacking and the spastic stuttering represented two symptoms which originated through similar causations and through an analogous mechanism. I have described this mechanism in a small essay: " Ein Fall von hypnotischer Heilung nebst Bemerkungen über den hysterischen Gegenwillen," *Zeitschrift für Hypnotismus,* Bd. I. At all events I shall return to it again.

she also exclaimed: "I'm afraid, so afraid, I believe I must die." What she was afraid of, whether it was of Dr. N., she did not know; she was just afraid. I put her in hypnosis before the consultant arrived, and she confessed that she was afraid that she had insulted me by the remark she made yesterday during the massage; it seemed to her impolite. Moreover, she was afraid of everything new and consequently, was afraid of the new Dr. N. She was readily calmed, and although she was startled now and then by Dr. N., she otherwise behaved well and showed neither the smacking nor the speech impediment. After he left, I again put her into hypnosis in order to remove the remnants of excitement resulting from his visit. She, herself, was satisfied with her behavior, and she put a great deal of hope in his treatment. I tried to show her by this example that one should not fear anything new, that it may also contain something good.[12]

In the *evening* she was very jolly and disburdened herself of many scruples expressed in the conversation before the hypnosis. In the hypnosis I asked her what event of her life had left the most lasting effect and returned most frequently in her memory. The death of her husband.—I made her relate this experience with all its details, which she did with signs of the deepest emotion, but all of it without any smacking or stuttering.

She told how she was in a place on the Riviera, which both of them loved. Once while crossing a bridge, he got a heart attack. He suddenly sank down, lay a few minutes as if lifeless, and then arose as if quite well. How shortly thereafter, while she was still in her confinement bed with her little girl, her husband, who was eating breakfast and reading the paper at a little tea table in front of her bed, suddenly arose, looked at her peculiarly, walked a few steps, and then dropped dead. She jumped out of bed, the physicians who responded to her call made every effort to revive him; she could hear it from the other room, but it was all in vain. She continued to relate how the child, who at that time was a few weeks old, became very sick and remained so for six months, during which she herself was sick with a high fever. And now her complaints against this child followed in chronological order, she forced them out with angry facial expressions, like talking of someone of whom one is tired. For some time this child was peculiar. She always cried and did not sleep, she then developed a paralysis of the left leg, the recovery from which was considered hopeless. At the age of four she had visions, she did not begin to walk and talk until quite late, so that for some time she was consdered idiotic. According to the physicians, she had suffered from cerebro-spinal meningitis, or what not. Here, I interrupted her and pointed out that this same child was now normal and blooming, and I then removed all possibilities of her seeing again these sad things by wiping away not only the plastic memories, but also the whole reminiscence, as if it had never

[12] All such instructive suggestions failed with Mrs. Emmy, as shown by the results.

been a part of her. I promised her that this would result in a cessation
of the feeling of anticipated misfortunes, which constantly annoyed her,
as well as of the pains of her whole body, of which she complained
particularly during the present recital, after she had mentioned nothing
of it for many days.[13]

To my surprise, immediately after this suggestion she began to talk
about Prince L., whose escape from an insane asylum was widely discussed at the time. She produced new ideas of anxiety concerning insane
asylums, stating that people were treated there with ice cold douches
on the head, that they were put into an apparatus and swung around
until they kept quiet. Three days before, while she first complained
of insane asylums after telling that patients were bound to chairs, I
interrupted her. I now realized that I gained nothing by it, that one
cannot possibly spare himself from listening to every point to the very
end. After this additional recital, I removed also this frightful new
picture. I appealed to her intelligence, saying that she really ought to
believe me rather than that foolish girl who told her such frightful
stories about happenings in mental hospitals. As I still heard some
stuttering in this last recital, I asked her again whence this came. No
answer—" Don't you know? "—" No "—" Why not? "—" Why? Because
I'm not allowed." (The last came out forcefully and angrily. I saw
in these utterances the success of my suggestion, but she also expressed
a wish to be awakened from the hypnosis, which I refused.)[14]

May 12th. Contrary to my expectation, she again slept poorly. I
found her in great anxiety, but at least without its usual physical signs.
She refused to tell what was wrong except that she had had bad dreams,
and that she still saw the same things. " How horrible if they should
be alive." During the massage she settled some thing through questioning, and then cheered up. She spoke about her social relations on
her estate on the Baltic, of the important men from the neighboring city
whom she was wont to invite as her guests, etc.

Hypnosis. She had terrifying dreams that the legs of the chairs

---

[13] This time my energy carried me a little too far. A year and a half later
when I saw Mrs. Emmy again in relatively fine health she complained that it
was remarkable that certain very important events of her life she could only
recall vaguely. She saw in this a proof of her failing memory. I had to guard
against giving her a special explanation for this amnesia. The striking success
of the therapy in this point was probably also due to the fact that I made her
relate this memory in great detail, more detailed than these notes show, when
ordinarily I was satisfied with a mere mention of the facts.

[14] This little scene I understood only the next day. Her untamed nature,
which revolted in the waking state as well as in the artificial sleep against
every force, made her angry because I took her story as completed, and interrupted her through my last suggestion. I have many other proofs for the fact
that she critically watched my work in her hypnotic consciousness. It is
probable that she wished to reproach me for the fact that I disturbed her story
today just as I disturbed her before in her lunatic asylum horrors; she did not,
however, trust herself to do so, but produced instead these additional thoughts,
as it were, independently, without betraying the associated mental trend. The
next day my mistake was disclosed to me through a hidden remark.

as well as the backs of stools were all snakes; a monster with a hawk's beak struck at her and bit her all over the body, then other wild animals sprang at her, etc. This immediately led to other animal deliria, which she, however, distinguished by adding that this was real and no dream. She also told how once desiring to grasp a ball of wool, it turned out to be a mouse, which scampered away. How once while taking a walk a large toad sprang at her, etc. I observed that my general prohibition had no effect and that I must remove individually every impression of anxiety.[15] By some path I came to the question of the origin of her stomach aches. I believed that stomach aches accompanied every attack of zoöpsia. Her quite unwilling answer was that she did not know. I gave her the task to recall it by the next morning. She then said rather morosely that I should not always ask her whence this and that came, but that I should let her recount what was in her mind. I agreed, and she continued without any introduction: "When they carried him out, I could not believe that he was dead." (She again referred to her husband, and I then recognized the cause of her depression, which she suppressed by withholding the rest of the story.) Following his death, she hated the child for three years, because she said to herself that she could have nursed her husband to health if she had not had to remain in bed on account of the child. And after her husband's death, she had nothing but annoyances and excitement. His relatives, who were always against the marriage, and were chagrined because the marriage turned out happily, spread rumors that she poisoned her husband, and they even thought of demanding an inquest. Through a nasty, shyster lawyer the relatives imposed upon her all sorts of legal processes. This scoundrel sent out agents to annoy her. He put abusive articles about her in the local papers, and then sent her the clippings. This treatment gave origin to her shyness of people and her hatred of strange men. After the calming words which I added to her story, she claimed that she felt serene.

May 13th. Again, she slept little on account of her stomach pains. Yesterday, she took no supper. She also complained of pains in the right arm. Her disposition, however, was good; she was cheerful, and since yesterday she treated me with special distinction. She asked my opinion concerning the most varied things which seemed to her important, and lapsed into a most disproportionate excitement when I, for example, had to look for her daughters who were needed at the massage. She also showed some smacking and grimacing.

Hypnosis. Last evening it suddenly flashed through her mind why the little animals, which she visualized, grew so gigantically. This happened to her for the first time at a theatrical performance in D., where

---

[15] Unfortunately I have failed to investigate in this case the meaning of the zoöpsia, and I have not attempted to distinguish the primary fear of animals, which is common to many neuropaths from childhood, from the symbolic.

a giant-like lizard was on the stage. This memory tortured her also very much yesterday.[16]

The return of the smacking was due to the fact that yesterday she had abdominal aches and made an effort not to betray them through sighing. Concerning the actual cause of the smacking (see p. 46), she knew nothing. She also recalled that I gave her the task to discover whence the stomach aches originated, but she did not know, and begged me to help her. I suggested that she might have at some time forced herself to eat after marked excitement. That turned out to be true. After the death of her husband, she lacked for a long time any desire for food, and ate only as a matter of duty. She then began to talk spontaneously about what most affected her: "I have said that I did not like the little one. I must add, however, that this was not noticed in my behavior. I have done everything that was necessary. Even now I reproach myself that I am fonder of the older one."

May 14th. She is well and cheerful, she slept until 7:30 A.M., and complains only of slight pains in the radial regions of her hand, and of aches in the head and face. The conversation before the hypnosis gained increasingly in significance. Today she had almost nothing frightful to discuss; she complained of pains and lack of feeling in the right leg and reflected that in 1871 she went through a pelvic inflammation, and when she scarcely recovered from it, she had to nurse her sick brother, and it was then that she got these pains, which at times produce a paralysis of the right foot.

During the *hypnosis* I asked her whether she was now able to mix with people, or whether she was still overcome with anxiety. She believed that she still felt unpleasant if someone stood behind her or close to her, and in this connection related other cases of unpleasant surprises through the sudden appearance of people. Thus, once when she took a walk with her daughters, two suspicious looking individuals appeared from behind a bush and insulted her. While in Abbazia during an evening's walk, a beggar suddenly appeared from behind a rock and knelt down before her. He probably was a harmless lunatic. She then told how someone broke into her isolated castle, which frightened her very much.

One could easily see that this fear of people was connected with the persecution to which she had been subjected after the death of her husband.[17]

---

[16] The visual memory of the large lizard attained this importance only through the temporal connection with the large affect to which she must have been subjected during this theatrical performance. But in the therapy of this patient, as I have already admitted, I was often satisfied with superficial findings, and in this case, too, I have not investigated any further. To be sure, one thinks here of hysterical macropsia. Mrs. Emmy had a high degree of shortsightedness and astigmatism and her hallucinations might have been provoked through the indistinctness of her visual perceptions.

[17] At that time, I was inclined to interpret all the symptoms of this hysteria on the basis of psychic origin. Today I would explain the tendency to anxiety in this woman who lived a continent life as *neurotic* (anxiety neurosis).

Evening. Apparently very cheerful, yet she received me with the exclamation: " I'm dying of fear, oh, I can hardly tell it to you, I hate myself." I finally discovered that Dr. Breuer paid her a visit, and as he arrived, she became frightened. When he noticed it, she assured him that it only happened this time, and that she was very sorry for my sake, that she had to betray now this remnant of her former anxiety! As a matter of fact, I had occasion to observe during the last few days how strict she was to herself; how ready she was to blame herself for the smallest negligence, as for example, if the sheets for the massage were not in the same place, or if the newspaper which I was to read while she was asleep was not spread out right before my eyes. After the first superficial strata of annoying reminiscences had been removed, her moral sensitiveness with a tendency to depreciation of her burdened personality came to the surface. Both in the waking state, as well as in the hypnosis, I preached to her a paraphrasing of the old saying, " minima non curat praetor," that between the good and the evil there was a very large group of indifferent little things for which no one should reproach himself. I believe, however, that these precepts made no deeper impression on her than on some ascetic monk of the middle ages, who saw the finger of God and the temptation of the Devil in every little experience that concerned him, and who was not in any position to view the world for a little while or from some small angle without associating everything with his own personality.

In the *hypnosis* she brought up individual supplements to her frightful images; thus, in Abbazia she saw gory heads on every wave. I made her repeat those precepts which I imparted to her in her waking state.

May 15th. She slept until 8:30, but became restless towards morning. She received me with a slight tic, some smacking, and some speech impediment. " I die of fear." On being questioned, she related that the Pension in which her children were living is on the fourth floor, which is reached by a lift (elevator). She requested yesterday that the children use the elevator also for descending, and now she reproached herself because she thought the elevator was not absolutely safe. The owner of the Pension himself said so. She wanted to know if I knew the history of Countess Sch., who was killed in Rome in just such an accident. I was well acquainted with the Pension and knew that the elevator was the private property of the proprietor, and it seemed hardly possible that this man, who boasted of this elevator in advertisements, should have warned against its use. I felt that we dealt here with an illusion of memory inspired by anxiety. I imparted my opinion to her, and without much effort she laughed over the improbability of her fear. Just for that reason I could not believe that that was the cause of her anxiety, and decided to question her about it in the hypnotic state. During the massage, which was resumed today after many days of interruption, she related a number of loosely connected stories, which might, however, have been true. As for example, about a toad which was found in the cellar of an eccentric mother, who took care of her child in a peculiar manner, about a woman who had to be locked up in an insane asylum on account of melancholia. In this way, she showed the kind of reminiscences that went through her mind when she was dominated by one of her uncomfortable moods. After she had disburdened herself in these recitals, she became very cheerful, talked about her life on her estate, about the relations she entertained with the most prominent men of German-Russia, and North Germany, and I found it quite hard to reconcile this enormous activity with the idea of a very nervous woman.

In the *hypnosis*, I, therefore, asked her why she had been so restless this morning. Instead of discussing her worry about the elevator, she informed me she was afraid that her menses might return and put a stop to the massage.[18]

[18] The origin of this was as follows: When she awoke in the morning she was in a state of anxiety, and in order to explain this state of mind she seized upon the nearest idea of anxiety which presented itself. On the afternoon of the previous day there was some talk about the elevator in the house where her children lived. The habitually worried mother asked the governess whether the older daughter, who could not walk very well because of the pain in the right ovary and right leg, was using the lift for descending. A memory deception permitted her then to connect the anxiety, of which she was conscious, with the idea of the lift. The actual reason for her anxiety she did not then find in her consciousness; that came out only after much hesitation when I questioned her about it in the hypnosis. It was the same process which Bernheim and others after him have studied in persons who perform post-hypnotically a command imparted to them in a state of hypnosis. As for example, Bernheim suggested to a patient that after awakening he would stick both his thumbs into his mouth. The patient actually did this, but excused himself by saying that since he bit himself the day before during an epileptic attack he felt pain in his tongue. Obeying a suggestion, a girl attempted to murder a court official, an absolute stranger to her. Having been caught and asked to explain her reason, she invented a story about some annoyance imposed upon her, which demanded revenge. There seems to be a need to bring psychic phenomena of which one is not conscious into casual relationships with others that are conscious. Whenever the real causation of the perception is withdrawn from consciousness, one strives unconsciously for another connection in which one believes, although it is false. It is quite clear that an existing splitting of the content of consciousness must markedly assist such *false connection*.

I wish to tarry a little longer at the above mentioned example of false connection because it may be designated as a model in more than one way. Above all, it is an illustration of the patient's behavior, which in the course of the treatment gave me repeated opportunities, to solve by means of the hypnotic explanations such false connections and the affects emanating from them. I wish to relate such a case in detail because it illuminates crassly enough the psychological situation in question. I proposed to Mrs. Emmy that instead of the customary lukewarm bath she should try a cool half-bath, which I thought would make her feel more refreshed. She implicitly obeyed this medical order, but always with the worst kind of suspicion. I have already reported that medical treatment had almost never given her relief. My suggestion to take cool baths was not given so authoritatively as to prevent her from mustering up courage to express such doubts as: " Every time, and as often as I have taken a cool bath, I have been melancholic throughout the whole day. But I

I made her tell me the history of the pain in her leg. The beginning of it was the same as yesterday, but there followed a long series of various cases of painful and irritating experiences, at the time that she had the pain in her leg, and through which influence it became more and more aggravated to the extent of a two-sided paralysis of the legs

will try it again if *you wish*. Please do not believe that I do not do what you tell me." For appearance's sake I waived my suggestions, but in the next hypnosis I suggested that she, herself, might propose the cool bath, now that she thought of it she might venture another trial, etc. Exactly what happened. She, herself, brought up the idea of taking cool baths, and in the next hypnosis sought to win me for this idea by many arguments. I gave in without much struggle. But on the day after this half-bath, I actually found her in deep depression. "Why do you feel this way today?——I really knew it beforehand. The cold baths always make you feel this way.——But you, yourself, asked for them. Now we know that you cannot tolerate them and we shall, therefore, return to lukewarm baths." In the hypnosis I then asked her: "Was it really the cool baths that depressed you so much?"——"Oh, the cool bath has nothing to do with it," was the answer, "but I read this morning in the paper that a revolution broke out in Santo Domingo. When there is unrest there, I always feel it here, because I have a brother in Santo Domingo who has given us a great deal of worry, and now I am worried that something might happen to him." Thus, the situation was settled between us. The next morning she took her cool half-bath as though it were self-evident, and continued to take it throughout many weeks without ever showing any depression.

One will have to admit that this example is also typical of the behavior of other neurotics when it is a question of suggestive therapy by a physician. Whether there is restlessness at Santo Domingo or elsewhere which evokes on a definite day a certain symptom, the patient is always inclined to trace the symptom back to the last influence of the physician. Of the two determinants which are required for associating such false connection, one, the suspicion, always seems to be present; the other, the splitting of consciousness, is substituted by the fact that most neurotics have in part no knowledge of the real reasons of their suffering (or at least the causal reason), and in part they intentionally do not wish to take cognizance of it because they are unwilling to be reminded of that which bears their own guilt.

One could suppose that the psychic determinants of not-knowing or of intentional neglect, which are rendered prominent in neurotics outside of hysteria, must be more favorable for the origin of a false connection than the existence of a splitting of consciousness, which in any case withdraws from consciousness the material for causal relation. Still, this splitting is rarely pure, and in most cases fragments of unconscious ideation lapse into everyday consciousness, and precisely these give occasion for such disturbances. Usually, it is the general sensation connected with the complex, the mood of anxiety, or of mourning, which, as in the above example, is consciously perceived, and for which a connection must be established in a consciously existing ideational complex, in the manner of a "compulsion to association." (*Cf.* the mechanism of *compulsive ideas,* which I have given in the *Neurolog. Centralblatt,* Nos. 10–11, 1894. Also, *Obsessions et Phobies, Revue Neurologique,* No. 2, 1895.)

Of the force of such an obsession to association, I have recently become convinced through an observation in another sphere. For a number of weeks I had to exchange my usual bed for another of a harder texture, upon which I probably dreamed more, or more actively, perhaps it was only difficult to attain the normal depth of sleep. I remembered all the dreams of the night during the first quarter of an hour after awakening, and I took the trouble to write them down in order to make an effort to interpret them. I succeeded in tracing with a loss of feeling. This same was true of the pains in the arm, which also began during her nursing, simultaneously with a cramp in the neck. Concerning these "cramps in the neck" I discovered only the following: They have taken the place of the peculiar states of restlessness with moodiness, which had existed before, and now consisted of an "icy pack" in the neck with stiffness and painful coldness in all

---

these individual dreams to two factors: (1) to the need of elaborating such ideas, at which I lingered only fleetingly during the day so that they were only touched but not settled, and (2) to the compulsion of connecting the things existing in the same state of consciousness with others. The senseless and contradictory part of the dreams could be traced to the free play of the last factor.

That the feeling which belongs to an experience with its content can regularly be brought in indirect relationship to the primary consciousness, I have learned from another patient, Mrs. Cecilia M., whom I studied more thoroughly than other patients mentioned here. From this lady I have collected the most numerous and convincing proofs of such a psychic mechanism of hysterical phenomena which concerns us in this work, but unfortunately I am prevented for personal reasons from giving a detailed account of this patient's history, to which I am now and then referring. Mrs. Cecilia M. was recently in a peculiar hysterical state, which is surely not unusual, although I do not know whether it has ever been recognized. It could be designated as an "hysterical annihilation psychosis." The patient had experienced numerous psychic traumas and suffered long years from a chronic hysteria with manifold manifestations. The causes for all these states were unknown to her and to others, and her excellently equipped memory showed the most striking gap: She herself complained that her life was as if broken up into fragments. One day there suddenly emerged an old reminiscence of the most plastic delineation with fresh and new feelings, and from then on she lived through anew for almost three years all the traumas of her life which were believed to have been long forgotten, and some that really were never recalled. All of them were accompanied by a frightful expenditure of suffering, and with a return of all the symptoms that she ever had. This "wiping out of old debts" embraced a period of thirty-three years and enabled us to recognize all her states, which often were very complicatedly determined. She could only get alleviation if she had the opportunity to talk away in the hypnosis the reminiscence with all the feeling and bodily manifestation that tortured her at the time. And when I was prevented from being present, and she was forced to talk to a person of whom she was ashamed, it happened a number of times that she related to that person everything very quietly, but subsequently reproduced the same thing in hypnosis before me with all the crying, weeping, and manifestations of despair that should have accompanied the story in the first place. After such a catharsis in the hypnosis, she was quite well and in touch with everything for a number of hours. In a short time the next reminiscence in order appeared, but the feelings belonging to it she sent to the surface hours before. She became irritable and anxious or despairing, without ever thinking that this feeling did not belong to the present, but to the state which would befall her next. During this transitional period she regularly made false connections, to which she held obstinately until the hypnosis. Thus, for example, she once received me with the question: "Am I not an outcast; is this not a sign of the deepest degradation that I told you this yesterday?" What she told me yesterday was not in any way appropriate for the justification of this condemnation; after a short discussion she could see it quite well, but the next hypnosis brought to the surface a reminiscence with which she deeply reproached herself twelve years ago, to which, to be sure, she no longer adhered.

the extremities, inability to talk and complete prostration. They usually lasted from six to twelve hours. My efforts to unravel this symptom complex on the basis of a reminiscence failed. The questions pointing to it, namely whether the brother whom she nursed once grabbed her by the neck in a delirium, were answered in the negative. She did not know whence these attacks came.[19]

Evening. She was very cheerful and developed a very delightful sense of humor. As to the elevator, it was not really as she told it to me, it was only a pretense that it was not to be used for descending. She asked many questions which showed nothing morbid. She had very annoying aches in her face, in the hand along the thumb, and in the leg. She felt stiffness and pains in the face when she sat quietly for a long time, or stared at a point. Lifting a heavy object caused pains in the arms.—The examination of the right leg showed fairly good sensibility on the upper part of the thigh, deep anesthesia in the lower part of the leg and foot, less in the gluteal and loin regions.

In the hypnosis she stated that she still had occasional ideas of anxiety, that something might happen to her children, that she could become ill, or that she might die, or that something might happen to her brother, who was now on his honeymoon, or that his wife might die because the married life of all siblings had been very short. No

---

[19] On subsequent reflection, I had to admit that this "neck cramp" might have been organically determined, analogous to the states of migraine. In practice one sees many of these states, which have not been described, and which have such striking resemblance to classic attacks of hemicrania that one would wish to broaden the latter concept, and to put the localization of the pain in the second place. It is well known that many neurotic women combine many hysterical attacks, such as twitching and deliria with their migraine attacks.

Concerning the pains in the arm and leg, I believe that we dealt here with a case of a not very interesting, but nevertheless a more frequent type of determination through accidental coincidence. She had such pains during the emotional period of nursing, which she felt more in consequence of the exhaustion, and these pains, which originally were only accidentally associated with these experiences, were then repeated in her memory as a physical symbol of the complex of associations. I shall be able to demonstrate this process by many more examples. The pains were probably originally of a rheumatic nature; to give this very abused word a definite sense, that is to say, pains, which are mainly located in the muscles in which one can demonstrate definite pressure feelings and change of consistency in the muscles. They manifest themselves mostly after prolonged rest or fixating of the extremity—that is, in the morning. They improve by exercising the painful part and can be made to disappear by massage. These myogenous pains, which are frequently found in many people, assume great significance in neurotics. Physicians who are not in the habit of testing the muscles by pressure of the finger also assume that these pains are of nervous origin, and thus add material for many indefinite hysterical neuralgias and for the so-called sciaticas, etc. I shall here only briefly refer to the relations of these pains to gouty disposition. The mother and two sisters of my patient suffered very much from gout or chronic rheumatism. Some of the pains of which she complained at the time might have been of that nature; I do not know. I did not at that time have any practice in diagnosing this state of the muscles.

other anxieties could be elicited. I removed her worriment, for which there was no cause. She promised to stop it " because you want it." I also gave her other suggestions for the pain in her legs, etc.

May 16th. She slept well, still complained of pains in the face, arms and legs, but was very cheerful. The hypnosis proved to be quite unfruitful. I administered Faradism for her anesthetic leg.

Evening. She became frightened as soon as I entered.—" It is a good thing you came. I am so frightened."—At the same time she showed all signs of fear, stuttering, and tic. I first let her tell me in the waking state what happened, whereby she excellently represented the fright with her curbed fingers and extended hands. While in the garden an enormously big mouse suddenly ran over her hand and disappeared as suddenly. It really scampered continuously to and fro (an illustration of a moving shadow?). On the trees there sat nothing but mice.— " Don't you hear the horses in the circus stamping? Nearby a man is groaning, I believe he suffers pain after the operation. Am I in Rügen, did I have such an oven there?"—She was evidently confused by the numberless thoughts which crossed her mind, and her effort to return to the present. Questioned about the present situation, as *e.g.,* whether her daughters had been here today, she could give no answer.

I then tried to unravel this condition in a state of hypnosis.

Hypnosis. " What were you afraid of?"—She repeated the story of the mice with all signs of terror. It seemed that when she went across the stairs there lay an abominable animal that immediately disappeared. I explained it as an hallucination. I told her not to be afraid of mice, that such fear is only seen in drunkards (whom she abhorred). I told her the story of Bishop Hatto, with which she was familiar, but she listened with the greatest of terror. " How did you happen to mention the circus?"—She heard distinctly close by how the horses stampeded in the stables, and thus became entangled in the harness, which could injure them. John was always in the habit of going out and untying them.— I disputed her statement concerning the nearness of the stables and the groaning of the neighbors. I asked her whether she knew where she was. She knew, but shortly before she imagined she was in Rügen.—How did she happen to remember this? " You said in the garden it was so hot in one place." This recalled to her the shadowless terrace in Rügen. What sad memories she had of her sojourn in Rügen.—She reproduced a series of them. There she got the most frightful pains in the arm and leg, she was very often out in fogs on excursions so that she lost her way. Twice while taking a walk she was chased by a bull, etc.—How did she come to this thought today? Yes, how?—She had written a great many letters. She wrote for three hours, which gave her a dull head.—I could, therefore, assume that the exhaustion brought on this attack of delirium, and that the contents of it were determined by such allusions as the shadowless place in the garden, etc. I repeated all the precepts which I was in the habit of giving to her, and left her sleeping.

May 17th. She slept very well. In the bran-bath, which she took today, she cried out many times because she mistook the bran for little worms. I heard this from the nurse. She herself did not like to tell it to me. She was almost exaggeratedly cheerful, but interrupted herself repeatedly with the exclamation, " Whee-ee," made grimaces which expressed terror and showed more stuttering than during the last days. She related that she dreamed last night that she was walking on nothing but leeches. The night before, she had terrifying dreams, she had to decorate so many dead people and lay them out in their coffins, but she would at no time put the cover on the top—apparently reminiscence of her husband (v.s.). She continued to tell that during her life she had experienced a great many adventures with animals, the most harrowing of all with a bat which entangled itself in her bedroom cupboard and which caused her to run out of the room undressed. To cure her of this anxiety her brother presented her with a beautiful brooch in the form of a bat, but she could not wear it.

In the *hypnosis* she stated: Her fear of worms had its origin in the fact that she once received a present of a beautiful needle-pillow and when she wished to use it, a swarm of little worms crept out of it, probably because it was filled with bran, which had not been quite dry. (Hallucination? Perhaps a fact.) I asked her for more animal stories. Once she took a walk with her husband in a park in St. Petersburg, and the whole path to the lake was strewn with toads, so that she had to turn back. She had gone through periods during which she could not shake hands with anyone for fear that her hand might turn into an abominable animal, a feeling which she had often experienced. I attempted to rid her of the animal fears by questioning her about each animal separately, whether she was afraid of it. To one, she answered, " No "; to another she said, " I must not be afraid of it." [20] I asked why she had twitched and stuttered so much today and yesterday. She always does that when she is afraid.[21]—But why was she so frightened yesterday?—In the garden all kinds of thoughts occurred to her which oppressed her. First of all, how could she stop herself from accumulating more things after the discharge from the treatment—I repeated to her again the three fundamental consolations, which I had already given her in the waking state: First, as a matter of fact, she has now become healthier and more capable of resistance. Second, she will get the habit of expressing herself against any offensive person. Third, a great many things which have hitherto oppressed her she will, henceforth, consider with indifference.—

[20] The method which I pursued was not very good as I did not follow it up exhaustively enough.

[21] On tracing back the two initial traumas the stuttering and smacking did not completely disappear, although both symptoms showed a striking decrease since then. The explanation for the incompleteness of the success was given by the patient herself (*cf.* p. 43). She became accustomed to smack and stutter whenever she became frightened. These symptoms, therefore, finally became connected not only with the initial traumas, but with a long chain of associated memories, which I failed to remove. It is a case which one sees frequently enough and which always spoils the elegance and completeness of the therapeutic results through the cathartic method.

Moreover, she was oppressed by the fact that she did not thank me for coming to her at such a late hour. She was afraid that her last relapse would make me lose patience with her. She was very much affected and frightened by the fact that the family physician had asked the gentleman in the garden whether he now had the courage to be operated on. His wife sat near by and she herself must have thought that this would be this poor man's last evening. With this last information, the depression seemed to have vanished.[22]

In the evening she was very cheerful and contented. The hypnosis, however, furnished no results. I occupied myself with the treatment of the muscular pains and the restoration of sensibility in the right leg, in which I was quite successful, although the restored sensation partially disappeared again after awakening. Before I left her, she expressed her surprise at the fact that she had had no cramp in the neck for so long a time when usually it appeared with every change of weather.

May 18th. She slept last night as she has not in many years, but since she had taken the bath, she complained of coldness in her neck and of a drawing feeling in the face, hands, and feet. Her features were tense and her hands were clenched. Hypnosis showed no psychic content for the " cramp in the neck," which later improved through massage in the waking state.[23]

[22] I learned here something for the first time, which I could confirm later in numerous cases: namely, that in hypnotic solutions of a new hysterical delirium the information obtained from the patient runs chronologically in the reverse order. He repeats first the impressions and streams of thought which came last and are least important, and only towards the end does he come back to the primary and most important causal impression.

[23] Her surprise of the evening before, that she had had no cramp in the neck for so long, was, therefore, a premonition of the coming state, which had already been in the process of developing, and known to her unconsciously. This remarkable form of premonition was something quite usual in the above mentioned Mrs. Cecilia M. Whenever she was in her best state of mind and said something like: " It is now a long time since I have feared witches at night," or: " How pleased I am that my eye-aches have stayed away so long," I was quite sure that next evening we would have to cope with the worst fears of witches, or that the next state would begin with the dreaded pains in the eyes. It was always as if that which was already lying fully completed in the unconscious was shining through and the unsuspecting " official " consciousness (to use Charcot's expression) elaborated the idea which came to the surface as a sudden thought into an expression of gratification, a lie which was quickly and surely enough punished. Mrs. Cecilia, a highly intelligent lady to whom I am grateful for much progress in the understanding of hysterical symptoms, called my attention to the fact that such occurrences might have given rise to the familiar superstitions of fearing to mention some ailment lest it might appear. One must not boast of any fortune without " knocking on wood," neither should one " paint the devil on the wall," lest he really come. As a matter of fact, one only boasts of fortune when misfortune already lurks, and one perceives the premonition in the form of a boast because the content of the reminiscence appears here earlier than the feeling belonging to it, because in consciousness there exists a pleasant contrast.

I hope that this abstract from the chronicle of the first three weeks will suffice to give an illustrative picture of the patient's state, of the mode of my therapeutic effort, and of its success. I shall now proceed to complete the history of the patient.

The hysterical delirium described last represented also the last marked disturbance in the behavior of Mrs. Emmy von N. As I did not originally look for morbid symptoms and their determination, but waited until something showed itself, or until the patient uttered some apprehensive thoughts, the hypnosis soon became unfruitful and was utilized mainly to impart some precepts that should always remain fresh in her mind, so as to protect her from merging into new and similar states at home. I was at that time entirely under the spell of Bernheim's book on suggestion, and expected more from such instructive influences than I would today. The health of my patient improved so markedly in a short time that she assured me that she had not felt like this since the death of her husband. I discharged her after altogether seven weeks of treatment to go to her home in the Baltic.

Not I, but Dr. Breuer, received information from her after seven months. Her good health continued for many months and then succumbed to new psychic shock. Her oldest daughter, while still in Vienna, imitated her mother's neck cramp and lighter hysterical states. She suffered above all from pains in walking as a result of a uterine retroflexion, and was treated at my suggestion by Dr. N., one of our most prominent gynecologists. He corrected this deformity through massage, so that she was free from all complaints for many months. When these symptoms reappeared at home, the mother consulted a gynecologist of a nearby university city, who prescribed a combined local and therapeutic procedure, which led, however, to a serious nervous breakdown of the child. In all probability this already showed the pathological disposition of this seventeen year old girl, which became manifest a year later in a change of character. The mother, who entrusted the child to the physician with her usual mixture of yielding and suspicion, hurled the most severe reproaches at herself after the unfortunate issue of this treatment. By a train of thought, which I have not investigated, she came to the conclusion that both of us, Dr. N. and myself, were to blame for her child's illness, because the serious illness of her child was rather lightly presented to her. Through an act of will she abrogated more or less the effect of my treatment and soon lapsed back into the state from which I freed her. A prominent physician from her city, to whom she appealed, and Dr. Breuer, with whom she corresponded, were able to make her see the innocence of the two defendants, but the aversion that she worked up towards me remained as an hysterical remnant after the explanation, and she declared that it would be impossible for her to put herself again under my care. Following the advice of that medical authority, she entered a sanitarium in North Germany, and at the request of Dr. Breuer I imparted to the physician in charge of the sanitarium whatever modification of hypnotic therapy proved effective in her case.

This attempt to transfer her to another physician failed completely. From the beginning, there was a misunderstanding between her and the physician, which culminated in resistance towards anything he had undertaken with her. She became worse, suffered from loss of sleep and lack of appetite, and recovered only after one of her friends, who visited her in the hospital, secretly abducted her to her home and nursed her there. Shortly thereafter, exactly one year after her first meeting with me, she was back in Vienna and put herself in my hands.

I found her much better than I imagined from the correspondence; she was flexible and free from anxiety, which showed that much remained of what I constructed before. The chief complaint was a frequent confusion, a " storm in the head," as she called it. Besides that, she suffered from insomnia, was subject to hours of crying, and became depressed at a definite hour of the day, at five o'clock. It was the time during which she was allowed to visit her daughter in the sanitarium during the winter. She stuttered and smacked very much, rubbed her hands together as if in a rage, and when I asked her if she saw any animals, her only answer was " Oh, keep quiet."

During the first attempt to put her in a hypnosis she clenched her fists and cried: " I want no antipyrin injection, I'd rather have my pains. I do not like Dr. R. I find him antagonistic." I recognized that she was in the midst of a reminiscence of a hypnosis while in the sanitarium, and I calmed her when I brought her back into the present situation.

In the very beginning of the treatment, I made an instructive discovery. I asked her since when the stuttering had returned, and she answered (in hypnosis) hesitatingly that she had noticed it since the fright that she had experienced during the winter at D. A waiter of the hotel in which she lived hid himself in her room. In the darkness she thought that this object was an overcoat, and when she got hold of it, the man suddenly "shot into the air." I removed this memory image, and from that time she actually hardly ever stuttered tangibly either in hypnosis or in the waking state. I do not know what induced me to put her to the test of this success. When I returned in the evening, I asked her apparently quite innocently what I should do to close the door in such a way that when I left her room, while she was asleep, no one could steal in. To my surprise, she became extremely frightened. She ground her teeth and rubbed her hands together, indicating in this way that she had been violently frightened, but I could not induce her to tell the story. I noticed that she had in mind the same story that she had told in the hypnosis in the forenoon, which I imagined I had. wiped away. In the next hypnosis she related everything circumstantially and truthfully. In her excitement during that evening she kept on walking to and fro, and finding herself at the open door of her chambermaid's room, she wished to enter and sit down. The chambermaid attempted to bar her way, but she insisted on going in, and as she stepped in, she noticed something dark against the wall, which turned out to be a man. It was apparently the erotic factor of this small adventure which first caused her to give this untruthful description. But experience had taught me that an incomplete recital in hypnosis had no remedial effect, and I, therefore, got into the habit of considering a story incomplete if it did not give any results. I gradually learned to read from the patient's mien whether she did or did not keep from me an essential part of the confession.

The work which I now took up with her consisted in the hypnotic adjustment of the unpleasant impressions which she received during the treatment of her daughter, and of her own sojourn in that sanitarium. She was full of suppressed rage against the physician who caused her to spell in hypnosis t-o-a-d, and she made me promise never to apply that word to her. I allowed myself a slight joke, the only quite harmless abuse of hypnosis of which I was guilty in this case, by suggesting in a rather humorous way that whenever she desired to pronounce the name of the sanitarium, which ended in "thal" (valley), she would get lost between the mountain, valley, forest, etc. . . . Precisely so it happened, and very soon the only speech impediment she showed was the uncertainty when she came to this name. Gradually, she was also freed of this paramnesia.

But I had to struggle much longer with the state she designated as " storm in the head " than with the remnant of this experience. When I first saw her in this state, she lay on a divan with distorted features in an incessant state of restlessness of her whole body, her hands always pressed to the forehead, calling longingly and despairingly the word, " Emmy," which was her own as well as her daughter's name. In the hypnosis she recounted that this state represented a repetition of so many attacks of despair which seized her during the treatment of her daughter, after she had reflected in vain for hours how the bad results of the treatment could be corrected. When she then felt that her thoughts were becoming confused, she got into the habit of calling loudly the name of her daughter in order to wake herself by it back into clearness. For, at that time, when the state of her daughter imposed new duties upon her and she felt that her nervousness was again gaining power over her, she resolved that whatever concerned this child must be kept away from the confusion, no matter what other confusions might revolve in her head.

After a few weeks, these reminiscences, too, were mastered, and Mrs. Emmy, though in perfect health, remained for some time longer under my care. Just at the end of her sojourn something happened, which I wish to relate in detail because this episode throws the clearest light on the character of the patient as well as on the mode of origin of her states.

I visited her once during her luncheon and surprised her as she was throwing something into the garden wrapped in a paper, which was caught by the janitor's children. To my question, she admitted that it was her (dry) dessert, which was wont to follow the same path every day. This gave me the opportunity to look at the remnants of the other courses, and I found that there was more left on the plates than she could have consumed. When questioned as to why she ate so little, she answered that she was not in the habit of eating more, that more food would do her harm, and that she had the same nature as her blessed father, who had also been a light eater. As to fluids, she stated that she could only digest thick fluids like milk, coffee, cocoa, etc., and that as often as she drank water or mineral water, she spoiled her stomach. This showed the unmistakable sign of a nervous selection. I took along a specimen of her urine, and I found that it was very concentrated, overloaded with salts.

I then considered it appropriate to advise her to take more fluids and also decided to increase her food. She was in no way strikingly thin, but it seemed to me that a little more nourishment would be worth while. When I prescribed during my next visit mineral water and forbade her from disposing of her desserts, she became somewhat excited. " I will do it because you desire it, but I can tell you beforehand that it will turn out badly because it goes against my nature; my father was also that way." To the question put in hypnosis, as to why she did not eat more and consume a full meal, and why she did not drink water, she answered sulkily: " I do not know." The next day the nurse informed me that Mrs. Emmy had managed to consume the whole meal and also drank a glass of mineral water. But I found her lying in bed, very moody, and in a very ungracious mood, and complaining of severe pains in the stomach. " But, I warned you, now all the success for which we have so long tormented ourselves is gone. I have spoiled my stomach as is always the case when I eat more or drink water, and I will have to starve myself for eight days or more until I can again tolerate anything." I assured her that she would not have to starve, and that it is quite impossible to spoil one's stomach in this way, that her pains were due to the anxiety with which she ate and drank. I did not seem to make the slightest impression upon her with this explanation, for when I tried shortly thereafter to put her to sleep, the hypnosis failed for the first time, and from the most raging look hurled at me, I recognized that she was in the midst of a perfect rage and that the situation was quite serious. I gave up the hypnosis and informed her that I was giving her twenty-four hours for reflection in order to accept my view that her stomach aches came only from her fear, and that after this period I would ask her whether she still thought that one can spoil one's stomach for eight days from a glass of mineral water, and a moderate meal, and if she answered in the affirmative, I would ask her to leave for home. This little scene was a marked contrast to our otherwise friendly relationship.

After twenty-four hours I found her very humble and mellow. To the question what she thought about the origin of her stomach aches, she answered: " I believe that they came from my fear, but only because you say so." I then put her in hypnosis and asked her again, " Why can't you eat more?"

The answer followed promptly, and again consisted of the following chronologically ordered series of motives from memory: " When I was a child, it often happened that because of my naughtiness I did not wish to eat my meat at the table. My mother was then always very strict and I was forced by severe punishment to eat everything from the same plate two hours later. The meat was then quite cold and the fat was so tough (disgust) . . . and I still see the fork before me, one of the prongs slightly bent. Now when I go to the table, I always see before me the plates with the cold meat and the fat. And then many years later I lived with my brother, who was an officer and who had a most foul disease. I knew that it was contagious and hence I was in mortal dread lest I make a mistake and use his set of dishes or his knife and fork (horror), yet I did eat with him in order that no one should notice that he was sick. Soon thereafter I nursed my other brother, who was tubercular, and we ate at his bedside and his spittoon always stood on the table, and quite open (horror) . . . and he had the nasty habit of spitting across the plate into the cup. I always felt such disgust, and yet I could not show it for fear of insulting him. And this spittoon always stands on the table when I eat and I always experience this same disgust when I eat." With this I cleaned away thoroughly the disgust. I then asked why she could not drink water. When she was seventeen years old, her family spent a few months in Munich, and almost all the members of her family contracted a catarrh of the stomach because of the bad drinking water. The others soon recovered through medical aid, but she never did. Nor did the mineral water, which was recommended, improve her condition. As the physician prescribed it, she immediately thought that that, too, would not help. Since then, the intolerance for plain and mineral water has repeated itself numerous times.

The therapeutic result of this hypnotic investigation was immediate and permanent. She did not starve for eight days, but ate and drank on the second day without the slightest complaint. Two months later, she said in a letter: " I eat very well and I have gained a lot. I have already consumed forty bottles of the water. Do you think I should continue it?"

I saw Mrs. Emmy von N. again in the spring of the next year on her estate near D. Her older daughter, whose name she used to call out during " the storm in the head " entered at this time into a phase of abnormal development. She showed an excessive ambition, which was disproportionate to her meager endowment. She became insubordinate and even violent towards her mother. I still had the confidence of the latter, and was requested to come there in order to give an opinion about this young girl's condition. I gained an unfavorable impression of the psychic change which took place in the child, and in giving the prognosis had to take into consideration that some half siblings of the patient (children of Mr. von N. by his first marriage) went to pieces from paranoia. Nor was there any lack of hereditary burdening on the mother's side of the family, although no members of her immediate family lapsed into a final psychosis. Mrs. von N., to whom I gave the required information without any reservation, took it quietly and understandingly. She looked stronger, and had a blooming appearance. The eight months since the ending of the last treatment had been passed in relatively excellent health; she was only slightly disturbed by the cramp in the neck and other insignificant complaints. The large extent of her duties, accomplishments and psychic interests I really learned during this many days' visit at her home. I also met the family physician, who did not have much to complain of about the lady. Thus, she was more or less reconciled to the " profession."

The patient was very much improved in health and functioned more capably, but the fundamentals of her character have changed little despite all instructive suggestions. She did not seem to have grasped the category of the " indifferent things," her tendency to self-torture was hardly less than during the period of treatment. Nor was the hysterical disposition quiescent during this good period; for example, she complained of an inability to take long railroad trips, which she had had to do during the last months. A pressing, hasty attempt to solve this hindrance yielded only a number of small disagreeable impressions, which she experienced on the last journey to D., as well as in the neighborhood. But in the hypnosis she seemed reluctant to give information, and it occurred to me even then that she was in the process of again withdrawing from my influence, and that the secret intention of the railroad inhibition lay in her desire to hinder another journey to Vienna.

During these days she also complained about gaps in her memory, " precisely in the most important events," from which I concluded that my work of two years ago had impressed itself sufficiently and lastingly.—When she conducted me one day through an alley, which led from her house to a bay, I ventured the question whether this alley was frequently covered with toads. As an answer, she met me with a punishing look, which was not, however, accompanied by any signs of fear, but which she supplemented with the following remark:

" But, here you find real toads." During the hypnosis in which I undertook to remove the railroad inhibition, she, herself, seemed to be dissatisfied with her answers, and expressed the fear that now she would not obey the hypnosis as much as she did before. I decided to convince her of the opposite. I wrote a few words on a piece of paper which I handed to her and said: " This noon you will again pour for me a glass of red wine as you did yesterday. As I will take the glass to my mouth, you will say: ' Oh, please pour also a glassful for me.' And as I reach for the bottle, you will call out: ' No thank you, I'd rather not!' Thereupon, you will put your hand in your pocket and draw out the note upon which these words are written." That was done in the forenoon. A few hours later the little scene was enacted precisely as I suggested it, and with such a natural process that none of the numerous guests noticed anything. She seemed visibly to struggle with herself when she asked me for the wine—for she never drank any—and after she put away the drink with apparent alleviation she felt in her pocket and drew out the note upon which one could read the last spoken word. She shook her head and looked at me with astonishment.

Since this visit of 1890, my information concerning Mrs. von N. became more scant. In a roundabout way I found out that the disagreeable state of her daughter, which caused her the most manifold painful emotions, finally undermined her health. In the summer of 1893 I received a short note from her in which she asked my permission to go to another physician for hypnosis, as she was again ailing and could not come to Vienna. At first I did not understand why my permission was needed until I recalled that in 1890 I protected her at her own request from being hypnotized by a stranger, and that she now wished to obviate the danger of becoming subjected to the painful compulsion of an unsympathetic physician. I, therefore, renounced in writing my exclusive prerogative.

Epicrisis

Without any previous deeper understanding of the value and significance of names, it is really not easy to decide whether a case belongs to hysteria or to the other (not purely neurasthenic) neuroses. In the realms of the commonly occurring mixed neuroses one still waits for the directing hand to set the landmarks and to render prominent the essential features characteristic of the disease. If we are still accustomed to diagnosing hysteria in the narrow sense following the similarity to the familiar typical cases, the designation of hysteria for the case of Mrs. Emmy von N. can hardly be disputed. The ease with which the deliria and the hallucinations came into being in an otherwise intact psychic activity, the alteration of personality and memory in artificial somnambulism, the anesthesia in the painful extremities, certain data of the anamnesis, the ovaritis, and similar symptoms, all leave no doubt concerning the hysterical nature of the disease, or at least of the patient. That the question should at all be raised is due to a definite character of the case, which may also offer occasion for an observation of general value. As was shown in our "preliminary communication" we have considered the hysterical symptoms as effects and remnants of excitements which have influenced the nervous system as traumas. Such remnants do not remain if the original excitement is discharged through abreaction and mental elaboration. We can no longer reject here the consideration of quantities (even if not measurable), and to conceive the process of hysteria, as if a sum of excitement had entered into the nervous system and was transformed into a lasting symptom in so far as it has not been utilized proportionately for action in the outside world. We are now in the habit of finding in hysteria that a considerable portion of the " sum of excitement " of the trauma changes into a purely physical symptom. It is that very feature of hysteria which stood in the way for so long a time of conceiving it as a psychic affection.

If for the sake of brevity, we choose to designate the term *"conversion,"* as the transformation of psychic excitement into chronic physical symptoms, which characterizes hysteria, we can say that in the case of Mrs. Emmy von N. there was a small amount of conversion. But as the original psychic excitement remained mostly in the psychic spheres, it was easy to see why it resembled other non-hysterical neuroses. There are cases of hysteria in which the conversion embraces the sum total of the excitement, so that the physical symptoms of hysteria seem to fuse with perfectly normal consciousness; more usually, however, there is an incomplete transformation, so that at least a part of the affect accompanying the trauma remains in consciousness as a component of the disposition.

The psychic symptoms of our case, which show a slight conversion hysteria, can be grouped as a change of disposition (anxiety, melancholic depression), phobias, and abulias (inhibitions of will). The two latter kinds of psychic disturbances which are conceived, however, by the French school of psychiatrists as stigmata of nervous degeneration, prove to be in our case prolifically determined by traumatic experiences, they are mostly traumatic phobias and abulias, as I shall show in detail.

As to the phobias, some surely correspond to the primary phobias of man, particularly of the neurotic; this is especially true of the fear of animals (snakes, toads, besides all vermin, as the master of which Mephistopheles boasted), the fear of storms, and others. But even these phobias were reinforced by traumatic experiences; thus, the fear of toads by the impressions from early youth when her brother threw a dead toad at her, to which she reacted with an attack of hysterical convulsions; the fear of storms, came from that fright which gave cause to the origin of the smacking, and the fear of fog from that walk in Rügen. At all events, the primary, so to speak, instinctive fear, which is taken as a psychic stigma, plays the main rôle in this group.

The other and more special phobias were also justified through particular experiences. The fear of an unexpected sudden fright was determined by the sudden experience of that most horrible impression in her life, when she saw her husband, apparently in the best of health, die suddenly of a heart attack. Fear of strange people, or fear of men in general, turned out to be a remnant of that period when she was subjected to persecutions by her family and was wont to see in every stranger an agent of her relatives, or it was determined by the thought that strangers knew about the things which were spread about her orally and in writing. The fear of the insane asylum and its inhabitants went back to a whole series of sad experiences in her family, and to descriptions which were imparted to the child by a stupid servant girl. Moreover, this phobia was also supported on the one hand by the primary instinctive fear of insanity entertained by healthy persons, and on the other hand, as in every nervous person, by the worry that she, herself, might become insane. Such special anxiety, as the one that someone stood behind her, was motivated by many frightful impressions of her childhood, and of later periods. Since the one special painful experience in the hotel, painful because it was connected with eroticism, the anxiety that a strange person might sneak in was particularly prominent. Finally, one of the phobias frequently seen in neurotics, namely, that she might be buried alive, can be fully explained by the belief that her husband was not dead when his body was carried away, a belief which manifests itself so touchingly in an inability to feel one's self suddenly cut off from all relationship with a beloved being. At all events, I believe that all those psychic factors can only explain the selection, but not the continuation of the phobias. The latter must be explained by the *neurotic* factors—that is, by the circumstance that the patient lived for so many years in sexual abstinence, which furnishes the most frequent causes for *tendencies to anxiety*.

The abulias (the incapacities and inhibitions of will) which existed in our patient, justify even less than the phobias the assumption of psychic stigmata as a result of a generally restricted, functional capacity. On the contrary, the hypnotic analysis of the case demonstrates that the abulias were here conditioned by a double psychic mechanism, which basically is again only one. The abulia is either simply the effect of a phobia, to wit, in all the cases in which the phobia is connected with a particular act, instead of with an expectation (to go out to visit people—the other case, that someone might sneak in, etc.), or the cause of the abulia, is the anxiety connected with the effect of the act. It would be incorrect to describe as a special symptom this form of abulia with its corresponding phobias, though one must admit that such a phobia can exist, if it is not of too high a grade, without leading to an abulia. The other form of abulia depends upon the existence of emotionally accentuated and unsolved associations, which resist connection to new associations, and especially to such as are unbearable. The most splendid example of such an abulia is offered by the anorexia of our patient. She ate so little only because it did not appeal to her, and she could not get any taste from the food because the act of eating was associated from her early age with memories of disgust, the affective sum of which had not yet become diminished. But it is impossible to eat simultaneously with both disgust and pleasure. The diminution of the disgust, which was connected with the meals from the first, did not take place because she had to suppress the disgust each time, instead of freeing herself from it through a reaction. As a child, she was forced to eat the cold meal through fear of punishment, and in more mature years she was prevented from expressing her emotions because of her regard for her brothers, with whom she had to take her meals.

I may here perhaps recall a small work, in which I attempted to give a psychological explanation of hysterical paralyses. There I came to the conclusion that the reason for these paralyses lies in the inadequacy of the ideation sphere, perhaps in an extremity for new associations. But the associative inadequacy, as such, is due to the fact that the idea of the paralyzed limb is involved in the traumatic memory with an unsettled affect. From examples of everyday life, I concluded that such an investment of an idea with undischarged affect always carries with it a certain amount of associative inadequacy or an incompatibility with new emotional investments [24] (cathexis).

Until this day I have not been able to demonstrate my former theories through hypnotic analysis of a case of motor paralysis, but I can refer to the anorexia of Mrs. von N. as proof that this mechanism concurs with some cases of abulias, and abulias are really nothing but expressions for very specialized, or " systematized " (following a French expression) psychic paralyses.

The psychic state of affairs of Mrs. von N. can essentially be characterized, if we render prominent two things: (1) The painful effects of traumatic experiences remained unsettled in her, the moodiness, the pain (from the death of her husband), the anger (from the persecution by relatives), the disgust (from the forced meals), the anxiety (from so many frightful experiences), etc.; and (2) She had a very vivid, active memory, which brought into actual consciousness, now spontaneously, and now through awakened stimuli of the present (e.g., the information of the revolution in Santo Domingo), fragment by fragment, all the traumas with their accompanying affects. My therapy followed the course of these memory activities, and sought to unravel and to settle, day by day, what the particular day brought to the surface, until the last stock of the disease-producing memories seemed exhausted.

To these psychic characteristics, which I consider as general findings in hysterical paroxysms, could be added some important considerations, which I shall postpone until I shall give some attention to the mechanism of the physical symptoms.

It is impossible to give the same deductions for all of the patient's symptoms; on the contrary, one discovers from this in itself not very prolific case that the physical symptoms of hysteria come about in various ways. First of all I take the liberty of attributing the pains to the physical symptoms. As far as I can see, some of the pains were certainly organically determined by the slight (rheumatic)

---

[24] Archives de Neurologie, Nr. 77, 1893. The author uses here for the first time the word *Besetzung* (occupation) in the sense of occupying, investing, or filling with a charge of energy a definite affective event. As this term was frequently used by Freud in his later works and gave rise to considerable ambiguity the word, cathexis, from the Greek, 'to occupy,' was coined about thirty years later to designate a concentration of energy in a particular channel.

changes in the muscles, tendons, and fascias, which produce so much more pain in the neurotic than in the healthy. Another part of the pains were most probably memory pains, symbolic memories of periods of excitement and sick nursing, which had taken up so much time in the life of the patient. These pains, too, might originally have been organically justified, but have since then become elaborated into neurotic aims. I base these statements concerning the pains of Mrs. von N. on experiences gained elsewhere, which I shall relate in a subsequent passage of this work; from the patient, herself, there was little explanation to be gained, especially about this point.

A part of the striking motor manifestations evinced by Mrs. von N. was simply an emotional expression, and easily recognized in this significance; thus, the extension of the hand with the spread out and curved fingers as an expression of fear, the same is also true of the play of features and similar signs. To be sure, it was a more vivid and more uninhibited expression of emotions than corresponded to the patient's former mimicry, to her education, and to her race. When not in an hysterical state, she was reserved, almost rigid in her emotional expressions. Another part of her motor symptoms was, in accordance with her statement, directly connected with her pain. She played restlessly with her fingers (1888), or rubbed her hands together (1889) in order not to cry out. This motivation vividly recalls Darwin's principles of " discharge of excitement " by which, for example, he explains the tail-wagging of dogs. To be sure, all of us substitute it when painfully stimulated by crying or some other motor innervation. Whoever resolves to keep his head and mouth quiet in the dental chair and not to interfere with his hands, at least drums with his feet.

Mrs. von N.'s tic-like movements form a more complicated manner of conversion. We refer to the smacking of her tongue and stuttering, the calling out of the name, " Emmy," in attacks of confusion, and to the compounded protective formula, " Keep quiet, don't speak, don't touch me " (1888). Of these motor expressions the stuttering and smacking can be explained by a mechanism which I have designated in a short contribution on the objectivity of contrast ideas.[25] This process could be explained even from our own example, in the following manner: The hysterical patient, exhausted from worry and vigilance, sits at the bed of her sick child and

[25] *Zeitschrift für Hypnotismus,* Band 1, 1893, " Objectivirung der Contrastvorstellung."

finally(!) falls asleep. She says to herself: " But now you must remain perfectly quiet, so that the child shall not be disturbed." This resolution probably awakened a contrast idea, or the apprehension that she might, nevertheless, make a noise, and that it would awaken the little one from the long desired sleep. Such contrast ideas against the resolution come into being in tangible degree also in us, when we are not sure of putting through an important resolution.

The neurotic, in whose self-consciousness one can seldom miss a trait of depression and anxious expectation, forms a larger amount of such contrast ideas, or he perceives them more easily; they appear to him also as more important. In the state of exhaustion in which our patient happened to be, this very contrast idea, which is ordinarily pushed aside, proved to be the stronger of the two. It was this idea which was objectivated, and to the horror of the patient, she then actually produced the dreaded noise. In order to explain the whole process, I also assume that the exhaustion was only partial; it concerned, as one would say in terms of Janet and his pupils, only the primary ego of the patient, but had not caused a weakening also of the contrasting idea.

Furthermore, I assume that it was the horror of the noise produced by the counter-will which endowed the moment with traumatic effectiveness, and fixed the noise itself as a physical memory symptom of the whole scene. Indeed, I believe that in the character of this very tic, consisting of many spasmodically emitted sounds separated from one another by pauses, and resembling mostly smackings, one can recognize the traces of the processes to which it owes its origins. It seems that there was a struggle between the resolution and the contrast idea, that is, the " counter-will," which furnished the tic with the cast of character, and which restricted the contrast idea to the unusual path of innervation of the speech muscles.

The spasmodic speech inhibition, or the peculiar stuttering, was the remnant of an essentially similar cause, only that here it was not the result of the final innervation, that is, the crying, but of the process of innervation itself, that is, the attempt of a cramp-like inhibition of the speech organs became raised in the memory to a symbol of the event.

Both symptoms, the smacking and stuttering, closely related through the history of their origin, remained henceforth associated, and through a repetition on a similar occasion, developed into constant symptoms. Later, however, they were adapted for further use.

Having originated under violent fright, they henceforth associated themselves (following the mechanisms of mono-symptomatic hysteria, which I will show in Case V) with every fear, even if the latter could not give cause for the objectivation of a contrast idea.

They were finally connected with so many traumas, and acquired so much right to reproduce themselves in memory, that without any further cause, following the manner of a senseless tic, they constantly interrupted speech. But the hypnotic analysis could then show how much meaning there was concealed behind this apparent tic, and even if it was not possible to bring both symptoms to full disappearance with one stroke by the Breuer method, this was due to the fact that the catharsis was extended only to the three principal traumas, and not to those of secondary association.[26]

[26] I could here give the impression that I put too much weight on the details of the symptom, and that I am losing myself in superfluous astrology. However, I have learned that the determination of hysterical symptoms really reaches back into the most delicate elaborations, and that one cannot easily attribute to them too much meaning. I shall cite an example which will justify my attitude. Months ago, I treated an eighteen year old girl from a family burdened by heredity, whose complicated neurosis showed its good share of hysteria. The first thing that I learned from her was a complaint of attacks of despair that had a twofold content; in the one, she felt a pulling and prickling on the lower part of the face, from the cheeks down towards the mouth, in the other the toes of both feet were spasmodically extended and moved restlessly to and fro. In the beginning, I, myself, was not inclined to attribute much significance to these details and it was quite in harmony with the former views of hysteria to see in these manifestations proof of an irritation in the cortical center. Where the centers of such parasthesia were we surely did not know, but it was known that such parasthesias initiated partial epilepsy, and contributed to the sensory epilepsy of Charcot. However, the situation was differently explained. When I became better acquainted with the girl, I once asked her directly what thoughts came to her mind. I told her that she should not be ashamed to tell, that there must be an explanation for these two manifestations. The patient became red in the face, and finally was led without hypnosis to the following explanation, the reality of which was fully confirmed by her companion, who happened to be present. Since the beginning of her menstruation she suffered for years from adolescent headaches, which made any continuous occupation impossible, and interrupted her education. Finally, when she became freed from this impediment, the ambitious but somewhat simple-minded child decided to work zealously in order to catch up with her sisters and casual friends. In doing this, she exerted herself beyond measure, and such an effort usually ended with an outbreak of despair over the fact that she overestimated her strength. She naturally was also in the habit of comparing herself physically with other girls, and felt unhappy when she discovered in herself a physical disadvantage. Her very prominent prognathism began to worry her, and she conceived the idea of correcting it by practicing for fifteen minutes at a time pulling down her upper lip over her protruding teeth. The failure of this childish effort once led her to an outbreak of despair, and from that time on, she gave as the content of one kind of her attacks a pulling and prickling from the cheeks downward.——No less transparent was the determination of the other attacks with the motor symptoms of extension and motion of her toes. I was informed that the first of these attacks appeared

Calling out the name, "Emmy," in attacks of confusion, which, according to the rules of hysterical attacks, reproduced the frequent states of helplessness during the treatment of her daughter, was connected through a complicated trend of thought with the content of the attack, and corresponded perhaps to a protective formula of the patient against this attack. In a looser utilization of its meaning, this call would probably have been adaptable as a tic. The complicated protective formula, "Do not touch me, etc. . . . ," had already attained this application, but the hypnotic therapy held back in both cases the further development of these symptoms. The call, "Emmy," which was quite newly developed, I still found in its native soil; that is, it was restricted to the attack of confusion.

Whether all these motor symptoms: the smacking, through the objectivation of a contrast idea, the stuttering, through a mere conversion of psychic motor excitement, the call, "Emmy," and the longer formula as a protective measure, may have originated through an intentional act of the patient in an hysterical paroxysm—all of them have this one thing in common, to wit, that in origin or continuity they are in demonstrable association with the traumas, for which they appear as symbols in the memory activity.

The patient's other physical symptoms were not at all of an hysterical nature. Thus, the neck cramps, which I conceived as a modified migraine, do not, as such, really belong to the neurosis, but

---

after a mountain-climbing party in a mountain resort, and the relatives were naturally inclined to attribute it to overexertion, but the girl gave the following information: One of the standing themes of mutual teasing among her brothers and sisters was to call attention to her undeniably large feet. Our patient, having been unhappy for a long time over this lack of beauty, strove to force her feet into the narrowest shoes, but her observant father would not allow this, and took care that she wore only comfortable footwear. She was quite dissatisfied with this arrangement, thought continuously of it, and got into the habit of playing with her toes in her shoes, like one does when one wishes to measure by how much the shoe is too big, and how much smaller a size one can wear, etc. During the mountain-climbing party, which she did not in any way find exerting, there was naturally another occasion to make remarks about her shoes, which were visible on account of her short skirt. One of her sisters said on the way, "But you are wearing particularly large shoes today." She then measured with her toes, and she thought so, too. The excitement over the unfortunately big feet no longer left her, and when she came home, she had the first attack in which her toes cramped and moved involuntarily as a memory symbol for the whole depressive trend of thought. I observe that we deal here with a symptom of attack and not with a permanent symptom. Moreover I wish to add that after this confession the attacks of the first kind ceased, whereas the second with the restless toes continued. There must surely have been a fragment connected with it, which has not been confessed.

Postscript: I also discovered later that this simple-minded girl worked overzealously to beautify herself because she wanted to please a young cousin.

must be put among the organic affections, though they regularly become connected with hysterical symptoms. In Mrs. von N. the neck cramps were utilized as hysterical attacks, whereas they exerted no influence over the typical forms of manifestations of the hysterical attacks.

I will now complete the characteristics of Mrs. von N.'s psychic state by taking up the demonstrable morbid changes of her consciousness. Just as through the neck cramps, she also lapsed into a delirium through painful impressions of the present,[27] or through forceful allusions to one of her traumas (judging by only few observations I cannot say anything different).—Such a delirium was swayed by a restriction of consciousness and by an associative force similar to that in the dream, in which hallucinations and illusions develop most easily, and in which weak and even contradictory conclusions are drawn. This state, comparable to a psychic alienation, probably took the place of her attack, something like an acute psychosis as an equivalent for the attack, which we would classify as an " hallucinatory confusion." Another similarity to the typical hysterical attack also lies in the fact that in most of them a fragment of the old traumatic memory could be demonstrated as the foundation of the delirium. The transition from the normal state into this delirium frequently proceeded quite imperceptibly. Thus, as she was speaking quite normally about more or less affective things and the conversation drifted to painful ideas, I suddenly noticed by her accelerated gestures, by the appearance of her speech formula, and similar signs, that she was in a state of delirium. In the beginning of the treatment the delirium continued throughout the whole day so that it was difficult to tell with certainty from individual symptoms, such as gestures, whether they belonged to the psychic state, as a symptom of the attack, or whether like the smacking and stuttering, they had developed into real permanent symptoms. It was often only possible to distinguish subsequently what occurred in the delirium, and what occurred in the normal state. The two states were actually separated by the memory, and she was then most surprised to hear what things had pieced together the delirium and the normally conducted conversation. How the two states permeated each other without one taking notice of the other was shown in the most remarkable way in my first conversation with her. Only once during this psychic see-sawing could one observe any impinging upon the normal conscious-

[27] *Cf.* the last delirium in the garden.

ness of the present, and that happened when she gave me an answer which originated in her delirium when she said that she was a woman of the last century.

The main reason for the superficiality of the analysis of this delirium was due to the fact that her condition improved so quickly that the deliria were soon sharply distinguished from her normal life, and confined themselves to the periods of her neck cramps. In contrast to this, I have gathered so much more experience concerning the behavior of the patient in the third psychic state, that is, in the artificial somnambulism. While she did not know in her normal state what psychic experiences she went through in her delirium and what in her somnambulism, she had full command over her memory in her somnambulism of all three states; here she was really most normal. If I disregard the fact that in a somnambulic state she was less reserved towards me than in the best hours of her ordinary life, as shown by the fact that she gave me information about her family and similar intimacies, whereas ordinarily she treated me as if I were a stranger, and when I also disregard the fact that she showed the full suggestibility of somnambulism, I must really say that in her somnambulism she was in a perfectly normal state. It was interesting to observe that this somnambulism showed no supernormal features, that it evinced all the psychic shortcomings which one expects in the normal state of consciousness. The behavior of the somnambulic memory may explain the following tests: While conversing with me, she once expressed her enthusiasm over a beautiful flower pot which decorated the vestibule of the sanitarium. " But what is the name of it, Doctor? " " Don't you know? " I knew both the German and the Latin names, but I have forgotten both." She was an excellent connoisseur of plants, whereas I admitted my botanical ignorance on such occasions. A few minutes later I asked her in hypnosis: " Do you know now the name of the plant in the vestibule? " The answer came without the slightest hesitation: " The German name is turk lily, and the Latin name I really have forgotten." On another occasion she told me during a period of well being about her visit to the catacombs of Rome, and could not recall two terms in the description, in which I could not assist her. I immediately thereafter found out in the hypnosis what words she meant. She did not know them even in the hypnosis. I, thereupon, said to her: " Don't think of it now, tomorrow between five and six in the afternoon in the garden, perhaps a little nearer to six, the names will suddenly come to you."

The next morning during a conversation which was quite foreign to the catacombs, she suddenly burst out: " Doctor, *crypt* and *columbarium.*" " Oh, these are the words which you could not recall yesterday. When did they flash through your mind?" " This afternoon in the garden shortly before I came up." I noticed that in this way she wished to show me that she was punctual to the exact time, for she was in the habit of leaving the garden at about six o'clock. Thus, even in her somnambulism she did not have at her disposal the whole bulk of her knowledge; here, too, there existed an actual and a potential consciousness. Often enough it happened that to my question in hypnosis, " Whence did this or that manifestation originate?" she wrinkled her forehead, and after a pause answered quietly, " That I do not know." I was in the habit of saying, " Just think and you will soon find out," and after a little while she could give me the desired information. But it also happened that nothing came to her mind and I had to leave her the task of recalling it the next day. This was invariably the case. This woman, who in everyday life avoided painfully every untruth, did not lie in the hypnosis either; but it often happened that she gave imperfect information and held back a fragment of the report until I forced her to complete it the next time. As mentioned above,[28] this was mainly due to a revulsion which the particular theme evoked, and which shut her mouth even in somnambulism. Despite these restricting features, the impression gained from her psychic behavior in somnambulism was one of uninhibited unfolding of her mental force and of a perfect mastery of her whole memory.

Her undeniably marked suggestibility in somnambulism was, nevertheless, very far from a morbid lack of resistance. On the whole, I must say that I really made no more impression upon her than I might have expected from such an investigation of the psychic mechanism of any person who would have listened to me with great confidence and with full mental clearness, except that Mrs. von N. could not offer me such a favorable psychic attitude when she was in her so-called normal state. Whenever, as in the case of the animal phobia, I was unsuccessful in showing her the causes of the conviction, or whenever I did not enter into the history of the psychic origin of the symptoms, but wished to produce results by means of

[28] P. 66.

authoritative suggestion, I have always observed the tense, unsatisfied expression in her features. And when I asked at the end, " Well, will you be afraid of these animals? ", the answer was " No, because you desire it." Such promising, which could have been based only on her yieldingness to me, produced no better results than the many general precepts which I imparted to her, instead of which I might just as lief have given her such a suggestion as, " Be in good health."

This same person who held on so stubbornly to her morbid symptoms in the face of suggestions, and only dropped them when confronted with psychic analysis or through conviction, was on the other hand, as passive as the best hospital medium when it concerned indifferent suggestions, things which had no reference to her disease. I have reported examples of such post-hypnotic obedience in the case history. I find no contradiction in this behavior. The right of the stronger idea had to assert itself even here. If one investigates the mechanisms of the pathological " fixed idea," one finds that it is founded on and supported by so many intensively effective experiences that one cannot be surprised that it can offer successful resistance to a suggested counter-idea, which again possesses only a certain force. If it would really be possible to blow away such justified experiences of intensive psychic processes through suggestion, we would surely deal with a very pathological brain.[29]

[29] In other cases I have gained a deep insight into these interesting contrasts between the most far-reaching somnambulistic obedience and the most stubborn persistence of the morbid symptoms because the latter were deeply founded and inaccessible to analysis. I treated unsuccessfully for over five months a young, active, and talented girl, who was afflicted with a severe disturbance of her gait. This patient showed analgesias and painful spots in both legs, a rapid tremor of the hands, she walked with heavy, short steps, her body bent forward swaying like in a cerebellar affliction, so that now and then she fell to the floor. Her state of mind, however, was strikingly cheerful. Because of this symptom-complex, one of our erstwhile Viennese authorities was led to make the diagnosis of multiple sclerosis. Another specialist recognized it as hysteria, which was favored by the complicated structure of the morbid picture at the onset of the disease (pains, faintings, amaurosis), and referred the patient to me for treatment. I made an attempt to improve her gait by means of hypnotic suggestions and treated also her legs by hypnosis, etc., but without success, although she was an excellent subject for somnambulism. One day as she again entered the office, swaying, supporting one arm on her father and the other on an umbrella, the tip of which was markedly worn off, I became impatient and screamed at her in the hypnosis, " You have carried on long enough, before noon tomorrow the umbrella you are holding in your hand will break and you will have to go home without an umbrella." I do not know how I came to the stupidity of directing any suggestion to an umbrella. Later, I was ashamed of it, but had no inkling that my smart patient would take it upon herself to save my reputation from her father who was a physician and witnessed this procedure. The next day, the father reported the following: " Do you know what she did yesterday? We were walking in the Ringstrasse.

When I studied the somnambulic state of Mrs. von N., weighty doubts arose in me for the first time about the correctness of Bernheim's statement: *Tout est dans la suggestion*—and about the thought of my keen-minded friend, Delboeuf: *Comme quoi il n'y a pas d'hypnotisme.* Nor can I understand today how my extended finger and the single repetition of " Sleep " could have created this special psychic state of the patient. I might have evoked this state, but I have surely not created it by my suggestions, for its characteristics, which were surely firmly established, surprised me very much.

How the somnambulic therapy was practised in this case can be readily seen from the case history. As is customary in hypnotic psychotherapy, I combated the existing morbid ideas through assurances, prohibitions, and the introduction of all kinds of counter ideas, but I was not satisfied with just that. I traced, therefore, the history of the origin of the individual symptoms in order to be able to combat the assumptions upon which the morbid ideas were constructed. During these analyses it regularly happened that the patient spoke under the stress of excitement about things the affects of which had hitherto gained discharge only through expressions of emotional feelings. How much of each therapeutic result could be attributed to this suggesting away *in statu nascendi,* and how much to the loosening of the affect through *abreaction* I cannot state, because I have allowed the two therapeutic factors to work together. Accordingly, this case could not be used as a strong proof that the cathartic method contains therapeutic efficacy. Nevertheless, I must say that only those morbid symptoms which were subjected to a psychic analysis were really removed permanently.

On the whole, the therapeutic result was considerable, but not

---

Suddenly, she became exaggeratingly cheerful and began to sing in the street: " We lead a free life . . ." and accompanied herself by beating time with the umbrella, and striking it against the sidewalk until it broke." She naturally had no idea that through her own good sense she transformed a foolish suggestion into a very successful one. When her condition had shown no improvement after assurance, command, and treatment in the hypnosis, I turned to psychic analysis and wanted to know what emotional state preceded the outbreak of her ailment. She then related in the hypnosis, but without any emotionalism, that shortly before her illness a young relative died, whose betrothed she had considered herself for many years. This information, however, changed nothing in her condition; accordingly, I said to her in the next hypnosis that I was quite convinced that the death of her cousin had nothing to do with her condition, that something else must have happened, which she did not mention. She then permitted herself to be drawn into one single allusion, but hardly had she uttered one word when she became mute and her elderly father, sitting behind her, began to sob bitterly. I naturally did not press the patient any further, nor have I ever seen her again.

permanent.   However, the patient's tendency to become sick in the same manner from new traumatic occurrences was not removed.   He who wishes to bring about a permanent cure of such hysteria must obtain a more detailed account of the causal relations of the phenomena than I had attempted at that time.   Mrs. von N. was certainly a neuropathic person, burdened by heredity; without such a disposition no hysteria could have probably developed.   Yet, a disposition alone does not make a hysteria, it requires other causes, and to be sure, as stated, adequate causes, that is, an etiology of a definite nature.   I have mentioned before that in Mrs. von N. the affects of so many traumatic experiences seemed to have been retained, and that a vivid memory activity then brought to the surface now this, and now that, trauma.   I will now venture to give the cause for this retention of the affects in Mrs. von N.   In the first place, it probably depended on her hereditary predisposition.   Her feelings were on the one hand very intensive; she was of a violent nature, capable of the greatest discharge of passions, and on the other hand, since her husband's death she lived in a state of complete psychic isolation, she was suspicious of her friends because of persecution by her relatives; and she watched jealously lest someone should gain too much influence over her.   The sphere of her duties was large and the psychic work which was imposed upon her she attended personally without the aid of a friend or a confidant.   She was almost isolated from her family, and labored under difficulties imposed upon her by her conscientiousness, her tendency to self-torture, and often also by her natural helplessness as a woman.   In fine, the mechanism of the *retention of large sums of excitement,* as such, cannot be ignored here.   It was based in part on the circumstances of her life, and in part of her own natural make-up.   Thus, her shyness to tell anything about herself was so great that none of her daily frequenters, as I learned with surprise during my visit in 1891, knew that she was a patient and I her physician.

Have I exhausted with these remarks the etiology of this case of hysteria?   I do not think so, for at the time of these two periods of treatment, I had not yet put to myself the question which could be answered only by an exhaustive explanation.   I now think that something else must have developed in the hitherto unchanged etiological relations to provoke an outbreak of the disease precisely in these last years.   I was also struck by the fact that of all the intimate information imparted by the patient, the sexual element, which is more responsible for traumas than anything else, was entirely lacking. Stimulations from these spheres hardly could have vanished without leaving any traumatic trace. What she allowed me to hear was probably an *editio in usum delphini* of her life's history. In her behavior the patient always displayed the most unartificial decency without any prudery. But when I think of the reverse with which she related in the hypnosis the little adventure about the hotel chambermaid, I suspect that this impetuous woman, capable of such strong feelings, must have mastered her sexual needs with no little struggle, and that her effort to suppress all these very strong impulses must have entailed much psychic exhaustion. She once confessed to me that she did not marry again because with her large fortune she could not trust herself to the unselfishness of her suitors, and that had she married, she would have reproached herself with harming the interests of her two children.

One more observation before I close the history of Mrs. von N. Both Breuer and myself knew her quite well and for quite a long time. We used to smile when we compared her character with the portrait of the hysterical psyche as found from the time of antiquity in books and as drawn by physicians. Just as our observation of Mrs. Cecilia M. had taught us that the severest form of hysteria is compatible with the richest and most original endowment—a fact which one gathers almost to the point of evidence from biographies of famous women in history and literature—so in Mrs. Emmy von N. we had a good example for the fact that the development of an irreproachable character and a well directed course of life is not incompatible with hysteria. She was a remarkable woman, whom we have learned to know, whose moral earnestness in the concept of her duties, whose very masculine intelligence and energy, whose high education and love for truth impressed both of us, while her kindly care of her dependents, her inner modesty, and the refinement of her company, stamped her as a most esteemed lady. To call such a woman " degenerate " is to distort this word beyond recognition. One does well to distinguish sharply those who are " predisposed " from those who are " degenerate "; otherwise, one will be forced to admit that mankind owes a great deal of its great accomplishments to the efforts of " degenerate " individuals.

I also admit that I could find nothing in the history of Mrs. von N. that would point to that " psychic inferiority " upon which P. Janet bases the origin of hysteria. According to Janet, the hysterical disposition consists in an abnormal narrowing of the field of consciousness (in consequence of hereditary degeneration), which leads to the neglect of whole series of perceptions, and in serious courses of this development, to the destruction of the ego, and to an organization of secondary personalities. Accordingly, after the subtraction of the hysterically organized psychic groups, the rest of the ego would also be less functionally capable than the normal ego. And as a matter of fact, Janet actually maintains that this ego, which is burdened in all hysterics by psychic stigmata, is condemned to monoideism, and is incapable of the ordinary volitional activity of life. It is my opinion that Janet has here unjustly raised the end-results of the hysterical change of consciousness to the rank of primary conditions of hysteria. This theme is worthy of a more thorough discussion in another place; but such functional inferiority was not observed in Mrs. von N. During the period of her most severe illness she was, and remained, capable of participating in the management of a large industrial undertaking, she never lost sight of the education of her children, and kept up a correspondence with mentally superior persons. In brief, she attended to all her duties so well that no one had any inkling of her illness. I would think, however, that such behavior would result in a palpable amount of psychic overexertion, and could not perhaps be maintained for a long time, and in our case had to lead to an exhaustion or to a secondary " misère psychologique." It is probable that such disturbances of her functional capacity began to make themselves already noticeable when I first saw her, but at all events, there existed a severe hysteria for many years before these symptoms of exhaustion manifested themselves.

Observation III. Miss Lucie R. (Freud)

Towards the end of 1892 a friendly colleague recommended to me a young lady whom he had been treating for chronic recurrent purulent rhinitis. It was later found that the obstinacy of her trouble was caused by a caries of the ethmoid. She finally complained of new symptoms which this experienced physician could no longer refer to local affections. She had lost all perception of smell and was almost constantly bothered by one or two subjective sensations of smell. This she found very irksome. In addition to this she was depressed in spirits, weak, and complained of a heavy head, loss of appetite, and an incapacity for work.

This young lady visited me from time to time during my office hours— she was a governess in the family of a factory superintendent living in the suburbs of Vienna. She was an English lady of rather delicate constitution, anemic, and with the exception of her nasal trouble was in good health. Her first statements concurred with those of her physician. She suffered from mild depression and lassitude, and was tormented by subjective sensations of smell. Of hysterical signs, she showed a quite distinct general analgesia without tactile impairment, the fields of vision showed no narrowing on coarse testing with the hand. The nasal mucous membrane was totally analgesic and reflexless. Tactile sensation was absent, and the perception of this sense organ was abolished for specific as well as for other stimuli, such as ammonia or acetic acid. The purulent nasal catarrh was just then in a period of improvement.

On first attempting to understand this case we felt that subjective sensations of smell must represent recurrent hallucinations interpreting persistent hysterical symptoms, that the mild depression was perhaps the affect belonging to the trauma, and that there must have been an episode during which the present subjective sensations were objective. This episode must have been the trauma, the symbols of which recurred in her memory as sensations of smell. Perhaps it would have been more correct to consider the recurring hallucinations of smell with the accompanying depression as equivalents of hysterical attacks. For the nature of recurrent hallucinations really makes them unsuitable for the rôle of chronic symptoms, which was hardly the question in this rudimentary case. But it was absolutely necessary that the subjective sensations of smell should show a specialization that could correspond to a very definite and real objective origin.

This expectation was soon fulfilled, for on being asked what odor troubled her most she stated that it was an odor of burned pastry. I could then assume that the odor of burned pastry really occurred in the traumatic event. It is quite unusual to select sensations of smell as memory symbols of traumas, but it was quite obvious why these were here selected. She was afflicted with purulent rhinitis, hence the nose and its perceptions were in the foreground of her attention. All I knew about the life of the patient was that she took care of two children whose mother died a few years ago from a grave and acute disease.

As a starting point of the analysis, I decided to use the "odor of burned pastry." I will now relate the history of this analysis. It could have occurred under more favorable conditions, but, as a matter of fact, what should have taken place in one session was extended over a number of them. She could only visit me during my office hours, during which I could devote to her but little of my time. One single conversation had to be extended for over a week as her duties did not permit her to come to me often from such a distance, so that the conversation was frequently broken off and resumed at the next session.

On attempting to hypnotize Miss Lucie R., she did not lapse into the somnambulic state. I, therefore, was obliged to forego somnambulism, and the analysis was made while she was in a state which did not perhaps differ much from the normal.

I feel obliged to express myself more fully about the point of the technique of my procedure. While visiting the Nancy clinics in 1889, I heard Dr. Lièbault, the old master of hypnotism, say "Yes, if we had the means to put everybody into the somnambulic state, hypnotism would then be the most powerful therapeutic agent." In Bernheim's clinic it almost seemed that such an art really existed, and that it could be learned from Bernheim. But as soon as I tried to practice it on my own patients, I noticed that at least my powers were quite limited in this respect. Whenever a patient did not sink into the somnambulic state after one or two attempts, I possessed no means to force him into it. However, the percentage of somnambulists in my experience was far below that claimed by Bernheim.

Thus, I had the choice either to refrain from using the cathartic method in most of the cases suitable for it, or to venture the attempt without somnambulism by using hypnotic influence in light or even doubtful cases. It made no difference of what degree (following the accepted scales of hypnotism) the hypnotism was, which did not correspond to somnambulism, for every line of suggestibility is independent of the other, and nothing prejudices the evocation of catalepsy, automatic movements and similar phenomena, for the purpose of facilitating the awakening of forgotten recollections. I soon relinquished the habit of deciding the degree of hypnotism, as in a great number of cases it incited the patient's resistance, and clouded the confidence which I needed for the more important psychic work. Moreover, in mild grades of hypnotism I soon tired of hearing, after the assurance and command, "You will sleep, sleep now!" such protests as, "But, Doctor, I am not sleeping." I was forced to bring in the very delicate distinction, saying, "I do not mean the usual sleep, I mean the hypnotic—you see, you are hypnotized, you cannot open your eyes"; or, "I really don't want you to sleep." I am convinced that many of my colleagues who use psychotherapy know how to get out of such difficulties more skilfully than I, they can, therefore, act differently. I, however, believe that if through the use of a word one can so frequently become embarrassed, it is better to avoid the word and the embarrassment. Wherever the first attempt did not produce either somnambulism or a degree of hypnotism with pronounced bodily changes, I dropped the hypnosis and demanded only "concentration," I ordered the patient to lie on his back and close his eyes as a means of attaining this "concentration." With little effort I obtained as profound a degree of hypnotism as was possible.

But as I gave up the use of somnambulism, I perhaps deprived myself of that prerequisite without which the cathartic method seemed inapplicable. For the latter is based on the assumption that in the altered state of consciousness the patients have at their disposal recollections and associations which do not apparently exist in their normal conscious state, and that wherever there is no somnambulic broadening of consciousness, it must also be impossible to bring about those causal relations which the patient gives the doctor as something unknown to him, that is, those pathogenic recollections " which are lacking from the memory of the patients in their usual psychic states or only exist in a most condensed state " (preliminary communication).

My memory helped me out of this embarrassment. I myself saw Bernheim demonstrate that the recollections of somnambulism are only manifestly forgotten in the waking state and can be readily reproduced by some urging, accompanied by hand pressure, which is supposed to mark another conscious state. He, for instance, imparted to a somnambulist the negative hallucination that he was no longer present, and then attempted to make himself noticeable to her by the most manifold and inconsiderate attacks, but was unsuccessful. After the patient was awakened, he asked her what he did to her during the time that she thought he was not there. She replied, very much astonished, that she knew nothing, but he did not stop there, he insisted that she would recall everything, and placed his hand on her forehead so that she should recall things, and behold, she finally related all that she did not apparently perceive in the somnambulic state, and about which she ostensibly knew nothing in the waking state.

This astonishing and instructive experiment was my model. I decided to proceed on the supposition that my patients knew everything that was of any pathogenic significance, and that all that was necessary was to force them to impart it. Whenever I reached a point where to my question, " Since when have you had this symptom? ", or " Where does it come from? ", I received the answer, " I really don't know this," I proceeded as follows: I placed my hand on the patient's forehead or took her head between my hands and said, " Through the pressure of my hands it will come into your mind, the moment that I stop the pressure you will see something before you, or something will flash through your mind which you must note, it is that which we are seeking. Well, what have you seen or what came into your mind? ".

On applying this method for the first time (it was not in the case of Miss Lucie R.) I was surprised to find just what I wanted, and I may say that it has since hardly ever failed me; it always showed me how to proceed in my investigations and enabled me to do all such analyses without somnambulism. Gradually, I became so bold that when a patient would answer " I see nothing," or " Nothing came into my mind," I insisted that it was impossible, that he probably had the right thought, but that he did not believe it and repudiated it, that I would repeat the procedure as often as he wished, and that every time he would see the same thing. Indeed, I was always right; the patients had not as yet learned to let their criticism rest. They repudiated the emerging recollection or fancy because they considered it as a useless, intruding disturbance, but after they imparted it, it was always shown that it was the right one. Occasionally, after forcing a communication by pressing the head three or four times I got such an answer as, " Yes, I was aware of it the first time, but did not wish to say it," or, " I hoped that it would not be this."

By this method it was far more laborious to broaden the alleged narrowed consciousness than by investigating in the somnambulic state, but it made me independent of somnambulism and afforded me an insight into the motives which are frequently decisive for the " forgetting " of recollections. I am in a position to assert that this forgetting is often intentional and desired, but it is always only *manifestly* successful.

It appeared to me even more remarkable that apparently long forgotten numbers and dates can be reproduced by a similar process, thus demonstrating an unexpected faithfulness of memory.

The insignificant choice which one has in searching for numbers and dates especially allows us to take to our aid the familiar axiom of the theory of aphasia, namely, that recognition is a lesser accomplishment of memory than spontaneous recollection.

Hence, to a patient who is unable to recall in what year, month, or day a certain event took place, enumerate the years during which it might have occurred as well as the names of the twelve months and the thirty-one days of the month, and assure him that at the right number or name his eyes will open themselves or that he will feel which number is the correct one. In most cases the patients really decide on a definite date and frequently enough (as in the case of Mrs. Cecilia N.) it could be ascertained from existing notes of that time that the date was correctly recognized. At other times and in different patients it was shown from the connection of the recollected facts that the dates thus found were incontestable. A patient, for instance, after a date was found by enumerating for her the dates, remarked, " This is my father's birthday," and added, " Of course, I expected this episode (about which we spoke) because it was my father's birthday."

I can only lightly touch upon this theme. The conclusion which I wish to draw from all these experiences is that the pathogenic important experiences with all their concomitant circumstances are faithfully retained in memory, even where they seem forgotten, as when the patient seems unable to recall them.[30]

[30] As an example of the technique mentioned above, that is, of investigating in a non-somnambulic state or where consciousness is not broadened, I will relate a case which I analyzed recently. I treated a woman of thirty-eight who suffered from an anxiety neurosis (agoraphobia, fear of death, etc.). Like many patients of that type, she had a disinclination to admit that she acquired this disease in her married state and was quite desirous of referring it back to her early youth. She informed me that at the age of seventeen when she was in the street of her small city she had the first attack of vertigo, anxiety, and faintness, and that these attacks recurred at times up to a few years ago when they were replaced by her present disease. I thought that the first attacks of vertigo, in which the anxiety was only blurred, were hysterical, and decided to analyze the same. All she knew was that she had the first attack when she went out to make purchases in the main street of her city.—— " What purchases did you wish to make? "——" Various things, I believe it was for a ball to which I was invited."——" When was the ball to take place? "——" I believe two days later."——" Something must have happened

After this long but unavoidable digression, I now return to the history of Miss Lucie R. As aforesaid, she did not sink into somnambulism when an attempt was made to hypnotize her, but lay calmly in

---

a few days before this which excited you and which made an impression on you."——" But I don't know, it is now twenty-one years."——" That does not matter, you will recall it. I will exert some pressure on your head and when I stop it, you will either think of or see something which I want you to tell me." I went through this procedure, but she remained quiet.——" Well, has nothing come into your mind?"——" I thought of something, but that can have no connection with it."——" Just say it."——" I thought of a young girl who is dead, but she died when I was eighteen, that is, a year later."——" Let us adhere to this. What was the matter with your friend?"——" Her death affected me very much, because I was very friendly with her. A few weeks before another young girl died, which attracted a great deal of attention in our city, but then I was only seventeen years old."——" You see, I told you that the thought obtained under the pressure of the hands can be relied upon. Well, now, can you recall the thought that you had when you became dizzy in the street?"—— " There was no thought, it was vertigo."——" That is quite impossible, such conditions are never without accompanying ideas. I will press your head again and you will think of it. Well, what came to your mind?"——" I thought, ' Now I am the third.' "——" What do you mean?"——" When I became dizzy, I must have thought ' Now I will die like the other two.' "——" That was then the idea, during the attack you thought of your friend, her death must have made a great impression on you."——" Yes, indeed, I recall now that I felt dreadful when I heard of her death, to think that I should go to a ball while she lay dead, but I anticipated so much pleasure at the ball and was so occupied with the invitation that I did not wish to think of this sad event." (Notice here the intentional repression from consciousness which caused the reminiscences of her friend to become pathogenic.)

The attack was now in a measure explained, but I still needed the occasional factor which just then provoked this recollection, and accidentally I formed a happy supposition about it.——" Can you recall through which street you passed at that time?"——" Surely, the main street with its old houses, I can see it now."——" And where did your friend live?"——" In the same street. I had just passed her house and was two houses farther when I was seized with the attack."——" Then it was the house which you passed that recalled your dead friend, and the contrast which you then did not wish to think about, that took possession of you."

Still, I was not satisfied; perhaps there was something else which provoked or strengthened the hysterical disposition in a hitherto normal girl. My suppositions were directed to the menstrual indisposition as an appropriate factor, and I asked, " Do you know when during that month you had your menses?"—— She became indignant: " Do you expect me to know that? I only know that I had them then very rarely and irregularly. When I was seventeen, I only had them once."——" Well, let us enumerate the days, months, etc., so as to find when it occurred."——She decided with certainty on a month and wavered between two days preceding a date which accompanied a fixed holiday.—— " Does that in any way correspond with the time of the ball?"——She answered quietly: " The ball was on this holiday. And now I recall that the only menses which I had had during the year occurred just when I had to go to the ball. It was the first invitation to a ball that I had received."

The combination of the events can now be readily constructed and the mechanism of this hysterical attack readily viewed. To be sure, the result was gained after painstaking labor. It necessitated on my side full confidence in the technique and in the individual leading ideas, in order to reawaken such details of forgotten experiences after twenty-one years in a sceptical and really awakened patient. But then everything coincided.

a degree of mild suggestibility, her eyes constantly closed, the features immobile, the limbs without motion. I asked her whether she remembered on what occasion the smell perception of burned pastry originated.—" Oh, yes, I know it well. It was about two months ago, two days before my birthday. I was with the children (two girls) in the school room playing and teaching them to cook, when a letter just left by the letter-carrier was brought in. From its postmark and handwriting, I recognized it as one sent to me by my mother from Glasgow and I wished to open it and read it. The children then came running over, pulled the letter out of my hand and exclaimed, ' No, you must not read it now, it is probably a congratulatory letter for your birthday and we will keep it for you until then.' While the children were thus playing, there was a sudden diffusion of an intense odor. The children forgot the pastry which they were cooking, and it burned. Since then, I have been troubled by this odor, it is really always present, but is more marked during emotional excitement."

" Do you see this scene distinctly before you ? "—" As clearly as I experienced it."—" What was there in it that so excited you ? "—" I was touched by the affection which the children displayed towards me."—" But weren't they always so affectionate ? "—" Yes, but I just got the letter from my mother."—" I can't understand in what way the affection of the little ones and the letter from the mother contrasted, a thing which you appear to intimate."—" I had the intention of going to my mother and my heart became heavy at the thought of leaving those dear children."—" What was the matter with your mother ? Was she lonesome that she wanted you, or was she sick just then and you expected some news ? "—" No, she is delicate, but not really sick, and has a companion with her."—" Why then were you obliged to leave the children ? "—" This house had become unbearable to me. The housekeeper, the cook, and the French maid seemed to be under the impression that I was too proud for my position. They united in intriguing against me and told the grandfather of the children all sorts of things about me, and when I complained to both gentlemen, I did not receive the support which I expected. I then tendered my resignation to the master (father of the children), but he was very friendly, asking me to reconsider it for two weeks before taking any definite steps. It was while I was in that state of indecision that the incident occurred. I thought that I would leave the house, but have remained."—" Aside from the attachment of the children, is there anything particular which attracts you to them ? "—" Yes, my mother is distantly related to their mother, and when the latter was on her death bed, I promised her to do my utmost to be a mother to them, and this promise I broke when I offered my resignation."

The analysis of the subjective sensation of smell seemed complete. It was once objective and intimately connected with an experience, a small scene, in which contrary affects conflicted, sorrow at forsaking the children, and the mortification which despite all, urged her to this decision. Her mother's letter naturally recalled the motives of this decision because she thought of returning to her mother. The conflict of the affects raised this factor to a trauma and the sensation of smell, which was connected with it, remained as its symbol. The only thing to be explained was the fact that out of all the sensory perceptions of that scene, the perception of smell was selected as the symbol, but I was already prepared to use the chronic nasal affliction as an explanation. On being directly questioned, she stated that just at that time she suffered from a severe coryza and could scarely smell anything, but in her excitement she perceived the odor of burned pastry, it penetrated the organically motivated anosmia.

As plausible as this sounded, it did not satisfy me; there was no acceptable reason why this series of excitement and this conflict of affects should have led to hysteria. Why did it not remain on a normal psychological basis? In other words, what justified the conversion under discussion? Why did she not recall the scenes themselves instead of the sensations connected with them which she preferred as symbols for her recollection? Such questions might seem superfluous and irrelevant when dealing with old hysterics in whom the mechanism of conversion is habitual, but this girl acquired hysteria for the first time through this trauma, or at least through this slight distress.

From the analysis of similar cases I already knew that in the process of hysterical development, one psychic determinant is indispensable; namely, that some idea must *intentionally be repressed from consciousness* and excluded from associative elaboration.

In this intentional repression I also find the reason for the conversion of the sum of excitement, be it partial or total. The sum of excitement which is not to enter into psychic association more readily finds the wrong road to bodily innervation. The reason for the repression itself could only be a disagreeable feeling, the incompatibility of one of the repressible ideas with the ruling ideational-mass of the ego. The repressed idea then avenges itself by becoming pathogenic.

From this I concluded that Miss Lucie R. had lapsed into that moment of hysterical conversion, which must have been one of the prerequisites of that trauma which she intentionally wished to leave in the dark, and which she took pains to forget. On considering her attachment for the children and her sensitiveness towards the other persons of the household, there remained but one interpretation which I was bold enough to impart to her. I told her that I did not believe that all these things were simply due to her affection for the children, but that I thought that she was rather in love with her master, perhaps unwittingly, that she really nurtured the hope of taking the place of the mother, and it was for that reason that she became so sensitive towards the servants with whom she had lived peacefully for years. She feared lest they would notice something of her hope and scoff at her.

She answered in her laconic manner: "Yes, I believe it is so."— "But if you knew that you were in love with the master, why did you not tell me so? "—" But I did not know it, or rather, I did not wish to know it. I wished to crowd it out of my mind, never to think of it, and of late I have been successful." [31]

" Why did you not wish to admit it to yourself? Were you ashamed because you loved a man? "—" Oh, no, I am not unreasonably prudish; one is certainly not responsible for one's own feelings. I only felt chagrined because it was my employer in whose service I was and in whose house I lived, and toward whom I could not feel as independent as towards another. What is more, I am a poor girl and he is a rich man of a prominent family, and if anybody should have had any inkling about my feelings, they would have ridiculed me."

After this I encountered no resistances in elucidating the origin of this affection. She told me that the first years of her life in that house were passed uneventfully. She fulfilled her duties without thinking about unrealizable wishes. One day, however, the serious and very busy, and hitherto very reserved, master, engaged her in conversation about the exigencies of rearing the children. He became milder and more cordial than usual, he told her how much he counted on her in the bringing up of his orphaned children, and looked at her rather peculiarily. It was in this moment that she began to love him, and gladly occupied herself with the pleasing hopes which she conceived during that conversation. However, as this was not followed by anything else, and despite her waiting and persevering no other confidential heart-to-heart talk followed, she decided to crowd it out of her mind. She quite agreed with me that the look which she noticed during the conversation was probably intended for the memory of his deceased wife. She was also perfectly convinced that her love was hopeless.

After this conversation I expected a decided change in her condition, but for a time it did not take place. She continued depressed and moody—a course of hydrotherapy which I prescribed for her at the same time refreshed her somewhat in the morning. The odor of burned pastry did not entirely disappear; though it became rarer and feebler, it appeared, as she said, only when she was very much excited.

The continuation of this memory symbol led me to believe that besides the principal scene it also represented many smaller side traumas and

---

[31] Another and better description of this peculiar state in which one knows something and at the same time does not know it, I could never obtain. It can apparently be understood only if one has found himself in such a state. I have at my disposal a very striking recollection of this kind which I can vividly see. If I make the effort to recall what passed through my mind at that time my output seems very poor. I saw at that time something which was not at all appropriate to my expectations, and I was not in the least diverted from my definite purpose by what I saw when, as a matter of fact, this perception should have deflected me from my purpose. I did not become conscious of this contradiction nor did I notice anything of the affect of the repulsion which was undoubtedly responsible for the fact that this perception did not attain any psychic validity. I was struck with that blindness in seeing eyes, which one admires so much in mothers towards their daughters, in husbands towards their wives, and in rulers towards their favorites.

I, therefore, investigated everything that might have been in any way connected with the scene of the burned pastry. We thus passed through the theme of family friction, the behavior of the grandfather and others, and with that the sensation of burned odor gradually disappeared. Just then there was a lengthy interruption occasioned by a new nasal affliction, which led to the discovery of the caries of the ethmoid.

On her return, she informed me that she received many Christmas presents from both gentlemen as well as from the household servants, as if they were trying to appease her and wipe away the recollection of the conflicts of the last months. These frank advances made no impression on her.

On questioning her on another occasion about the odor of burned pastry, she stated that it had entirely disappeared, but instead she was now bothered by another and similar odor like the smoke of a cigar. This odor really existed before; it was only concealed by the odor of the pastry, but now it appeared as such.

I was not very much pleased with the success of my treatment. What occurred here is what a mere symptomatic treatment is generally blamed for, namely, that it removes one symptom only to make room for another. Nevertheless, I immediately set forth to remove this new memory symbol by analysis.

This time I did not know whence this subjective sensation of smell originated, nor on what important occasion it was objective. On being questioned, she said, " They constantly smoke at home, I really don't know whether the smell which I feel has any particular significance." I then proposed that she should try to recall things under the pressure of my hands. I have already mentioned that her recollections were plastically vivid, that she was of the " visual type." Indeed, under the pressure of my hands a picture came into her mind—at first, only slowly and fragmentarily. It was the dining room in which she waited with the children for the arrival of the gentlemen from the factory for dinner.— " Now we are all at the table, the gentlemen, the French maid, the housekeeper, the children and I. It is the same as usual."—" Just keep on looking at that picture. It will soon become developed and specialized."—" Yes, there is a guest, the chief accountant, an old gentleman, who loves the children like his own grandchildren, but he dines with us so frequently that it is nothing unusual."—" Just have patience, keep on looking at the picture, something will certainly happen."—" Nothing happens. We leave the table, the children take leave and go with us to the second floor as usual."—" Well? "—" There really is something unusual, I now recognize the scene. As the children leave, the chief accountant attempts to kiss them, but my master jumps up and shouts at him, ' Don't kiss the children! ' I then experienced a stitch in the heart, and as the gentlemen were smoking, this odor remained in my memory."

This, therefore, was the second, deeper seated scene, which acted as a trauma, and left the memory symbol. But why was this scene so effective? I then asked her which scene happened first, this one or the one of the burned pastry—" The last scene happened first by almost two months."—" Why did you feel the stitch at the father's interference? The reproof was not meant for you."—" It was really not right to rebuke an old man in such a manner, who was a dear friend and a guest; it could have been said more clamly."—" Then you were really affected by your master's impetuosity? Were you perhaps ashamed of him, or did you think, ' If he could become so impetuous towards an old friend and guest over such a trifle, how would he act towards me if I were his wife?' "—" No, that is not it."—" But still it was about his impetuosity?"—" Yes, about the kissing of the children, he never liked that." Under the pressure of my hands there emerged a still older scene, which was the real effective trauma and which bestowed on the scene of the chief accountant the traumatic effectivity.

A few months before a lady friend visited the house, and on leaving kissed both children on the lips. The father, who was present, controlled himself and said nothing to the lady, but when she left, he was very angry at the unfortunate governess. He said that he held her responsible for this kissing; that it was her duty not to tolerate it; that she was neglecting her duties in allowing such things, and that if it ever happened again, he would entrust the education of his children to someone else. This occurred while she believed herself loved, and waited for a repetition of that serious and friendly talk. This episode shattered all her hopes. She thought: " If he can upbraid and threaten me on account of such a trifle, of which I am entirely innocent, I must have been mistaken, he never entertained any tenderer feelings towards me, else he would have been more considerate."—It was evidently this painful scene that came to her as the father reprimanded the chief accountant for attempting to kiss the children.

On being visited by Miss Lucie R. two days after the last analysis, I had to ask her what pleasant things happened to her. She looked as though transformed, she smiled, and held her head aloft. For a moment I thought that after all I probably mistook the situations, and that the governess of the children had now become the bride of her master. But she soon dissipated all my suppositions by saying, " Nothing new has happened. You really do not know me. You have always seen me while I was sick and depressed. Usually I am always cheerful. On awaking yesterday morning my burden was gone and since then I have felt well."—" What do you think of your chances in the house?"— " I am perfectly clear about that. I know that I have none, and I am not going to be unhappy about it."—" Will you now be able to get along with the others in the house?"—" I believe so, because most of the trouble was due to my sensitiveness."—" Do you still love the master?"—" Certainly I love him, but that does not bother me much. One can think and feel as one wishes."

I now examined her nose and found that the pain and the reflex sensations had almost completely reappeared. She could distinguish odors, but she was uncertain when they were very intense. What part the nasal trouble played in the anosmia, I must leave undecided.

The whole treatment extended over a period of nine weeks. Four months later I accidentally met the patient at one of our summer resorts—she was cheerful and stated that her health continued to be good.

Epicrisis

I would not like to underestimate the aforesaid case even though it only represents a minor and light hysteria with but few symptoms. On the contrary, it seems to me instructive that even such a slight neurotic affliction should require so many psychic determinants, and on more exhaustive consideration of this history, I am tempted to put it down as an illustration of that form of hysteria which even persons not burdened by heredity may acquire, if they have the *suitable* experiences for it. It should be well noted that I do not speak of a hysteria which may be independent of all predisposition; such form probably does not exist, but we speak of such a predisposition only after the person became hysterical, as nothing pointed to it before. A neuropathic disposition as commonly understood is something different. It is determined even before the disease by a number of hereditary burdens, or by a sum of individual psychic abnormalities. As far as I know, none of these two factors could be demonstrated in the case of Miss Lucie R. Her hysteria may, therefore, be called acquired, and by and large presupposes nothing more than a very marked susceptibility to acquire hysteria, a characteristic about which we know scarcely anything. In such cases the greatest emphasis lies in the nature of the trauma and naturally in connection with the reaction of the person to the trauma. It is an indispensable condition for the acquisition of hysteria, that there should arise a relation of incompatibility between the ego and an idea that comes in contact with it. I hope to be able to show in another place how a variety of neurotic disturbances originate from the different procedures which the " ego " pursues in order to free itself from that incompatibility. The hysterical form of defense, for which a special adaptation is required, consists in a conversion of the excitement into physical innervation. The gain brought about by this process consists in the crowding out of the unbearable idea from the ego consciousness, which then contains instead the physical reminiscences produced by conversion—in our case the subjective sensation of smell—and suffers from the affect which more or less distinctly connects itself with these reminiscences. The situation thus produced can no longer be changed, for the resistance which would have striven for the adjustment of the affect was eliminated through repression and conversion. Thus, the mechanism producing hysteria corresponds on the one hand to an act of moral faint-heartedness, on the other hand it presents itself as a protective process at the command of the ego. There are many cases in which it must be admitted that the defense against the increased excitement through the production of hysteria may actually have been most expedient, but more frequently one will naturally come to the conclusion that a greater measure of moral courage would have been of more advantage to the individual.

Accordingly, the real traumatic moment is that in which the conflict thrusts itself upon the ego and the latter decides to banish the incompatible idea. Such banishment does not annihilate the opposing idea, but merely crowds it into the unconscious. When this process occurs for the first time, it forms a nucleus, or a point of crystallization for the formation of a new psychic group separated from the ego, around which, in the course of time, everything collects which is in accord with the opposing idea. The splitting of consciousness in such cases of acquired hysteria is thus desired and intentional, and is often initiated by at least one arbitrary act. But as a matter of fact, something different happens than the individual expects, he would like to eliminate an idea as though it never came to pass, but he only succeeds in isolating it psychically.

The traumatic factor in the history of our patient corresponds to the scene created by her master on account of the kissing of the children. For the time being this scene remained without any palpable effects, perhaps it initiated the depression and sensitiveness, but I leave this open; the hysterical symptoms, however, commenced later in moments which can be designated as "auxiliary," and which may be characterized by the fact that in them there was a simultaneous inter-fusion of both separated groups just as in the broadened somnambulic consciousness. The first of these factors in which the conversion took place in Miss Lucie R. was the scene at the table when the chief accountant attempted to kiss the children. The traumatic memory helped along, and she acted as though she had not entirely banished her attachment for her master. In other cases we find that these different factors coalesce and the conversion occurs directly under the influence of the trauma.

The second auxiliary factor repeated almost precisely the mechanism of the first. A strong impression transitorily reëstablished the unity of consciousness, and the conversion took the same route that was opened to it the first time. It is interesting to note that the symptom which occurred second concealed the first so that the latter could not be distinctly perceived until the former was eliminated. The reversal of the succession of events, to which also the analysis had to be adapted seemed quite remarkable. In a whole series of cases I found that the symptoms which came later covered the first, and only the last thing in the analysis contained the key to the whole.

The therapy here consisted in forcing the union of the dissociated psychic groups with the ego consciousness. It is remarkable that the success did not run parallel with the accomplished work, the cure resulted suddenly only after the last part was accomplished.

OBSERVATION IV. MISS KATHARINA (FREUD)

During the vacation of 189– I made an excursion to the High Tauern (Eastern Alps) in order to forget medicine for a while, and especially the neuroses. I almost succeeded when one day I deviated from the main street to climb an out of the way mountain, which was famous for a beautiful view and for its well kept inn. After exhaustive wandering, I reached the top, and after refreshment and rest, I sat there sunk in the reflection of an enchanting view. I was so forgetful of myself that at first I was loath to refer to myself the question: " Is the gentleman a doctor?" The question was, however, directed to me by a girl of about 18 years. who had displayed a sulky expression while serving my meal, and who was addressed by the hostess as " Katharina." Judging by her dress and bearing, she could not be a servant, but most probably was a daughter or a relative of the hostess.

Having regained my senses, I said " Yes, I am a doctor. How do you know that?"

" You registered in the guestbook, and then I thought if the doctor now had a little time . . ., you see I am nervous, and I have already consulted a doctor in L. . . . , who also gave me something, but it has not done me any good."

Well, I was back in the midst of neuroses, for it could hardly be anything else in this large and robust girl with the morose features. It interested me that neuroses should flourish so well at a height of over 2,000 meters, and I, therefore, continued questioning her.

The conversation which then developed between us I shall now reproduce as it impressed itself upon my memory. I shall also endeavor to reproduce her peculiar expressions.

" What are you complaining of?"

" I have so much difficulty in breathing. Not always, but sometimes it catches me so that I believe I am choking."

At first that did not sound like nervousness, but it soon became probable that it might well be a substitutive designation for an anxiety attack. Out of the whole complex of sensations she stressed unduly one of the factors, the difficulty of breathing.

" Sit down and describe to me how such a state of ' difficulty in breathing ' feels."

" It suddenly comes upon me. There is first a pressure on my eyes. My head becomes so heavy and it hums so that I can hardly bear it, and then I become so dizzy that I believe I am falling, and then my chest begins to press together so that I cannot get my breath."

" And do you feel nothing in the throat? "

" The throat becomes laced together as if I choked."

" And you feel nothing else in the head? "

" Yes, it hammers as if it would split."

" Yes, and doesn't that frighten you? "

" I always feel, ' Now, I must die,' and I am otherwise courageous, I go everywhere alone, into the cellar and down over the whole mountain, but on the day that I have this attack, I do not trust myself anywhere. I always believe that someone stands behind me and suddenly grabs me."

It was really an anxiety attack, and to be sure, initiated by the signs of an hysterical aura, or better expressed, it was an hysterical attack, the content of which was anxiety. Might it not have an additional content?

" When you have the attack, do you always think of the same thing, or do you see something before you? "

Perhaps we have here found a way by which we can advance quickly to the nucleus of the situation.

" Do you recognize the face? I mean is it a face which you have really once seen? "

" No."

" Do you know how you got these attacks? "

" No."

" When did you first get them? "

" The first time two years ago when I was still with my aunt on the other mountain. She had an inn there before; we have now been here for a year and a half, but they always come again."

Should I attempt an analysis here? To be sure, I did not dare to transplant hypnosis to this height, but perhaps we will succeed with simple conversation. I must have been fortunate in my guessing. I have often seen anxiety in young girls as a result of fear which strikes the virginal mind when the world of sexuality reveals itself to it for the first time.[32]

---

[32] I shall quote here the case where I first recognized this causal relation. I treated a young woman for a complicated neurosis, who repeatedly refused to admit that she contracted her anxiety in her married life. She argued that already as a girl she had suffered attacks of anxiety which ended with fainting.

I, therefore, said: "If you do not know it, I will tell you what I believe is the cause of your attacks. At that time, two years ago, you had seen or heard something which embarrassed you much, something that you would rather not have seen."

Thereupon, she exclaimed: "Heavens, yes, I caught my uncle with my cousin Francisca!"

"What is the story about this girl? Will you tell it to me?"

"One can tell everything to a doctor. You may know, therefore, that my uncle, the husband of my aunt, whom you saw, at that time kept an inn with my aunt on the mountain. Now they are divorced and it is my fault that they are divorced, because through me it became known that he had something to do with Francisca."

"Yes, how did you come to discover this?"

"It was this way. Two years ago, two gentlemen once came up the mountain and wanted to get something to eat. My aunt was not at home and Francisca, who always did the cooking, could not be found anywhere. Nor could we find my uncle. We looked for them everywhere until the boy, Alois, my counsin, said "In the end Francisca will be found with father." Then we both laughed, but we thought nothing bad thereby. We went to the room where my uncle lived and that was locked. That seemed peculiar. Then Alois said: "On the path there is a window from which you can look into the room. We got on the path, but Alois would not go to the window. He said he was afraid. Then, I said 'You stupid boy; I will go. I am not afraid of anything.' Nor did I think of anything bad. I looked in, the room was quite dark, but then I saw my uncle and Francisca, and he was lying on her."

"Well?"

"I immediately left the window and leaned against the wall and got the difficulty in breathing which I have had since then. My senses left me. My eyes closed tight and my head hammered and hummed."

"Did you tell it to your aunt immediately on the same day?"

"Oh, no, I said nothing."

"But why were you so frightened when you found them both together? Did you understand anything? Did you know what had happened?"

"Oh, no. At that time I understood nothing. I was only sixteen years old. I do not know what frightened me."

"Fräulien Katharina, if you could now recall what went through your mind at the time that you got the first attack, what you thought at that time, it would help you."

But I remained firm in my conviction. When we became better acquainted, she one day suddenly said, "Now, I will also tell you whence my anxiety states came as a young girl. At that time I slept in a room next to my parents; the door was open and a night light was burning on the table. There I saw a number of times how my father went into my mother's bed and I heard something which excited me very much. Thereupon, I got my attacks."

" Yes, if I could, but I was so frightened that I forgot everything."
(Translated in the language of our "preliminary communication,"
it means: The affect itself created the hypnoid state, the products of
which remained in the ego consciousness without any associative
relations.)

" Tell me, Katharina, is the head that you always see with the difficulty of breathing the head of Francisca, as you saw it then at
that time?"

" Oh, no, hers is not so horrible, and moreover, it is a man's head."

" Or, perhaps, it is your uncle's?"

" But, I did not even see his face distinctly. It was too dark in
the room, and why should he at that time have had such a terrifying
face?"

" You are right." (The leads suddenly seemed closed. Perhaps
something will be found on continuing the story.)

" And what happened later?"

" Well, the two of them must have heard some noise. They soon
came out. I felt quite bad the whole time. I always had to think
about it. Then, two days later it was Sunday when there was a lot
to do and I worked the whole day, and Monday morning I again had
dizziness and vomiting and remained in bed, and for three days I
vomited continually."

We have often compared the hysterical symptomatology to picture
writing, the reading of which we understood only after we discovered
some bi-lingual cases. According to this alphabet, vomiting signified
disgust. I, therefore, said to her: " If you vomited three days later,
I believe you felt disgust when you looked into the room."

" Yes, I surely was disgusted," she said reflectingly, " But, at what?"

" Perhaps you saw something naked. How were these two persons
in the room?"

" It was too dark to see anything and both of them had their clothes
on. Yes, if I only knew at what I was disgusted at that time."

Nor did I know, but I requested her to keep on relating what came
to her mind with the assured expectation that something would come
to her mind, which I needed for the explanation of the case.

She then related that she finally told the aunt of her discovery because
she found that the latter had changed and she imagined that there was
some secret behind it; thereupon, there ensued angry scenes between the
uncle and the aunt, and the children heard things that opened their eyes
to some things, which they had better not have heard. Finally, the
aunt decided to leave the uncle with Francisca, who, meanwhile had
become pregnant, and departed with the children and her niece to take
over the management of another inn. But then to my astonishment,
she dropped this thread and began to relate two series of older stories,
which went back to two or three years behind the traumatic event.
The first series contained occasions during which the same uncle had
made sexual advances to her when she was only 14 years old. She

told how she once made a tour with him in the winter into the valley, when they stayed overnight at an inn. He remained in the inn drinking and playing cards, while she, becoming sleepy, retired early into the room which they occupied together. She did not sleep soundly when he came up, but then she fell asleep again only to awake suddenly and "feel his body" in bed. She jumped up, reproached him: "What are you up to, uncle? Why don't you remain in your bed?" He attempted to joke about it, and said, "Go, you stupid goose, be quiet. You don't even know how good this is." "I don't want anything good from you. You don't even let me sleep." She remained standing at the door, ready to flee out to the path, until he stopped and fell asleep. Then, she returned to bed and slept until morning. From the mode of her defense it would seem that she did not recognize the attack as sexual. Being asked whether she knew what he was up to, she answered "At that time, no," but it became clear to her much later. She was irritated because she was disturbed in her sleep, and because she had never heard of such things.

I had to report this event in detail because it has great importance for everything that is to follow.—She then related other experiences of later times, how she had to defend herself against him in an inn when he was very drunk, etc. But to my question whether she had experienced on these occasions anything similar to the difficulty in breathing which happened later, she answered with certainty that she had experienced the pressure on the eyes and in the chest on each occasion, but not as strongly as at the scene of the discovery.

Immediately after the conclusion of this series of memories she began to relate a second series, which treated of events wherein her attention was called to something between her uncle and Francisca. She related how she and the whole family once spent a night in their clothing on a haystack. She was awakened, as a result of some noise, and she believed that she observed that the uncle, who was lying between her and Francisca, moved away and Francisca changed her position. She spoke of how at another time she spent the night in the village, N. She and her uncle were in one room and Francisca next door to them. During the night she suddenly awoke and saw a long, white form at the door in the act of turning the door knob:

"Heavens, uncle, is that you? What are you doing at the door?"—"Be quiet, I am only looking for something."—"But, you can only go out by the other door."—"I just made a mistake," etc.

I asked her whether at that time she had any suspicions. "No, I thought nothing about it. It struck me as peculiar, but I made nothing out of it."—Whether she had anxiety on this occasion?—She believed yes, but at the present time she was not so sure of it.

After she finished these two series of stories, she stopped. She looked as if changed. The sulky, suffering features were vivified, her look was cheerful, she felt lighter and elated. Meanwhile, the understanding of her case dawned upon me; what she related last, seemingly without any plan, explains excellently her behavior at the scene of the discovery. At that time she carried with her two series of experiences which she recalled, which she did not understand, and which did not help her in drawing any conclusion. At the sight of the pair in the act of coitus, she immediately connected the new impression with these two series of reminiscences, she began to understand and simultaneously to reject. There then followed a short period of elaboration, "the incubation," and thereupon came the conversion symptoms, the vomiting as a substitute for the moral and physical disgust. With this the riddle was solved. She was not disgusted at the sight of the two, but at a reminiscence which this sight awakened in her and explained everything. This could only be the memory of the nightly attack when she "felt her uncle's body."

After this confession was finished, I said to her: "Now I know what you thought at the time that you looked into the room. You thought ' Now, he does with her what he wished to do with me on that night and the other time.' It disgusted you, because you recalled the feeling how you awakened in the night and felt his body."

She answered: "It is very probable that this disgusted me and that I thought of it at that time."

"Just tell me exactly now that you are a grown up girl and know everything."

"Yes, now certainly."

"Tell me exactly what did you really feel that night of his body?" But she gave me no definite answer. She smiled perplexed, as if convinced, and like one who must admit that as we have now come to the bottom of the thing, there is nothing more to be said about it. I can imagine the kind of tactile sensation which she later learned to interpret. Her features, too, seemed to express that she agreed with my assumption. But I could not penetrate any deeper into her. At all events, I owe her gratitude for the fact that it was so much easier to talk with her than with the prudish ladies of my city practice, for whom all the *naturalia* are *turpia*.

With this the case would be explained, but wait, whence came the hallucination of the head, which returned in the attack and which inspired her with fear? I asked her about it. As if this conversation had also broadened her understanding, she answered promptly: "Yes, I know that now. The head is the head of my uncle. I recognize it now, but I did not at the time. Later, when all the quarrels were taking place, the uncle expressed a senseless rage against me. He always said that it was all my fault. If I had not blabbered, it would have never come to a divorce. He always threatened that he would do something to me, and when he saw me from a distance, his face became tense with rage and he ran at me with a raised hand. I always ran away from him and always had the greatest anxiety that he might grab me without my seeing him. The face which I then always saw was his face in a rage."

This information reminded me of the fact that the first symptom of the hysteria, the vomiting, had disappeared, but that the anxiety attack remained and was filled with a new content. Accordingly, we dealt with an hysteria, a great part of which was abreacted. For soon thereafter, she actually informed her aunt of her discovery.

Have you also related the other stories to your aunt, how he appeared to you?

"Yes, not right away, but later when it was already a question of divorce. My aunt then said: 'We will keep that to ourselves. If he makes any difficulties at the divorce, then we will bring it up.'"

I can understand that from that last period the exciting scenes in the house piled up, when her ailment ceased to awaken her aunt's interest, who was now entirely taken up with her quarrel—that from exactly that time of accumulation and retention, there remained the memory symbol.

I hope that our conversation has done some good to this girl, whose sexual sensibilities were so prematurely traumatized. I did not see her again.

Epicrisis

I have no objection to offer should anyone consider the history of the solution of this case of hysteria as given in this case history more as one of guessing than analysis. To be sure, the patient accepted as probable everything I interpolated into her report, but she was, nevertheless, in no position to recognize it as something that she had experienced. It is my opinion that such recognition on her part would have necessitated the use of hypnotism. If I assume that I had guessed correctly and now attempted to reduce this case to the scheme of an acquired hysteria, as shown in Case History III; it is obvious that we should compare the two series of erotic experiences with traumatic factors, the scene of the discovery of the pair, with an auxiliary factor. The similarity lies in the fact that in the first there originated a content of consciousness, which, having been excluded from the mental activity of the ego, remained preserved, while in the latter scene a new impression forced an associative connection of this separately existing group with the ego. On the other hand, there are also deviations, which cannot be disregarded. The reason for the isolation is not the will of the ego as in Case III, but rather the ignorance of the ego, which does not yet know how to cope with sexual experiences. The case of Katharina is typical in this respect, for in every hysteria based on sexual traumas one finds that experiences from a fore-sexual period, which produced no effect on the child, later, as memories, receive traumatic force, when the young girl or the woman gains understanding of her sexual life. The splitting-off of psychic groups is, as it were, a normal process in the development of adolescence, and it is quite comprehensible that their later reception into the ego offers advantageous occasions for psychic disturbances. Moreover, I wish to give expression in this place to a doubt: whether the splitting of consciousness through ignorance is really different from the one through conscious rejection, and whether adolescents do not frequently possess more sexual knowledge than one supposes or than they, themselves, believe.

A further deviation in the psychic mechanism of this case lies in the fact that the scene of the discovery, which we have designated as " auxiliary," deserves also the name, " traumatic." It exerted influences through its own content, and not just through the awakening of the preceding traumatic experience; it unites the characters of an " auxiliary " and a " traumatic " factor. However, I see no reason for giving up in this coincidence an abstract separation, which in other cases corresponds also to a temporal separation. Another peculiarity of Katharina's case, which was, however, known for some time, is shown in the fact that in the conversion the production of the hysterical phenomena did not immediately follow the trauma, but only after an interval of incubation. Charcot had a predilection for calling this interval the " period of psychic elaboration."

The anxiety which Katharina showed in her attacks was hysterical, *i.e.,* it was a reproduction of that anxiety, which appeared at each of the sexual traumas. I am also desisting here from elucidating the process which I have recognized regularly and pertinently in an unusually large number of cases; namely, that the mere presentiment of sexual relations in virginal persons, evokes an affect of anxiety.

Observation V. Miss Elisabeth v. R. (Freud)

In the fall of 1892 I was requested by a friendly colleague to examine a young lady who had been suffering from pains in her legs for over two years, so that she walked badly. He also added to his request that he had diagnosed the case as hysteria, though none of the usual symptoms of the neurosis could be found. He stated that he knew very little of the family, but that the last few years had brought them much misfortune and little pleasure. First the patient's father died, then the mother underwent a serious operation on her eyes, and soon thereafter a married sister succumbed to a chronic cardiac affection following childbirth. Our patient had taken an active part in all the afflictions, especially in the nursing of the sick.

I made no further progress in the case after I had seen the twenty-four year old patient for the first time. She seemed intelligent and psychically normal, and bore her affliction with a cheerful mien, thus vividly recalling the " belle indifference " of hysterics. She walked with the upper part of her body bent forward, but without any support; her walk did not correspond to any known pathological gait, and it was in no way strikingly bad. She complained only of severe pains and of early fatigue in walking as well as standing, so that after a brief period she had to seek rest in which the pains diminished, but by no means disappeared. The pain was of an indefinite nature—one could assume it to be a painful fatigue. The seat of the pain was quite extensive, but indefinitely circumscribed on the superficial surface of the right thigh. It was from this area that the pains radiated and were of the greatest intensity. Here, too, the skin and muscles were especially sensitive to pressure and pinching, while needle pricks were rather indifferently perceived. The same hyperalgesia of the skin and muscles was demonstrable not only in this area, but over almost the entire surface of both legs. The muscles were perhaps more painful than the skin, but both kinds of pains were unmistakably most pronounced over the thighs. The motor power of the legs was not diminished, the reflexes were of average intensity, and as all other symptoms were lacking, there was no basis for the assumption of a serious organic affection. The disease developed gradually during two years and changed considerably in its intensity.

I did not find it easy to determine the diagnosis, but for two reasons I concluded to agree with my colleague. First, because it was rather strange that such a highly intelligent patient should not be able to give anything definite about the character of her pains. A patient suffering from an organic pain, if it is not accompanied by any nervousness, will be able to describe it definitely and calmly; it may perhaps be lancinating, appear at certain intervals, and extend from this to that location, or in his opinion it may be evoked by this or that influence. The neurasthenic [33] in describing his pain gives the impression as being occupied with some difficult mental problem, something far beyond his powers. His features are tense and distorted as though under the domination of a painful affect, his voice becomes shriller, he struggles for expression, he rejects all designations that the physician makes for his pains, even though they are undoubtedly afterwards found to be correct. He is ostensibly of the opinion that language is too poor to give expression to his feelings. These sensations are something unique, they never existed before, so that they cannot be exhaustively described. It is for this reason that he never tires of constantly adding new details, and when he has to stop, he is distinctly controlled by the impression that he was unsuccessful in making himself understood to the physician. All this is due to the fact that his pains absorb his whole attention. In the case of Miss v. R. we had just the opposite behavior and we had to conclude from this that she attributed sufficient significance to the pain, but that her attention was concentrated

[33] A hypochondriac afflicted with anxiety neurosis.

on something else of which the pains were only the accompanying phenomena, perhaps on thoughts and sensations which were connected with pain.

A still greater determination for the conception of the pain must, however, be found in a second factor. If we irritate a painful area in a patient suffering from an organic disease or neurasthenia, his physiognomy will show a definite expression of discomfort or of physical pain, the patient winces, refuses to be examined, and assumes a defensive attitude. But if anyone pinched or pressed Miss v. R.'s hyperalgesic skin or muscles of her legs, her face assumed a peculiar expression approaching nearer pleasure than pain, she cried out and—I had to think of a perhaps pleasurable tickling—her face reddened, she threw her head backward, closed her eyes, and her body bent backward; all this was not very distinct, but sufficiently marked so that it could only agree with the conception that her affliction was a hysteria and that the irritation touched a hysterogenic zone.

Her mien was not adequate to the pain, which the pinching of the muscles and skin were supposed to excite. It probably harmonized better with the contents of the thoughts which were behind the pain and which were evoked in the patient through a stimulation of those parts of the body associated with them. I have repeatedly observed similar significant expression from stimulation of hyperalgesic zones in unmistakable cases of hysteria. The other gestures evidently corresponded to the slightest suggestion of an hysterical attack.

We could not at that time find any explanation for the unusual localization of the hysterogenic zone. That the hyperalgesia chiefly concerned the muscles, gave material for reflection. The most frequent affliction which could produce diffuse and local pressure sensitiveness of the muscles is rheumatic infiltration, or the common chronic muscular rheumatism, concerning which aptitude to mask nervous ailments I have spoken. The consistency of the painful muscles in Miss v. R. did not contradict this assumption, as there were many hard cords in the muscle masses, which seemed to be especially sensitive. There was probably also an organic change in the muscles, in the assumed sense, upon which the neurosis leaned, and the significance of which was markedly exaggerated by the neurosis.

The therapeutic procedure was, therefore, based on the assumption of a mixed affection. We recommended systematic massage and faradization of the sensitive muscles regardless of the pain it produced, and in order to remain in contact with the patient, I treated her legs by means of strong Franklin sparks. To her question whether she should force herself to walk, we answered decidedly in the affirmative.

We thus attained a slight improvement. She particularly liked the painful shocks of the " influence machine," and the stronger they were, the more they seemed to remove her pains. My colleague, meanwhile, prepared the soil for the psychic treatment, and when after four weeks of this sham treatment, I proposed it and explained to the patient the procedures and its effects, I found a ready understanding and only a slight resistance.

The work which I then began, turned out to be the most arduous undertaking that ever fell to my lot, and the difficulty of giving an account of this work ranks well with the obstacles that had to be overcome. For a long time, too, I did not understand the connection between the history of the disease and the affliction, which should really have been caused and determined by this series of events.

When one undertakes a cathartic treatment, he at first asks himself whether the patient understands the origin and cause of her suffering. If that is so, one does not need any special technique to cause her to reproduce the history of her ailment. The interest shown in her, the understanding which we foreshadow, the hope of recovery extended to her, all these induce the patient to give up her secrets. In the case of Miss Elisabeth, it seemed probable right from the very beginning that she was conscious of the reasons for her suffering, that she had only a secret but no foreign body in consciousness. On looking at her one had to think of the poet's words, " That mask indicates a hidden meaning." [34]

At first I could, therefore, dispense with hypnosis, reserving it, however, for future use should conditions arise in the course of the confession for which explanation the memory would not suffice. Thus, in this first complete analysis of an hysteria which I had undertaken I attained a process of treatment which I later raised to a method and intentionally used as a process of clearing stratum by stratum the pathogenic psychic material, which we were pleased to compare with the technique of excavating a buried city. At first I let the patient relate what was known to her, paying careful attention wherever a connection remained enigmatical, or where a link in the chain of causation seemed to be lacking. Later, I penetrated into the deeper strata of memory by using for those locations hypnotic investigations or a similar technique. The presupposition of the whole work was naturally based on the expectation that a perfect and sufficient determination could be demonstrated. The methods of the deeper investigation will soon be discussed.

The history which Miss Elisabeth gave was quite dull and was woven of manifold painful experiences. During this recital she was not in a hypnotic state; I merely asked her to lie down and keep her eyes closed. I, however, made no objection if from time to time she opened her eyes, changed her position, or sat up. Whenever she entered more deeply into a part of her history, she seemed to lapse spontaneously into a condition resembling a hypnotic state. She then remained motionless and kept her eyes firmly closed.

I shall now reproduce the results of the most superficial stratum of her memory. As the youngest of three daughters she spent her youth with her parents, to whom she was devotedly attached, on their estate in Hungary. Her mother's health was frequently disturbed by an affliction of the eyes, as well as by a nervous ailment. It thus happened that she

---

[34] It will be shown that I was, nevertheless, mistaken.

became especially and devotedly attached to her jovial and broadminded father, who was wont to say that his daughter took the place of both a son and friend with whom he could exchange thoughts. As much as the girl gained in mental stimulation in consequence of this intercourse, it did not escape the father that her psychic constitution deviated from that ideal which one so much desires to see in a girl. Jocosely he called her "pert and disputatious." He warned her against being too confident in her judgments, against her tendencies to tell the truth regardless of everybody, and expressed his opinion that she would find it difficult to get a husband. As a matter of fact, she was very discontented with her girlhood; she was filled with ambitious plans, she wished to study or to obtain a musical education, and revolted at the thought of being forced to give up her ambitions and sacrifice her freedom of judgment for the sake of marriage. Meanwhile, she was proud of her father, of the regard and social position of her family, and jealously guarded everything connected with these matters. The indifference with which she treated her mother and older sisters, as will be shown, was considered by her parents to be due to the blunter side of her character.

The age of the girls impelled the family to move into the metropolis, where for a time Elisabeth enjoyed a richer and gayer social life. But then came the calamity which destroyed the happiness of the home. The father either concealed or overlooked a chronic cardiac affection, and one day he was brought home in an unconscious state after the first attack of œdema of the lungs. This was followed by an illness of one and a half years, during which Elisabeth took the most prominent part in nursing him. She slept in her father's room, awoke at night at his call, watched over him faithfully during the day, and forced herself to appear cheerful while he went through a hopeless condition with amiable resignation. The beginning of her affection must have been connected with this period of her nursing, for she could recall that during the last half year of this care she had to remain in bed on one occasion for a day and a half on account of severe pain in her right leg. She maintained, however, that these pains soon passed away and excited neither worry nor attention. As a matter of fact, it was not before two years after the death of her father that she began to feel sick and unable to walk on account of pain.

The void which her father left in the life of this family consisting of four women, the social solitude, the cessation of so many relations which promised stimulation and pleasure, the increased infirmity of the mother, all these beclouded the patient's emotional attitude, but simultaneously aroused a warm desire that the family might soon find a substitute for the lost happiness, and impelled her to concentrate her entire devotion and care on the surviving mother. At the end of the year of mourning the eldest sister married a talented and ambitious man of notable position, who seemed to have been destined for a great future by virtue of his mentality, but who, however, soon developed a morbid sensitiveness and egotistic perseveration of moods, and dared to show his disregard for the old lady in the family circle. That was more than Elisabeth could endure. She felt it her duty to take up the cudgels against her brother-in-law whenever he gave occasion for it, whereas the other women took lightly the outburst of his excited temperament. She felt it a painful disillusionment that the reconstruction of the old family happiness could be impeded by such a disturbance, and she could not forgive her married sister because, due to feminine docility, the latter firmly avoided espousing either cause. Thus, a whole series of scenes remained in Elisabeth's memory, which were connected with a number of partially unuttered grievances against her first brother-in-law. But her greatest grievance against him was the fact that for the sake of a prospective promotion he moved his small family to a distant city in Austria, and thus helped to increase her mother's isolation. On this occasion Elisabeth distinctly felt her inability and helplessness to afford her mother a substitute for her lost happiness, as well as the impossibility of following out the resolution she made on the occasion of her father's death.

The marriage of the second sister seemed more promising for the future welfare of the family. The second brother-in-law, although not of the same mental caliber as the first, was a man after the heart of delicate ladies, and his behavior reconciled Elisabeth to the institution of marriage and to the sacrifices it entailed. What is more, the second couple remained near her mother, and the child of this brother-in-law and the second sister became Elisabeth's pet. Unfortunately, the year during which the child was born was clouded by another event. The visual affliction of the mother demanded many weeks' treatment in a dark room, in which Elisabeth participated. Following this, an operation proved necessary and the excitement connected with this occurred at the same time as the first brother-in-law made preparations to move. Finally, the operation, having been skilfully performed, proved successful, and the three families met at a summer resort. There Elisabeth, exhausted by the worries of the past months, had the first opportunity to recuperate from the effects of the suffering and anxiety to which the family had been subjected since the death of her father.

But just during this sojourn in the summer resort, Elisabeth became ill with pain and weakness. These pains, which had been noticeable for a short while some time previously, manifested themselves severely for the first time after taking a warm bath at a small spa. A long walk, actually half a day's hike a few days previously, was thought to have had some connection with the onset of the pains, so that it was quite easy to gain the impression that Elisabeth at first became "fatigued," and then "caught cold."

From now on Elisabeth became the patient in the family. Following the advice of the physician, she spent the rest of the summer in Bad Gastein, whither she went with her mother, but not without having a new worriment to think about. The second sister was again pregnant, and the information as to her condition was quite unfavorable, so that Elisabeth could hardly decide to take the journey to Gastein. After barely two weeks at Gastein both mother and sister were recalled because things were not well with the patient at home.

An agonizing journey, which for Elisabeth was full of pain and anxious expectations, was followed by certain signs at the railroad station which forbode the worst, and then, on entering the sick room, they were confronted with the reality—that they had arrived too late to take leave of the dying one.

Elisabeth not only suffered from the loss of this sister, whom she dearly loved, but almost as much from the thoughts instigated by her death, and from the changes which it entailed. The sister had succumbed to heart trouble, which was aggravated by the pregnancy.

The idea then came to her mind that heart trouble was the paternal inheritance of the family. It was then recalled that in her early girlhood the deceased went through an attack of chorea with a slight heart affection. The members of the family then blamed themselves and the physicians for permitting the marriage, and they could not help reproaching the unfortunate widower for endangering his wife's health through two successive pregnancies without any pause. The sad thought that after the rare conditions for a happy marriage had been found, that this happiness should have terminated in this way, constantly occupied Elisabeth's mind. Moreover, she again saw everything go to pieces that she had planned for her mother. The widowed brother-in-law was inconsolable and withdrew from his wife's family. It seemed that his own family from whom he was estranged during his short and happy married life took advantage of the opportunity to draw him back into their own circle. There was no way of maintaining the former union; out of regard for his unmarried sister-in-law, it would have seemed improper to live together with his mother-in-law, and as he refused to relinquish his child, the only legacy of the deceased, to the two ladies, they accused him for the first time of heartlessness. Finally, and this was not the least painful, Elisabeth received some definite information concerning a disagreement between the two brothers-in-law, the cause of which she could only surmise. It seemed that the widower made some financial demands, which the other brother-in-law considered unjustifiable; indeed, in view of the mother's recent sorrow, he could only designate it as a wicked extortion. This then was the history of the ambitious and lovable young woman. Resentful of her fate, embittered over the failure of her little plans to restore the family luster; of those dear to her, some were dead, some away, and some estranged—without any inclination to seek refuge in the love of a strange man, she lived thus for a year and a half away from almost all social relations nursing her mother and her pains.

If one could forget greater suffering, and wished to read one's self into the psychic life of a girl, one could hardly deny Miss Elisabeth a sincere human sympathy. But what about the physician's interest in this sorrowful tale and its relation to her painful and weak gait; what about the prospects of explaining and curing this case by the knowledge which we may perhaps obtain from these psychic traumas?

For the physician the confession of this patient was at first a great disappointment. For, to be sure, it was a history composed of banal mental shocks, from which we could neither explain why the patient became afflicted with hysteria, nor how the hysteria assumed the form of the painful abasia. It explained neither the causation nor the determination of the hysteria in question. We could perhaps assume that the patient had formed an association between her psychically painful impressions and bodily pains, which she accidentally perceived simultaneously, and that now she utilized in her memory the physical sensation as a symbol for the psychic. What motives she had for this substitution and in what moment this came about remained unexplained. To be sure, these were questions, whose nature was not hitherto familiar to physicians. For it was customary to content one's self with the information that the patient was constitutionally hysterical, and that under the intensive pressure of any kind of excitement she could develop hysterical symptoms.

This confession offered even less for the explanation than for the treatment of the case. One could not conceive what beneficial influence Miss Elisabeth could derive from recounting sad, familiar family experiences of the past years to a stranger, who could give her in return only moderate sympathy, nor could one observe any improvement after the confession. During the first period of the treatment the patient never failed to repeat to her physician: "I continue to feel ill, I have the same pains as before," and when she accompanied this by a crafty and malicious glance, I could perhaps recall the words which old Mr. v. R. was wont to say about his favorite daughter: "She is frequently pert and disputatious," but after all I had to confess that she was right.

Had I given up the patient at this stage of the psychic treatment, the case of Miss Elisabeth v. R. would have been of no importance whatever for the theory of hysteria. But I continued my analysis because I felt sure that an understanding of the causation, as well as the determination of the hysterical symptoms could be gained from the deeper strata of consciousness.

I, therefore, decided to put the direct question to the broadened consciousness of the patient as to what psychic impression was connected with the origin of the pain in the legs.

For this purpose the patient should have been put into deep hypnosis. But fortunately I was forced to realize that all my procedures in that direction could not put the patient in any other state of consciousness than that in which she gave me her confession. Still, I was very pleased that this time she abstained from triumphantly remonstrating with the words: "You see I really do not sleep. I cannot be hypnotized." In such despair I conceived the idea of making use of the trick of pressing the head, the origin of which I have thoroughly discussed in the preceding observation of Miss Lucie. This was done by requesting the patient to unfailingly inform me of whatever appeared before her mind's eye or flashed through her memory at the moment of the pressure. She was silent for a long time, and then admitted that on my pressure she thought of an evening in which a young man had accompanied her home from some social affair, of the conversation that passed between them, and of her feelings on returning home to nurse her father.

With this first mention of the young man a new shaft was opened, the content of which I then gradually brought out. We dealt here rather with a secret, for with the exception of a mutual friend, no one knew anything of the relationship and the hopes connected with it. It concerned the son of an old friendly family, who formerly lived in the neighborhood.

The young man, being an orphan, attached himself with great devotion to her father, who guided him in his career, and this veneration for the father was naturally extended to the ladies of the family. Numerous reminiscences of joint readings, exchange of views, and remarks which had been repeated to her, marked the gradual growth of her conviction that he loved and understood her, and that a marriage with him would not impose upon her the sacrifice that she feared. Unhappily, he was only slightly older than she, and as yet far from independent. She, however, firmly resolved to wait for him.

With the serious illness of her father, and the necessity of nursing him, these relations became less frequent. The evening, which she recalled first, really marked the height of her feelings, but even then there was no exchange of ideas between them on the subject. It was only at the urging of her family that she consented to leave the sick bed that evening and attend the social affair, where she was to meet him. She wished to hasten home early, but she was forced to remain, and only yielded on his promising to accompany her home. At no time had she entertained such a tender regard for him as during this walk, but after returning home at a late hour in this blissful state and finding the condition of her father aggravated, she bitterly reproached herself for having sacrificed so much for her own amusement. It was the last time that she left her sick father for a whole evening, and thereafter she saw her friend only rarely. After the death of her father he seemed to hold himself aloof out of respect for her sorrow, and business affairs later took him to other regions. Gradually, she came to the realization that his interest in her was suppressed by other feelings and that he was lost to her. This failure of her first love pained her as often as she thought of it.

In this relationship and in the above mentioned scene to which it led, I had to seek the causation of the first hysterical pain. A conflict, or a state of incompatibility arose through the contrast between the happiness which she had not at that time denied herself, and the sad condition in which she found her father upon her arrival home. As a result of this conflict, the erotic ideas were repressed from the associations and the affect connected with them was utilized in aggravating or reviving a simultaneously (or somewhat previously) existing physical pain. It was, thus, the mechanism of a *conversion for the purpose of defense,* as I have shown circumstantially in another place.[35]

[35] Die Abwehr-Neuropsychosen, Neurologisches Centralblatt, 1 June, 1894.

To be sure, we have room here for all kinds of observations. I must stress the fact that I did not succeed in demonstrating from her memory that the conversion took place at the time of her returning home. I, therefore, investigated for similar experiences which might have occurred while she was nursing her father, and I evoked a number of scenes, among which was one during which she had to jump out of bed with bare feet in a cold room to respond to the repeated calls of her father. I was inclined to attribute to this moment a certain significance, for in addition to complaining of pain in her legs, she also complained of tormenting sensations of coldness. Nevertheless, here, too, I could not with certainty lay hold of the scene which could be designated as the scene of conversion. This led me to admit that there was some gap in the explanation until I recalled that the hysterical pains in the legs were really not present at the time she nursed her father. From her memory she recalled only a single attack of pain lasting a few days, to which at that time she paid no attention. I then directed my attention to the first appearance of the pains. Here I was successful in awakening a definite memory. Just at that time a relative visited her; she could not receive him because she was ill in bed, and he had the misfortune to find her ill on another occasion two years later. But the search for the psychic motive of these first pains failed as often as it was repeated. I believed that I could assume that these first pains were due to a slight rheumatic attack and really *had no psychic basis,* and I could also discover that this organic trouble was the model for the later hysterical imitation, at all events that it occurred *before* the scene of being accompanied home. That these mild organic pains should have continued for some time without her paying much attention to them was quite possible when we consider the nature of the situation. The obscurity resulting from this, namely, that the analysis pointed to a conversion of psychic excitement into bodily pain at a time when such pain was certainly not perceived and not recalled— this problem I hope to be able to solve in later considerations and by other examples.[36]

With the discovery of the motive for the first conversion we began a second more fruitful period of the treatment. In the first place, very soon afterward the patient surprised me with the statement that she now knew why the pains always radiated from that definite location on the right thigh, and were most painful there. This was the exact place upon which her father's leg rested every morning while she changed the bandages of his badly swollen leg. That occurred hundreds of times, and strange to say, she did not think of this connection until today. She, thus, gave me the desired explanation for the origin of an *atypical* hysterogenic zone. Furthermore, during our analysis her painful legs always " joined in the discussion." I mean the following remarkable state of affairs: The patient was as a rule free from pain when we began our work, but as soon as I evoked some recollection by question or by

---

[36] I can neither exclude nor prove that this pain, especially of the thighs, was of a *neurasthenic* nature.

pressure of the head, she at first reported some pain, usually of a very vivid nature, and then winced and placed her hand on the painful area. This awakened pain remained constant as long as the patient was dominated by the recollection, reaching its height when she was about to utter the essential and critical part of her communication, and disappeared with the last words of the statement. I gradually learned to use this awakened pain as a compass. Whenever she became mute, but still claimed to have pains, I knew that she had not told me everything, and urged her to continue the confession until the pain was " spoken away." Then only did I awaken a new recollection.

During this period of " abreaction " the patient's condition showed such a striking improvement both somatically and psychically that I used to remark half jokingly that during each treatment I carried away a certain number of pain motives, and that when I had cleaned them all out, she would be well. She soon reached a stage during which she had no pain most of the time; she consented to walk a great deal and to give up her hitherto self-imposed isolation. During the analysis I followed up, now the spontaneous fluctuations of her condition, and now some fragments of her sorrowful tale, which I felt was not sufficiently exhausted. In this work I made some interesting discoveries, the principles of which I could later verify in other patients.

In the first place, it was found that the spontaneous fluctuations never occurred unless provoked associatively by the events of the day. On one occasion she heard of an illness in the circle of her acquaintances, which recalled to her a detail in the illness of her father. On another occasion the child of her deceased sister visited her and its resemblance to its mother recalled many painful incidents. On still another occasion it was a letter from her absent sister showing distinctly the influence of the inconsiderate brother-in-law, and this awakened a pain, which made her crave to relate a family scene not reported before.

As she never reproduced the same pain motives twice, we seemed to be justified in the expectation that the stock would in time become exhausted, and I did not in any way prevent her from getting into situations conducive to evoking new memories, which had not yet come to the surface. Thus, for example, I asked her to visit the grave of her sister, or I urged her to go in society where she was apt to meet her youthful friend, who happened to be in the city.

In this manner I obtained an insight into the mode of origin of a hysteria, which could be designated as *mono-symptomatic*. I found, for example, that the right leg became painful during our hypnosis when we dealt with memories relating to the nursing of her father, to her young friend, and to other things which occurred during the first part of the pathogenic period; while the pain in the left leg appeared as soon as I evoked the memory of her lost sister, of both brothers-in-law, in brief, of any impression relating to the second half of the history. My attention having been called to this by this constant behavior, I went further in my investigations and gained the impression that the detailization went perhaps still further and that every new psychic cause of painful feeling might have some connection with a differently located pain area in the legs. The original painful location on the right thigh referred to the nursing of her father, and as the result of new traumas the painful area then grew by apposition, so that strictly speaking, we had here not one single physical symptom connected with multiform psychic memory complexes, but a multiplicity of similar symptoms which on superficial examination seemed to be fused into one. To be sure, I have not followed out the demarcations of the individual psychic causes corresponding to the pain zones, for I found that the patient's attention was turned away from these relations.

But my interest was further directed to the mode of construction of the whole symptom-complex, of the abasia, upon this painful zone, and with this view in mind, I asked such questions as this: " What is the origin of the pains in walking, standing, or lying? " She answered these questions partially uninfluenced, partially under the pressure of my hand. We, thus, obtained two results. In the first place, she grouped all the scenes connected with painful impressions according to their occurrence, sitting, standing, etc. Thus, for example, she *stood* at the door when her father was brought home with his cardiac attack, and in her fright remained as though rooted to the spot. To this first quotation, " fright while *standing*," she connected more recollections up to the overwhelming scene when she again *stood* as if pinned near the death bed of her sister. The whole chain of reminiscences should justify the connection of the pains with the standing up and could also serve as an association proof, except that one must be mindful of the fact that in all these events another factor must be demonstrated, that which had directed the attention—and consequently the conversion—precisely, to the standing (walking, sitting, etc.). The explanation for this direction of attention could hardly be sought in other connections than in the fact that walking, standing, and lying are connected with functions and conditions of those members which here bore the painful zones; namely, the legs. We could then easily understand the connection between the astasia-abasia and the first scene of conversion in this history.

Among the scenes which, according to this review, had made the *walking* painful, one became most prominent. It referred to a walk she had taken in large company at the watering place, which apparently lasted too long. The deeper circumstances of this occurrence revealed themselves only hesitatingly and left many a riddle unsolved. She was in an especially good humor and gladly joined the circle of friendly persons; it was a lovely day, not too warm; her mother remained at home, her older sister had already departed, the younger one felt indisposed, but did not wish to mar her pleasure. The husband of the second sister at first declared that he would remain at home with his wife, but finally went along for her (Elisabeth's) sake. This scene seemed to have a great deal to do with the first appearance of the pains, for she recalled that she returned home from the walk very fatigued and with severe pains. She could not, however, say definitely whether she had perceived the pains before this. I took for granted that if she had suffered any pain she would hardly have resolved to enter upon this long walk. On being questioned whence the pains originated on this walk, she answered rather indefinitely that the contrast between her solitude and the married happiness of her sick sister, of which she was constantly reminded by the behavior of her brother-in-law, was painful to her.

Another scene closely related to the former as regards to time played a part in connection with the pains on *sitting*. It was a few days later, her sister and brother-in-law had already departed and she found herself in a tense and longing mood. She arose in the morning and ascended to the top of a small hill, which they were frequently wont to visit together, and which afforded a very pretty view. There she sat down on a stone bench and gave free play to her thoughts. Her thoughts again revolved on her lonesomeness, the fate of her family, and she now frankly admitted that she entertained the eager wish to become as happy as her sister. After this morning's meditation, she returned home with severe pains. In the evening of the same day she took the bath, after which the pains definitely appeared and continued persistently.

We could further ascertain with great certainty that the pains on walking and standing diminished in the beginning *on lying down*. Only after she heard of her sister's illness and left Gastein in the evening, spending a sleepless night in the sleeping car, tormented simultaneously by worrying over her sister and by violent pains—it was only then that the pains appeared for the first time while she was lying down, and throughout that time, *lying down* was even more painful than walking or standing.

In this way the painful sphere grew by apposition, first, because every new pathogenically affecting theme occupied a new region of the legs; second, every one of the impressionable scenes left a trace because it produced lasting, always more cumulative cathexes [37] of the different functions of the legs, thus connecting these functions with the sensations of pain. There was unmistakably, however, still a third mechanism which furthered the production of astasia-abasia. When the patient finished the recitation of a whole series of events with the plaint that she then perceived pain on "*standing alone*," and when in another series, referring to the unfortunate attempt of bringing about new conditions in the family, she was not tired of repeating that the painful part of it was the feeling of her helplessness, the sensation that she "*could make no headway*," I then had to think that her reflections, too, influenced the formation of the abasia, and I had to assume that she directly sought a *symbolic* expression for her painfully accentuated thoughts and had found it in the aggravation of her pains. That somatic symptoms of hysteria could originate through such symbolization we have already asserted in our preliminary communication, and I shall give some examples of conclusive evidence in the epicrisis to this history. In Miss Elisabeth v. R.

[37] v.s.

the psychic mechanism of the symbolization was not in the foreground, it had not produced the abasia, but everything pointed to the fact that the already existing abasia had in this way undergone a considerable reën-forcement. Accordingly, this abasia as I encountered it in the stage of development, could not only be compared to a psychically associative paralysis of function, but also to a symbolic paralysis of function.

Before I continue with the history of my patient I will add something about her behavior during the second period of the treatment. Through-out this whole analysis I made use of the method of evoking pictures and ideas by pressing her head, a method, therefore, which would be inappli-cable without the full coöperation and voluntary attention of the patient. At times her behavior left nothing to be desired, and at such periods it was really surprising how promptly and how infallibly the individual scenes belonging to one theme succeeded each other in chronological order. It was as if she read from a large picture book, the pages of which passed in review before her eyes. At other times there seemed to be inhibitions, the nature of which I could not at that time surmise. When I applied pressure, she maintained that nothing came into her mind; I repeated the pressure and told her to wait, but still nothing would come. At first, when such obstinacy manifested itself, I determined to discon-tinue the work and to try again later, as the day seemed unpropitious. Two observations, however, caused me to change my procedure. Firstly, because such failure of this method occurred only when I found Elisabeth cheerful and free from pain and never when she had a bad day; secondly, because she frequently made assertions of seeing nothing after the lapse of a long pause during which her tense and absorbed mind betrayed to me some inner psychic process. I, therefore, decided to assume that the method never failed, that under the pressure of my hands Elisabeth had each time perceived some idea or had seen some picture, but that she was not always ready to impart it to me and attempted to suppress what was conjured up. I could think of two motives for such conceal-ment; either Elisabeth subjected the idea that came to her mind to an unjustified criticism thinking it not sufficiently important or unfit as an answer to the question, or she feared to say it because that state-ment was too disagreeable to her. I, therefore, proceeded as if I were perfectly convinced of the reliability of my technique. Whenever she asserted that nothing came into her mind, I did not let that pass. I assured her that something must have come to her, but that perhaps she was not attentive enough, that I was quite willing to repeat the pressure. I also told her not to entertain any doubts concerning the correctness of the idea which presented itself to her mind, be it suitable or not, and I ended by saying that I knew well that something did come which she concealed from me and that as long as she would continue to do so, she would not get rid of her pains. Through such urging I came to the realization that no pressure remained unsuccessful. I then had to assume that I correctly recognized the state of affairs, and indeed, I won perfect confidence in my technique through this analysis. It often happened that she did not make a statement until after the third pressure, and then added, " Why I could have told you that the first time."—" Indeed, why did you not say it? "—" I thought that is was not correct," or " I thought that I could avoid it, but it recurred each time." During this difficult work I began to attach a profounder significance to the resistance [38] which the patient showed in the reproduction of her recollections, and I carefully noted these occasions in which it was especially striking.

I now come to the description of the third period of our treatment. The patient felt better, she was psychically unburdened and less restrained in her behavior, but the pains were manifestly not removed, and reappeared from time to time with the old severity. The imperfect cure went hand in hand with the imperfect analysis; as yet, I did not know in what moment and through what mechanisms the pains originated. During the repro- duction of the most manifold scenes of the second period and the observa- tion of the patient's resistance towards the reproduction, I had a definite suspicion which I did not dare use as a basis for my action. An acci- dental observation turned the issue. While working with the patient one day, I heard the steps of a man in the adjacent room and a rather pleasant voice asking some questions. My patient immediately arose requesting me to discontinue the treatment for the day because she heard her brother- in-law, who had just arrived, asking for her. Before this disturbance she was free from pains, but now she betrayed by her mien and gait the sudden appearance of violent pains. This strengthened my suspicion and I decided to elicit the decisive explanation.

I therefore questioned her again concerning the circumstances and causes of the first appearance of the pains. Her thoughts were directed to the summer resort in that watering place where she had been before making the journey to Gastein. A number of scenes were reproduced which had already been treated less exhaustively. They recalled her frame of mind at that time, the exhaustion following the worriment about her mother's vision, and the nursing of her mother during the time of the operation, and her final despair at being unable as a lonesome girl to enjoy or accomplish anything in life. Until then she felt strong enough to dispense with the help of a man, but now she was overcome by a feeling of her womanly weakness, a yearning for love in which, to put it in her own words, her " obdurate self began to soften." In such humor the happy marriage of her younger sister made the profoundest impression on her. She thought how affectionately he cared for her, how they under- stood each other by a mere glance, and how sure they seemed to be of each other. It was truly regrettable that the second pregnancy followed so closely upon the first, her sister knew that this was the cause of her suffering, but how willingly she endured it, and all because he was the cause of it. The brother-in-law did not at first wish to participate in the walk which was so intimately connected with Elisabeth's pain;

---

[38] The mechanisms of resistance, which the author now counts among the great pillars of psychoanalytic technique, are mentioned here for the first time. [Translator.]

he preferred to remain home with his sick wife, but the latter urged him with a glance to go because she thought that it would give Elisabeth pleasure. Elisabeth remained with him throughout the whole walk; they spoke about the most varied and intimate things; she found herself in thorough accord with all he said, and she became overwhelmed with a desire to possess a man like him. This was followed by a scene a few days later, when, on the morning after their departure, she visited the point commanding the beautiful view which had been their favorite walk. There she seated herself upon a stone and again dreamed of her sister's happiness and of a man like her brother-in-law who could engage her affections. When she arose, she had pains which again disappeared, and only in the afternoon after having taken the warm bath did they reappear, remaining ever since. I attempted to investigate the thoughts which occupied her mind while taking the bath, but all I could obtain was that the bathroom recalled her absent sister because she had lived in the same house.

For some time the state of affairs must have been clear to me. The patient seemed absorbed in painfully-sweet recollections, so that she was wholly unconscious of the drift of her thoughts and continued to reproduce her reminiscences. She spoke of the time in Gastein, the worry connected with the expectations of the letter, finally the information of her sister's illness, the long wait until the evening when she could finally leave Gastein, the journey with its tormenting uncertainties during a sleepless night—all these moments were accompanied by a violent aggravation of the pain. I asked her if during the journey she thought of the sad possibility which she afterward found realized. She answered that she carefully avoided the thought, but that in her opinion her mother expected the worst from the very beginning. This was followed by the reminiscences of her arrival in Vienna—the impressions which she received from the relatives at the station, the short journey from Vienna to the neighboring summer resort where her sister lived, the arrival in the evening, the hasty walk through the garden to the door of the little garden pavilion—a silence in the house, the oppressive darkness, the fact of not having been received by the brother-in-law. She then recalled standing before the bed seeing the deceased, and in the moment of the awful certainty that the beloved sister had died without having taken leave of them and without having her last days eased through their nursing—in that very moment another thought flashed through Elisabeth's brain, which now peremptorily repeated itself. The thought, which flashed like dazzling lightning through the darkness, was, " Now he is free again, and I can become his wife."

Of course, now everything was clear. The analyst's effort was richly repaid. The ideas of " defense " against an unbearable idea, the origin of hysterical symptoms through conversion of psychic into physical excitement, the formation of a separate psychic group by an act of the will, which led to the defense—all these were in that moment palpably presented before my eyes. Thus, and thus alone did things happen here.

This girl entertained an affectionate regard for her brother-in-law, against the acceptance of which into her consciousness her whole moral being struggled. She succeeded in sparing herself the painful consciousness that she was in love with her sister's husband by creating for herself instead bodily pains, and at the moment when this certainty wished to thrust itself into her consciousness (while she walked with him, during that morning reverie, in the bath, and before her sister's bed) her pains originated through a successful conversion into the somatic. At the time she came under my care the isolation from her awareness of the group of ideas referring to this love affair had already been accomplished, else I believe that she would never have agreed to this mode of treatment. The resistance with which she repeatedly opposed the reproduction of the traumatically effective scenes really corresponded to the energy with which the unbearable idea had been crowded out from the associations.

For the therapist there now came a sorry time. The effect of the resumption of that repressed idea was crushing for the poor child. When I summed up the whole situation with these prosaic words: " You were really for a long time in love with your brother-in-law," she complained of the most horrible pains; she made another despairing effort to reject the explanation, saying that it was not true, that I suggested it to her, it could not be, she was incapable of such baseness, and that she would never forgive herself for it. It was quite easy to prove to her that her own information allowed no other interpretation, but it took a long time before the two reasons that I offered for consolation, namely, that one is not responsible for one's feelings, and that her behavior, her sickness under those circumstances was sufficient proof of her moral nature—I say it took a long time before these consolations made an impression on her.

I was now forced to pursue more than one course in order to alleviate the patient. In the first place, I wished to give her the opportunity to rid herself by abreaction of the material long since accumulated. We investigated the first impressions of the relations with her brother-in-law, the beginning of those unconsciously kept affectionate regards. We found here all those little indications and forebodings which on retrospection showed a fully developed passion. In his first visit to the house he mistook her for his destined bride and greeted her before he greeted her older and more homely sister. One evening they entertained each other so vivaciously and seemed to understand each other so well that the bride interrupted them with this half serious remark: " You two, indeed, would have suited each other very nicely." On another occasion while at a social gathering where none knew of the engagement, the conversation drifted to the young man, and a young lady indiscreetly remarked about a blemish in his figure, a juvenile joint affliction. The bride herself remained calm while Elisabeth flew into a passion, and with an ardor which even she herself could not afterwards understand defended the straight form of her future brother-in-law. While we worked our way through these reminiscences, it became clear to Elisabeth that her affection for her brother-in-law had slumbered in her for a long time, perhaps since the beginning of their relations, and had concealed itself so long under the mask of a mere kinsmanlike affection, as only her very delicate family feeling would allow.

This abreaction benefited her much, but I was able to give her still more relief by taking a friendly interest in her present state of affairs. With this object in view I sought an interview with Mrs. v. R., whom I found to be an intelligent and refined lady, whose courage to face life, however, was somewhat impaired through the last misfortunes. From her I learned that the accusation of rude extortion, which the older brother-in-law had brought against the widower, and which was so painful to Elisabeth, had to be retracted on closer investigation. The character of the young man remained untarnished; it was merely a mis-understanding, an easily conceived difference of opinion concerning the valuation of money that could arise between the merchant, to whom money is only a working tool, and the official—that is all there was to this seemingly so painful incident. I begged the mother to give Elisabeth all explanations that she might hereafter need, and to offer her in the future that opportunity for unburdening her mind to which I had accustomed her.

Naturally I was also anxious to know what chance there was for the fulfillment of the girls's present conscious wish. Here things were less favorable! The mother stated that for some time she had had an inkling of Elisabeth's affections for her brother in-law; of course, she did not know that it had existed during the lifetime of her sister. Whoever saw them both in friendly intercourse—of late, to be sure, only seldom—could enter-tain no doubt of the girl's anxiety to please him. However, neither she, the mother, nor the advisers of the family showed any particular inclina-tion to bring about a matrimonial union between the two. The health of the young man had not been very good and had received a setback through the death of his beloved wife, and it was not at all certain that he had sufficiently recovered from the shock to enter into a new marriage. It was quite probable that this was the reason for his reserve, perhaps also because he was not sure of his position and wished to avoid all obvious gossip. With such a reserve on both sides the solution for which Elisabeth was yearning was likely to fail.

I informed the girl of everything that I had heard from her mother and had the satisfaction of seeing her benefited by the explanation con-cerning the money affair. On the other hand, I urged her to bear calmly the uncertainties of her future which could not be dismissed. The advancing summer forced us to bring the treatment to an end. She now felt better, and since we had discussed the causes to which the pain could be traced, she no longer complained of pain. We both felt that the work had been finished, although I felt that the abreaction of the suppressed love was really not as complete as it should have been. I regarded her as cured and urged her to continue independently the solution after the way had been cleared for it, to which she agreed. She left with her mother for a summer resort where they were to join the older sister and her family.

I still have something more to report about the further course of Miss Elisabeth v. R.'s disease. A few weeks after our parting I received a despairing letter from her mother informing me that at the first attempt to draw Elisabeth into a conversation about her love affairs she became very excited and refused to talk, and since then had suffered from violent pains. She was very indignant at my having betrayed her confidence and was perfectly inaccessible, so that the treatment seemed a complete failure. She wished to know what was to be done, for of me she would hear nothing. I made no reply. It was to be expected that after she had been relieved from my discipline she would make another attempt to reject her mother's interference and return to her reserve. I was, however, quite certain that everything would adjust itself and that my efforts had not been in vain. Two months later they returned to Vienna and the colleague to whom I was grateful for the case informed me that Elisabeth was perfectly well, and that her behavior was normal although occasionally she had slight pains. Since then she has repeatedly sent me similar messages, each time promising to visit me, which she has never done. This is quite characteristic of the personal relationship formed during such treatment. My colleague assured me that she could be considered cured. The relation of the brother-in-law to the family had not changed.

In the spring of 1894 I was informed that she would be present at a private ball to which I could gain access. I did not let the opportunity escape me and saw my former patient gliding along in a rapid dance. Since then, following her own inclination, she married a stranger.

Epicrisis

I have not always been a psychotherapist, but like other neuropathologists I was educated to methods of focal diagnoses and electrical prognosis, so that even I myself am struck by the fact that the case histories which I am writing read like novels, and as it were, dispense with the serious features of the scientific character. Yet, I must console myself with the fact that the nature of the subject is apparently more responsible for this issue than my own predilection. Focal diagnosis and electrical reactions are really not important in the study of hysteria, whereas a detailed discussion of the psychic processes, as one is wont to hear it from the poet, and the application of a few psychological formulæ, allows one to gain an insight into the course of events of hysteria. Such case histories should be considered like psychiatrical ones, but they have the advantage over the latter in the fact that they give the intimate connection between the history of the disease and the morbid symptoms, a thing for which we are still looking in vain in the histories of other psychoses.[39]

With the description of the treatment I endeavored to interweave the explanations which I gave about the case of Miss Elisabeth v. R., and it will perhaps not be superfluous to summarize here the essential features. I have discussed the character of the patient and the features which repeat themselves in so many hysterics, and which we really cannot consider as degenerative. I mentioned the talent, the ambition, the moral sensitiveness, the immense yearning for love which found its gratification in the family, the independence of her nature reaching beyond the womanly ideal, which manifested itself largely in obstinacy, pugnaciousness, and shut-in-ness. According to the information of my colleague, no hereditary taints could be shown on either side of the family. Her mother, to be sure, suffered for years from some indefinite neurotic depression, but her brothers and sisters, her father and his family belonged to the even-tempered and not to the nervous type. There was no serious case of psychosis in any near relatives.

Her nature was influenced by painful emotions, the foremost of which was the debilitating influence of a long attendance upon her beloved sick father.

That nursing of the sick plays such a significant rôle in the histories of hysterias has its good reasons. A number of effective factors, which one finds here, are quite obvious; thus, the disturbance of the physical health through interrupted sleep, neglect of nourishment, and the reaction of a constantly gnawing worriment on the vegetative functions. The most important factor, however, is in my estimation to be found elsewhere. He whose mind is occupied with the hundred different tasks of nursing which succeed each other continuously for weeks and months, gets into the habit, on the one hand, of suppressing all signs of his own emotions, and on the other hand, his attention is soon turned away from his own impressions because he has neither the time nor the strength to do them justice. Thus, the nurse accumulates in himself an overabundance of affective impressions which he or she barely perceives clearly enough; at any rate, they are not dissipated by abreaction; that is, he or she creates for himself the material for a *retention hysteria*. If the patient

[39] This situation no longer obtains in present-day psychiatry. Beginning with the Zurich School under the stimulation of Bleuler the descriptive psychiatry of Kraepelin long ago gave way to the interpretative psychiatry of the present.

recovers, these impressions naturally lose their value, but if he dies and one goes into a period of mourning during which only that which refers to the deceased seems of value, the impressions waiting for discharge appear in turn, and after a brief pause of exhaustion the hysteria, the germ of which originated during the nursing, bursts forth.

The same fact of subsequent adjustment to traumas accumulated during nursing is occasionally also encountered where the general impression of being sick does not ensue, but where the mechanism of hysteria, nevertheless, can be noticed. Thus, I have known a highly gifted but slightly nervous lady whose whole personality suggests the hysteric, yet she never became a burden to the doctor and was never forced to interrupt the exercise of her duties. This lady had nursed three or four of her dear ones until they died, which caused her each time a complete physical exhaustion, yet these sad duties have never made her sick. However, shortly after the death of the patient she begins her work of reproduction in which she reviews the scenes of the disease, and of the death. Each day—one might say, at her leisure—she goes over again every impression, crying over it, and consoling herself. Such adjustment continues through her daily occupations without any confusion of the two activities. Everything passes before her chronologically. Whether the memory work of one day precisely corresponded to a day of the past, I am unable to say. I presume that it depends on the leisure which is left to her by the current affairs of the household.

Aside from this " after crying," which follows these demises after short intervals, this lady periodically observed the anniversaries of the various catastrophies, and here her vivid visual reproductions and her affective manifestations follow faithfully the dates. Thus, for example, I found her in tears, and on sympathetic inquiry as to what occurred on that day, she half irritably remarked, " Nothing on that day except that Professor N. was again here and gave us to understand that things were hopeless—at that time I had no time to cry." She referred to the last illness of her husband, who died three years before. It would have been very interesting to know whether she always repeated the same scenes on these recurring anniversaries, or whether, as I suppose, in the interest of my theory, other details presented themselves each time for abreaction. I was, however, unable to find anything definite about this; the wise and courageous woman was ashamed of the intensity with which those reminiscences acted upon her.[40]

I repeat that this woman was not sick and that subsequent abreaction, despite all resemblance, is still not a hysterical process; one may ask why after one nursing there results a hysteria and after another none. It cannot lie in the personal predisposition, for the lady whom I have here in mind showed it in the most prolific manner.

I now return to Miss Elisabeth v. R. While nursing her father, there occurred for the first time an hysterical symptom in the form of a pain in a definite location on the right thigh. The mechanism of this symptom is fully explained on an analytic basis. It occurred in a moment during which the ideas of her duties towards her sick father came into conflict with the content of her erotic yearning, which she then entertained. Under vivid self-reproach she decided in favor of the former and created for herself the hysterical pain. According to the conception explained by the theory of conversion in hysteria, the process could be described as follows: She repressed the erotic idea from her consciousness and changed the sum of the

[40] To my surprise, I once discovered that such subsequent abreaction—through other impressions than nursing—may form the content of an otherwise enigmatic neurosis. It was the case of a pretty girl of nineteen, Miss Matilda H., whom I first saw with an incomplete paralysis of the legs, and months later I was again called because her character had changed. She was depressed and tired of living, lacked all consideration for her mother, and was irritable and inapproachable. The whole picture of the patient did not seem to me to be that of an ordinary melancholia. She could easily be put into a somnambulic state, and I made use of this peculiarity to impart to her each time commands and suggestions to which she listened in her profound sleep and responded with profuse tears, but which, however, caused but little change in her condition. One day while hypnotized she became talkative and informed me that the reason for her depression was the breaking of her betrothal many months before. She stated that on closer acquaintance with her fiancé the things displeasing to her and her mother became more and more evident in him. On the other hand, the material advantages of the engagement were too tangible to make the decision of a rupture easy; thus, both of them hesitated for a long time. She then lapsed into a condition of indecision in which she allowed everything to pass apathetically and finally her mother pronounced for her the decisive " no." Shortly afterwards she awoke as from a dream and began to occupy herself fervently with the thoughts about the broken betrothal, she began to weigh the pros and cons, a process which she continued for some time. She continued to live in that time of doubt, and entertained daily the moods and the thoughts, which would have been appropriate for that day. The irritability against her mother could only be explained by circumstances that existed at that time. Next to this mental activity she found her present life a mere phantom, just like a dream. I did not again succeed in getting the girl to talk—I continued my exhortations during deep somnambulism. I saw her each time burst into tears without, however, receiving any answer from her. But one day, it was near the anniversary of the engagement, the whole state of depression disappeared. This was attributed to the success of my great hypnotic cure.

affect into somatic sensations of pain. Whether this first conflict occurred only once, or repeated itself, is not clear. The latter is more probable. Quite a similar conflict—of a higher moral significance, and even better demonstrated by the analysis—repeated itself after years and led to the aggravation of the same pain and to its dissemination beyond its original limits. Again, it was an erotic idea which came into conflict with all her moral conceptions, for her affection for her brother-in-law, both during the life and after the death of her sister, and the thought that she should yearn just for this man, was very disagreeable to her. This analysis gives detailed information about this conflict which represents the pivotal point in the history of her malady. The patient's affection for her brother-in-law might have begun to germinate long ago, but in favor of its development was the physical exhaustion from the recent nursing, and her moral exhaustion from years of disillusionment, which then began to break down her reserve, and caused her to confess to herself the need of the love of a man. During a relationship which extended over weeks (in that summer resort) this erotic desire attained full development simultaneously with the pain, and analysis shows that during that time the patient was in a special psychic state, which in conjunction with the desire and pain, seems to afford an understanding of the process in the sense of the conversion theory.

I must place reliance on the statement that the patient's affection for her brother-in-law, intensive as it was, was not *clearly known* to her except on certain rare occasions, and then only momentarily. If that were not so, she would have become conscious of the incompatibility between this desire and her moral ideas, and would have had to endure the same mental agonies which I saw her suffer after our analysis. Her reminiscences gave us no information concerning such suffering, these she spared herself, and as a result, the love itself did not become clear to her. At that time, as well as during the analysis, her love for her brother-in-law existed in the form of a foreign body in her consciousness without entering into any relationship with her other ideation. In reference to this love there existed the peculiar condition of knowing and simultaneously not knowing; it was the condition of the split-off psychic group. When we assert that this love was not " clearly known " to her, we mean exactly what we say. We do not mean a lower quality or a lesser degree of consciousness, but a separation of the free associative mental process from the rest of the ideational content.

How did it happen that such an intensively accentuated group of ideas could be kept so isolated? For generally the rôle of an idea in the association actually increases with the size of its affect.

This question can be answered if we take into account two facts which we can use as if proven: (1) That the hysterical pain originated simultaneously with the formation of these separate psychic groups, (2) that the patient exerted great resistance against the attempt to bring about the association between the separate psychic groups and the rest of the content of consciousness, and when the union was, nevertheless, effected, she felt excessive psychic pain. Our conception of hysteria brings together these two factors with the fact of the splitting of consciousness, by asserting that (2) contains the indication of the *motive* for the splitting of consciousness, while (1) shows the *mechanism* of the same. The motive was that of *defense,* or the striving of the whole ego to get into harmony with this ideation group, and the mechanism was that of *conversion;* that is, instead of psychic pains which she spared herself, there appeared physical pains. A transformation was thus initiated, which resulted in a *gain* insofar as the patient had escaped an unbearable psychic state; to be sure, this gain was obtained at the cost of a psychic anomaly, a splitting of consciousness and physical suffering. the pains, upon which an astasia-abasia was constructed.

To be sure, I can give no directions as to how one can produce in himself such a conversion. Apparently it is not done as one intentionally performs an arbitrary action; it is a process which takes place in a person under the impulse of the motive of defense, if he has a tendency for it in his organization, or if it is brought about by temporary modification.

One has the right to examine the theory more closely and ask: "What is it then that becomes transformed into physical pains?" The cautious reply will be: "Something out of which psychic pains could have and should have been formed." If one wishes to venture further and attempt a kind of algebraic formulation of the ideational mechanism, one might perhaps attribute to the ideational complex of this desire (which remained unconscious) a certain amount of affect and designate the latter quality as the thing converted. A direct deduction of this conception would be that through such conversion the "unconscious love" forfeits so much of its intensity that it becomes reduced to a weak idea, and its existence as a separate psychic group could be possible only through this weakening. However, the present case is not capable of throwing light on this delicate matter. It probably corresponds only to an imperfect conversion. From other cases it seems quite probable that there are also perfect conversions, and that in these the unbearable idea actually becomes "*repressed*" as only an idea of very little intensity could be repressed. After an associative union has been reëstablished, the patients assure us that since the origin of the hysterical symptoms their unbearable ideas had never occupied their minds.

I have stated above that on certain occasions, though only transitorily, the patient consciously recognized the love for her brother-in-law. Such a moment occurred when, for example, at the deathbed of her sister the thought flashed through her mind, " Now he is free and I can become his wife." I must discuss the significance of these moments for the conception of the whole neurosis. However, I think that in the assumption of a " defense hysteria " there is already the requisite that at least one such moment should have occurred. For consciousness really does not know in advance when such an unbearable idea will present itself. For the unbearable idea, which is later excluded with its appendage for the formation of a separate psychic group, must have been originally in the mental activity, else there would have been no conflict to lead to its exclusion.[41] Just such moments should be designated as "*traumatic.*" It is in them that the conversion takes place, and results in the splitting of consciousness and the hysterical symptoms. Everything tends to show that in Miss Elisabeth v. R. there were a number of such moments (the scenes of the walking, morning meditation, bath, and at the bedside of her sister), and perhaps new moments of this kind also occurred during the treatment. The multiplicity of such traumatic moments is made possible by the fact that an experience similar to the one which first initiated the unbearable idea, introduces new emotions to the separated psychic groups and thus transitorily abolishes the success of the conversion. The ego is forced to occupy itself with this suddenly reënforced and flared-up idea, and must later restore the former state through new conversions. Miss Elisabeth, who was in constant relation with her brother-in-law, must have been particularly exposed to the appearance of new traumas. A case whose traumatic history had been finished in the past would have been more desirable for this discussion.

[41] It is different in a hypnoid hysteria. Here the content of the separate psychic groups may never have been in the ego consciousness.

I must now occupy myself with the point which I have designated as a difficulty for the understanding of this case history. On the analytical basis I assumed that the first conversion took place in the patient while she nursed her father, at the time when her duties as a nurse came into conflict with her erotic yearnings, and that this process was the model for the later ones which led to the outbreak of the disease in the Alpine spa. But, according to the patient's statement she had *not at all suffered from any pains and weakness* at the time of the nursing, and the period following it, which I designated as the "first period." To be sure, during the illness of her father she was once bedridden for a few days with pains in her legs, but it is doubtful whether this attack already belonged to the hysteria. A causal relation between these first pains and any psychic impressions could not be demonstrated by analysis; it is possible, even probable, that at that time we dealt with a common rheumatic muscular pain. But if we should assume that this first attack of pain was the result of an hysterical conversion in consequence of the rejection of erotic thoughts which then existed, the fact, nevertheless, remains that the pains disappeared after a few days, so, that the patient actually behaved differently than she seemed to show during the analysis. During the reproduction of the so-called first period, all her statements concerning the illness and death of her father, the impressions relating to her first brother-in-law, etc., all these were accompanied by manifestations of pain, while at the time she really experienced these impressions she felt no pains. Is this not a contradiction which is likely to diminish considerably the confidence in the explanatory value of such an analysis?

I believe that I can explain the contradiction by assuming that the pains—the product of the conversion—did not originate while the patient experienced the impressions during the first period, but subsequently, that is, in the second period when the patient reproduced these impressions in her mind. The conversion did not follow the fresh impressions, but the memories of the same. I even believe that such a process is not at all unusual in hysteria and regularly participates in creating hysterical symptoms. Nevertheless, as such an assertion does not seem plausible, I shall attempt to make it more credible by citing other experiences.

During a similar analysis it once happened that a new hysterical symptom was formed during the treatment so that I could attempt its removal on the day after its origin.

I will describe the essential features of the history of this patient. They are simple, but not without interest.

Miss Rosalia H., twenty-three years old, who for a number of years made great efforts to educate herself as a singer, complained that her beautiful voice did not obey her in certain notes. She felt choking and tightening sensations in the throat, so that the tones sounded strained, and her teacher could, therefore, not yet permit her to appear in public. Although this imperfection affected only her middle notes, it could not be explained on the basis of a defect of her vocal organs, for at times this disturbance did not show itself and her teacher was very pleased with her, but at other times, the slightest excitement, seemingly without any provocation, evoked the choking sensation, and prevented free expansion of the voice. It was not difficult to recognize in this annoying sensation an hysterical conversion. Whether there was really a contracture of certain muscles of the vocal chords could not be verified.[42] In the hypnotic analysis, which I undertook with this girl, I found out the following concerning her vicissitudes and the ailments occasioned through them. She became an orphan at an early age and was brought up by her aunt, who had many children, and she had to share the life of a most unfortunate family existence. The husband of this aunt, seemingly a pathological personality, abused his wife and children in the most brutal manner, and what especially pained her was his unconcealed sexual preference for the servant and nurse girls in the house. This became even more obnoxious as the children grew older. When her aunt died, Rosalia became the protectress of the orphaned children who were harassed by their father. She took her duties seriously, fought through all conflicts, and had to exert her greatest efforts to suppress the manifestations of her contempt for her uncle. It was then that the choking sensation in her throat originated. Whenever she was compelled to swallow an affront, whenever she had to remain silent on hearing a provoking accusation, she perceived a scratching

[42] I had under observation another case in which a contracture of the masseters made it impossible for the artist to sing. The young lady in question through painful experiences in the family was forced to go on the stage. While rehearsing in Rome, in great excitement, she suddenly perceived the sensation of being unable to close her opened mouth and sank fainting to the floor. The physician, who was called, closed her jaws forcibly, but since that time the patient had been unable to open her jaws more than a finger's breadth and had to give up her newly chosen profession. When she came under my care, many years later, the motives for that excitement apparently had been over for some time, for massage in a light hypnosis sufficed to open her mouth widely. The lady has since then sung in public.

in her throat, the tightening and failure of her voice; in brief, she had all the localized sensations in her larynx and pharynx which now disturbed her in singing. It was conceivable that she sought the possibility of making herself independent in order to escape the excitement and painful impressions which were daily occurrences in her uncle's house. An efficient music teacher took an unselfish interest in her, assuring her that her voice entitled her to choose the profession of singing. She began secretly to take lessons of him, and because she often went for her lessons with the choking sensation in her throat, following some violent scene in the house, a connection was formed between the singing and the hysterical paresthesia for which a way was prepared by the sensitiveness of the vocal organs during singing. The apparatus of which she should have had free control was filled with the remnants of innervation from those numerous scenes of suppressed excitement. Since then she has left her uncle's house and has moved to another city, so as to be away from the family, but her ailments were not benefited by it. No other hysterical symptoms were discovered in this pretty and unusually bright girl.

I endeavored to cure this "retention-hysteria" by a reproduction of all the exciting impressions and by subsequent abreaction. I afforded her the opportunity of railing against her uncle in long speeches and of telling him the bare truth to his face, etc. The treatment benefited her, but unfortunately she lived here under quite unfavorable conditions. She had no luck with her relatives. She was the guest of another uncle who treated her with friendliness, but just for that reason she incurred the displeasure of her aunt. The latter believed that her husband evinced too marked an interest in his niece and made it a point of opposing the girl's stay in Vienna. She, herself, in her youth was obliged to relinquish a desire of becoming an artist and was now jealous of her niece because she had the opportunity to develop her talent, not considering that it was not mere desire, but a wish to become independent which led her niece to take this step. Rosalia felt so uncomfortable in the house that she, for instance, did not dare to sing or play the piano when her aunt was within hearing distance, and carefully avoided either singing or playing anything for her aged uncle—her mother's brother—whenever her aunt was home. While I was endeavoring to efface the traces of the old excitements, new ones originated through these relations with her hosts, and finally interfered with the success of my treatment and prematurely interrupted the cure.

One day the patient came to me with a new symptom hardly twenty-four hours old. She complained of a disagreeable prickling sensation in the fingertips, which had manifested itself every few hours since the day before, and forced her to make very peculiar jerky movements. I could not see the attack; otherwise, I would have guessed the cause from seeing the motions of the fingers, but I immediately endeavored to trace through hypnotic analysis the causation of this symptom (it was really a minor hysterical attack). As the whole thing existed only for a short time, I hoped to be able to explain it and quickly remove it. To my surprise, she reproduced without any hesitation in chronological order a whole row of scenes beginning in her early childhood. All these had perhaps the same characteristics in the fact that she had suffered an injustice without defense, something which could make her fingers jerk; for example, scenes like the one of being forced to hold out her hand in school while the teacher struck it with a ruler. But they were all banal causes, to which I would have gladly opposed the right to enter into the etiology of hysterical symptoms. It was different, however, with one scene of her early girlhood, which was connected with the others. The bad uncle who suffered from rheumatism asked her to massage his back. She did not dare refuse him. He was in bed while she was doing it and he suddenly threw off the covers, jumped up, and attempted to grab her and throw her down. She naturally stopped the massage and in a moment escaped and locked herself in her own room. She evidently did not like to recall this experience and could not say whether she had seen anything when the man suddenly exposed himself. The sensations in the fingers could be explained as due to the suppressed impulse to punish him, or it might simply have originated from the fact that she was at that time massaging him. Only after this scene did she begin to talk about the one which she experienced yesterday after which the sensitiveness and jerkiness of the fingers appeared as a recurring memory symbol. The uncle with whom she now lived begged her to play something for him. She sat at the piano ond accompanied herself singing, believing that her aunt was out. Suddenly she appeared in the doorway, Rosalia jumped up, closed the piano, and flung away the sheet of music. We can guess what memories came to her mind, and the train of thought which she tried to ward off at that moment, for the exasperation brought on by the unjust accusation should have really urged her to leave the house, but on account of her illness she was forced to remain in Vienna and had no other shelter. The movement of the fingers which I saw during the reproduction of this scene resembled a continuous jerking, as if one literally and figuratively would reject something like throwing away a sheet of music or rejecting an unreasonable demand.

She was quite positive in her assurance that she did not perceive the symptom before, that it was not caused by the scenes previously related. Was there anything else to be assumed except that the scene experienced yesterday had in the first place awakened the recollection of a former similar content, and that it then developed into a memory symbol for the whole group of recollections? The conversion was on the one hand furnished with newly experienced affects, and on the other, with recollected affects.

When we consider this state of affairs, we must admit that in the origin of hysterical symptoms such a process is the rule rather than the exception. Whenever I seek for the determinants of such states, I frequently find not a single but a group of similar traumatic motives.[43] In some of these cases it could be ascertained that this particular symptom had already existed for a short time after the first trauma and then subsided, but reappeared after the next trauma and became fixed. Yet, no real distinction can be made between those of temporary appearance and those which remained entirely latent causations. In a large majority of cases it was also found that the first traumas had left no symptoms, while a later trauma of the same kind produced a symptom for the origin of which the coöperation of the former motives could not be dispensed with, and for the solution of which it required a consideration of all the motives. Translating this into the language of conversion theory, this undeniable fact of the summation of traumas and the erstwhile latency of the symptoms simply means that the conversion can be brought about from a fresh, as well as from a remembered, affect, and this assumption fully explains the contradiction which seems to exist in the history and analysis of Miss Elisabeth v. R.

For there is no question that normal persons continue to carry in their consciousness a large number of ideas with unadjusted affects. The assertion which I have just defended merely approximates the behavior of hysteria to that of the normal. It is apparently reduced to

[43] Compare here the nice examples of Mrs. Emmy in Case History II.

a quantitative factor; it is simply a question of *how many* such affective strains an organization can endure. Even an hysterical person will be able to retain a certain amount in an unadjusted state, but if through a summation of similar motives it increases beyond the individual's endurance, the impetus for conversion is formed. It is, therefore, no singular theory, but almost a postulate to say that the formation of hysterical symptoms may also be brought about at the cost of recollected affects.

I have now occupied myself with the *motive* and *mechanism* of this case of hysteria, it still remains to discuss the *determination* of the hysterical symptoms. Why should just the pains in the legs have been selected to represent the psychic pains? The circumstances of the case point to the fact that this somatic pain was not created by the neurosis, but was merely utilized, aggravated, and retained by it. I will add that in most of the cases of hysterical algias into which I have been able to gain an insight, the conditions were similar, that is, there was to begin with always a real organically founded pain. It is always the most common, the most widespread pain of humanity that seem to be most frequently called upon to play a part in hysteria. Among the most common are the periosteal and the neuralgic pains of the teeth, headaches which originate from so many different sources, and not in a lesser degree the so often mistaken rheumatic pains of the muscles. The first attack of pain which Miss Elisabeth v. R. had while she nursed her father I consider to have been organically determined, for I received no information when I investigated for its psychic motive, and I admit that I am inclined to attribute differential diagnostic significance to my methods of evoking hidden memories, if they are carefully applied. This original rheumatic pain [44] became the memory symbol for her painful psychic excitements, and as far as I can see, for more than one reason. First and principally, because it existed in consciousness almost simultaneously with the other excitements, and second because it was or could be connected in many ways with the ideation content of that time. At all events, it was perhaps a remote consequence of the nursing, of her want of exercise, and of the poor nutrition entailed by her duties. But this hardly became clear to the patient, and what is more important is that she had to perceive it during important moments of the nursing, as for example, when she jumped out of bed in the cold room to respond to her father's call. Even more decisive for the

---

[44] But perhaps spinal neurasthenic?

direction taken by the conversion must have been the other manner of associative connection, namely, the fact that for many days one of her painful legs came in contact with the swollen leg of her father during the changing of the bandages. The location on the right leg distinguished by this contact henceforth remained the focus and starting point of the pains; it was an artificial hysterogenic zone, the origin of which can be plainly seen in this case.

If anyone should be surprised at the associative connection between physical pain and psychic affect, thinking it to be too manifold and artificial, I should answer that such surprise is just as unfair as to be surprised over the fact " that just the richest people in the world possess most of the money." Where prolific connections do not exist, there is naturally no formation of hysterical symptoms, and conversion does not find its way. I can also state that in reference to determinations the case of Miss Elisabeth v. R. belongs to the simpler ones. In the case of Mrs. Cecilia M. particularly, I had to solve the most intricate knots of this kind.

I have already discussed in the case history how the astasia-abasia of our patient was built up on those pains after a definite path was opened to the conversion. But, there, too, I have expressed the opinion that the patient created or aggravated the disturbance of function through symbolization. For her dependence and helplessness to change anything in the circumstances she found a somatic expression in the astasia-abasia, and the expressions "to make no headway," "to have no support," etc., formed the bridge for this new act of conversion. I will endeavor to support this conception by other examples.

Conversion on the basis of coincidence in otherwise existing associative connections seems to exert the least claims on the hysterical predisposition; on the other hand, conversion through symbolization seems to require a higher grade of hysterical modification, a fact also demonstrated in Miss Elisabeth in the later stages of her hysteria. The nicest examples of symbolization I have observed in Mrs. Cecilia M., whom I can call my most difficult and most instructive case. I have already mentioned that unfortunately this case history does not lend itself to detailed reproduction.

Among other things Mrs. Cecilia also suffered from a most violent facial neuralgia, which appeared suddenly two or three times during the year and persisted for from five to ten days, resisting every remedy, and then ceased as if cut off. It limited itself to the second and third branches of the trigeminus, and as there was undoubtedly an excess of urates in the urine, and as a not very "clear acute rheumatism" played a certain part in the patient's history, it was reasonable to assume that we dealt with a gouty neuralgia. This opinion was also shared by the consulting physicians who saw every attack. The neuralgia was treated by the methods in vogue, such as electric penciling, alkaline waters and purgatives, but it always remained uninfluenced until it found it convenient to make room for another symptom. In former years—the neuralgia was fifteen years old—the teeth were accused of preserving it and were condemned to extraction, and one fine morning under narcosis the execution of seven of the culprits took place.[45] This did not run so smoothly, as the teeth were so firm that most of the roots were left behind. This cruel operation was followed by neither temporary nor permanent relief. At that time the neuralgia raged for months. Even while under my care whenever she had neuralgia, the dentist was called and he always declared he found diseased roots. He started to get ready for an extraction, but usually he was soon interrupted, for the neuralgia suddenly ceased, and with it the desire for the dentist. During the intervals the teeth did not ache at all. One day just while another attack was raging, I put the patient into a hypnotic condition and placed an energetic interdiction on the pains, and from that moment they ceased. I then began to doubt the genuineness of this neuralgia.

About a year after this hypnotic remedial success, the condition of Mrs. Cecilia M. took a new and surprising turn. There suddenly appeared other states than those that had been characteristic of the last years, but after some reflection the patient declared that all these conditions had existed before and were really scattered over the long period of her disease (thirty years). Indeed, a surprising abundance of hysterical incidents were unrolled which the patient was able to localize correctly in the past and soon the frequently very entangled mental connections, which determined the sequence of these incidents, became recognizable. It was like a series of pictures with an explanatory text. *Pitres,* on describing his *délire ecmnésique,* must have had in mind a similar case. The way such an hysterical condition belonging to the past was reproduced was most remarkable.

---

[45] It is remarkable how history repeats itself. Lest there should be some misunderstanding, I wish to remind the reader that the above was written in 1893, and the theory of focal infection especially of the teeth was brought out as something new in psychiatry only about ten years ago. [Translator.]

In the first place, while the patient was in the best of condition, there appeared a pathological mood of special coloring, which was regularly mistaken by the patient and was referred to a banal occurrence of the last hours. This increasing obnubilation of consciousness was followed by hysterical symptoms, such as hallucinations, pains, convulsions, and long declamations, and finally an event of the past attached itself to this hallucinatory manifestation which could explain the initial mood and determine the occasional symptoms. With this last part of the attack lucidity returned, the symptoms disappeared as if by magic, and good health again existed—until the next attack, which was half a day later. Usually I was called at the height of this condition. I induced hypnosis, evoked a reproduction of the traumatic events, and by artificial aid I curtailed the attack. Having gone through with the patient many hundreds of such cycles, I obtained the most instructive explanations concerning the determinants of hysterical symptoms. The joint observation with Breuer of this remarkable case was also the chief motive for the publication of our " preliminary communication."

In this connection it finally also came to the reproduction of the facial neuralgias, which I myself had still treated as actual attacks. I was desirous of knowing whether we would find here a psychic causation. When I attempted to evoke the traumatic scene, the patient soon imagined herself in a period during which she felt marked psychic sensitiveness against her husband. She related a conversation with him and a remark that he made which annoyed her very much. She then suddenly grasped her cheek, crying aloud with pain, and said, " That was like a slap in the face."—With this, both the attack and the pain came to an end.

There is no doubt that here, too, we dealt with a symbolization. She had felt as if she really received a slap in the face. Now everybody will ask how the sensation of " a slap in the face " can lead to the manifestation of a trigeminal neuralgia, to its limiting itself to the second and third branches, and to its being aggravated on opening the mouth, and on mastication (not on talking!).

The following day the neuralgia reappeared, but this time it could be solved by the reproduction of another scene, the content of which equally showed a supposed insult. This process continued for nine days, and from the result it seemed that for years irritations, especially through words, produced new attacks of this facial neuralgia by way of symbolization.

But finally we also succeeded in reproducing the first attack of the neuralgia which occurred more than fifteen years before. Here, there was no symbolization, but a conversion through coincidence. It was a painful sight which recalled to her mind a reproach, and this caused her to repress another series of thoughts. We had here, then, a case of conflict and defense, and the origin of the neuralgia in this moment could not be further explained if we did not wish to assume that she suffered at that time from slight toothache or facial pains, a thing not improbable, as she was then in the first months of pregnancy.

The result of the explanation showed that this neuralgia became the mark of a definite psychic excitement through the usual road of conversion, but that it could be awakened later through associative accusations from mental life and symbolic conversions. It was really the same procedure as we encountered in Miss Elisabeth v. R.

I will now introduce another example which will illustrate the efficacy of symbolization under other determinants. On one occasion Mrs. Cecilia M. was tormented by a violent pain in her right heel, she had stinging sensations on every step, which made walking impossible. The analysis conducted us to a time when the patient was in a foreign sanitarium. For eight days she kept to her room, and for the first time the house physician was to take her to the dining room. The pain came on while the patient took the physician's arm on leaving the room. It disappeared during the reproduction of this scene while she remarked at at that time she feared lest she would not make the " proper impression " on this strange society [46] (" rechte Auftreten " equals ' proper stepping ').

This seems a striking, almost comical example for the origin of hysterical symptoms through symbolization by means of a verbal expression. But closer investigation of the circumstances of that moment favors another conception. The patient suffered at that time from actual pains in her feet on account of which she remained in bed, and we can only assume that the fear, which obsessed her on taking the first steps, produced from the simultaneously existing pains the one symbolically appropriate symptom in the right heel, in order to form it into a psychic algia and to assist it to maintain itself for a long time.

Notwithstanding the fact that the mechanism of symbolization in these examples seems to be pushed into second rank, which certainly

[46] The literal translation of *Auftreten* is " to press down by treading."

agrees with the rule, I have still other examples at my disposal which seem to demonstrate the origin of hysterical symptoms through symbolization only. One of the best is the following example which again refers to Mrs. Cecilia M. At the age of fifteen she once lay in bed watched by her austere grandmother. The girl suddenly cried out, complaining of having perceived a pain in the forehead between the eyes, which thereafter continued for weeks. On analyzing this pain, which was reproduced after almost thirty years, she stated that her grandmother gazed at her so " piercingly " that it seemed as if her look penetrated deeply into her brain. She was really afraid of being looked upon suspiciously by this old lady. On reproducing this thought she burst into loud laughter and the pain ceased. Here I find nothing other than the mechanism of symbolization which in a way stands midway between the mechanism of *auto-suggestion* and that of *conversion*.

The study of Mrs. Cecilia M. gave me the opportunity to gather a collection of such symbolizations. A whole series of physical sensations, which were otherwise looked upon as organically determined, were of psychic origin, or at least lent themselves to psychic interpretation. A certain number of her experiences were accompanied by a piercing sensation in the region of the heart (" I felt a stitch in my heart "). The piercing headache of hysteria was undoubtedly, in her case, to be interpreted as a mental pain (" something sticks in my head "), and it disappeared each time when the problem in question was solved. The sensation of the hysterical aura in the throat, when it manifested itself during an annoyance, ran parallel with the thought, " I have to swallow that." There was a whole series of parallel, running sensations and ideas, in which it was now the sensation evoking the idea as an interpretation, and now the idea which produced the sensation by symbolization, and not seldom it remained obscure, which of the two elements was the primary one.

In no other patient was I able to find such a prolific application of symbolization. To be sure, Mrs. Cecilia M. was quite an unusual person, of a special artistic temperament, whose highly developed sense of form manifested itself in producing very beautiful poems. I maintain, however, that if an hysteric creates through symbolization a somatic sensation for an emotionally accentuated idea, it is due less to individual and arbitrary things than one supposes. When during an offending harangue she takes literally such phrases as " stitch in the heart " or " slap in the face," and perceives them as real occurrences, she practices no facetious misuse, but only revives the sensations to which these phrases owe their existence. For how does it happen that in speaking of an aggrieved person we use such expressions as " he experienced a ' stitch in his heart '," if the mortification was not actually accompanied by a precordial sensation that could be so interpreted and recognized? Is it not probable that the phrase, " to swallow something," applied to an unreturned insult, really originates from the sensation of innervation appearing in the pharynx when one forces back his speech, thus preventing a reaction to the insult? All these sensations and innervations belong to the " expression of the emotions," which, as Darwin taught us, originally consisted of sensible and expedient actions; at present most of them may be so weakened that their verbal expression seems to us like a figurative transformation, but very probably all this was once meant literally, and hysteria is justified in reconstructing the original literal sense for its stronger innervation. Indeed, perhaps it is improper to say that it creates such sensations through symbolization, perhaps it has not taken the usage of speech as a model, but like it draws it from a common source.[47]

[47] In conditions of profounder psychic changes we apparently find a symbolic stamp of the more artificial usage of language in the form of emblematic pictures and sensations. There was a time in Mrs. Cecilia M. during which every thought was changed into an hallucination, and which solution frequently afforded great humor. She at that time complained to me of being troubled by the hallucination that both her physicians, Breuer and I, were hanged in the garden on two nearby trees. The hallucination disappeared after the analysis revealed the following origin: The evening before Breuer refused her request for a certain drug. She then placed her hopes on me, but found me just as inflexible. She was angry at both of us, and in her affect she thought " They are worthy of each other, the one is a *pendant* of the other! "

CHAPTER III

THEORETICAL MATERIAL

By Dr. J. Breuer

In the "preliminary communication," which introduces these studies, we have presented the views to which we were led by our observations; and I believe that essentially we can adhere to them. But the "preliminary communication" is so short and scanty that for the most part we could only indicate what we meant. May we, therefore, be permitted now that we have illustrated our views with case histories to discuss these in detail. Naturally, we shall not, and cannot here deal with the "whole problem of hysteria," but those points which have been insufficiently proven and only feebly stressed in the "preliminary communication" will receive a more exhaustive, more intelligible, as well as a more restricted discussion.

In these discussions there will be little talk of the brain and nothing at all of molecules. Psychic processes will be dealt with in psychological language, for it cannot really be done in any other way. If instead of "idea" we should say "cortical irritation," the latter expression will only convey some sense through the fact that we will recognize in the disguise our old acquaintance, and thus quietly restore the "idea." For while ideas with all their nuances are familiar to us as objects of our experience, "cortical irritations" impress us more as a postulate, as an object of future and hoped for cognition. Such substitution of terms seems only an aimless masquerade.

We may, therefore, be pardoned for making almost exclusive use of psychological terminology.

Just now I must also request your consideration for other things. Wherever a science marches rapidly forward, thoughts which have at first been expressed by individuals soon become common property. Thus, no one who attempts to demonstrate today his views on hysteria and its psychic foundation can avoid expressing and repeating a multitude of other people's thoughts, which have passed over from individual to common possession. It is hardly possible always to verify who expressed them first. There is also the danger that one

133

will consider a product of his own that which has already been said by others. We may, therefore, be excused if we give here only few citations, and if we do not sharply distinguish between that which is ours and that which belongs to others. What will be discussed in the following pages makes the least claim to originality.

I. *Are All Hysterical Phenomena Ideogenic?*

In the " preliminary communication " we spoke of the psychic mechanisms of " hysterical phenomena " and not of " hysteria," because we did not wish to claim unrestricted validity for either the former or for the psychic theories of the hysterical symptoms in general. For we do not believe that all the manifestations of hysteria come into being in the manner presented by us, nor do we feel that they are all ideogenic, *i.e.,* that they are all determined by ideas. In this we differ from Moebius,[1] who, in 1888, proposed the following definition: " Hysterical are all these morbid manifestations which are caused by ideas." This statement was later explained by the fact that only a part of the morbid phenomena corresponds contently to the causative ideas, namely, those symptoms which were produced by suggestion from within or from without, as, for example, when the idea, not to be able to move the arm, conditions a paralysis of the same. Another part of the morbid phenomena may, indeed, be caused by ideas, but need not contently correspond to them; as for example, when (as happened in one of our cases) the paralysis of the arm was produced by the sight of snake-like objects.

Moebius does not perhaps wish to advocate with this definition a change in the nomenclature, he does not imply that hereafter only those ideogenic morbid phenomena which are determined by ideas should be called hysterical, but he really means that all hysterical morbid manifestations are ideogenic. To put it in his own words: " Because ideas are very frequently the cause of hysterical manifestations, we believe that they are always so." He calls this a conclusion by analogy, but I would prefer to call it a generalization, the justification for which must first be investigated.

It would seem that before entering into any discussion one should first decide what we understand by hysteria. I consider hysteria something that was empirically discovered, it is a morbid picture which discovered through observation just like tuberculosis of the

---

[1] Möbius, Über den Begriff der Hysterie, Wiederabgedruckt, in " Neurologische Beiträge," I Heft, 1894.

lungs. Such empirically discovered diseases become refined, deepened, and explained through the progress of further cognition, but they shall not and cannot be destroyed thereby. Thus, etiological investigation has shown that the various partial processes of phthisis may be determined by various morbid processes, the tubercle through *Koch's bacillus,* the tissue breakdown, the cavity formation, or the septic fever through other microbes. Nevertheless, tubercular phthisis remains a clinical entity, and it would be wrong to destroy it by adjudging it only as the " specific tuberculosis " conditioned by the tissue destruction of *Koch's bacillus,* and to separate it from all the others.—In the same way we must also preserve the clinical entity of hysteria, even if it turns out that its phenomena are conditioned by various causes, some through a psychic mechanism, while others through different causes.

According to my conviction, this is really the case. Only one part of the hysterical mechanism is ideogenic, and Moebius' assumption, judging from his definition, tears asunder the clinical entity of hysteria, indeed also the entity of one and the same symptom in one and the same patient.

We would be quite justified to draw the analogous conclusion to Moebius' analogous conclusion, namely, that : " Because ideas and perceptions very often evoke an erection, we assume that they alone always do this, and that even peripheral stimuli can release that vasomotor process only through detours over the psyche." We know that this is a mistake, yet this conclusion is surely based on as many facts as Moebius' statement about hysteria. Analogous to a large number of physiological processes, such as saliva and tear secretions, changes of the heart action and similar ones, it may be assumed as possible and probable that the same process can be released through ideas, as well as through peripheral or other stimuli, but not through psychic stimuli. The contrary must first be proved, and we are still far from it. Indeed, it seems certain that many of the phenomena designated as hysterical are not solely caused by ideas.

Let us consider a very ordinary case. As a result of every affect in the throat, chest, and face, a woman gets first a macular and then a patchy erythema. As this is conditioned by ideas, it is, according to Moebius, an hysterical phenomenon. But as the same erythema also appears, albeit in lesser dissemination, through irritation of the skin, through touch, etc., this would, therefore, not be hysterical. Thus, a perfectly unified phenomenon would now belong to hysteria and the next time it would not. It is also doubtful whether this belongs to the vasomotor erethisms or whether it really belongs to the specific hysterical manifestations, or whether it would not be better to put it under simple "nervousness." But, according to Moebius, that disintegration of a unified process must take place in any case, and only that erythema which is affectively determined could be designated as hysterical.

The same is also the case in hysterical algias which are of such practical importance. They are surely very frequently conditioned by ideas, they are "pain hallucinations." But when we examine them more thoroughly we find that a marked vividness of imagination is not enough to produce them, but that their origin depends on an especially abnormal state of the pain conducting and sensitive apparatus, just as an abnormal irritability of the vasomotors is required for the production of the affective erythemas. The term, "pain hallucinations," surely designates the nature of this neuralgia in the most pregnant manner, but it also impels us to classify it under the views which we have formulated concerning hallucinations in general. To discuss these exhaustively is not in place here. But I profess the opinion that the "idea" of the memory picture alone, without the incitement of the perception-apparatus, despite its greatest vividness and intensity, would in itself never attain that character of objective existence which constitutes an hallucination.[2]

This holds true for sensory hallucinations and still more for pain hallucinations. For it seems impossible for a healthy person to furnish the memory of a bodily pain with that vividness or even with a slight resemblance to the real feeling which can be readily attained through optical and acoustic memory pictures. I believe that even in the normal hallucinatory state of the healthy person, that is, in

[2] This perception apparatus, including the cortico-sensory spheres, must be different from the organ which preserves and reproduces sensory impressions as memory pictures. For the main determinant of the function of the perception apparatus lies in the quickest *restitutio in statum quo ante;* otherwise, no other correct perception could take place. On the other hand, the condition of memory lies in the fact that there is no such restitution, but that every perception creates permanent changes. It is impossible that one and the same organ should suffice for both contradictory conditions; the mirror of a reflection telescope cannot at the same time be a photographic plate. I agree with Meynert in the sense that the stimulation of the perception apparatus—not with the definite statement that the irritation of the subcortical centers—furnishes the hallucination the character of objectivity. But if the organ of perception should become stimulated by the memory picture, we must assume that there is a changed stimulus contrary to the normal, which makes the hallucinations possible.

sleep, pains are never dreamed unless there exists a real sensation of pain. The " retrograding " irritation of the perception apparatus emanating from the organ of memory is normally even more difficult when it concerns ideas of pain than visual and auditory sensations. If pain hallucinations appear in hysteria with such ease, we must, therefore, assume that there is an anomalous irritation of the pain sensing apparatus.

This appears not only through ideas, but also through peripheral stimuli brought into existence precisely as in the above considered vasomotor erethisms.

It is an every day observation that in normally nervous persons peripheral pains of pathological processes, though in themselves not of a painful nature, may produce pain in other organs. Thus, we have headaches as a result of some insignificant changes in the nose and the adjacent sinuses, intercostal and brachial neuralgias from endocarditis, etc. If a patient is endowed with that abnormal sensitiveness which we have to assume as a condition for pain hallucinations, this predisposition is also, as it were, at the disposal of the above mentioned irradiations. But even those which occur in nonnervous persons sometimes become more intensive, and then form such irradiations, which we find in only nervous patients, but which are, however, conditioned by the same mechanisms as the others. Thus, I believe that an ovaritis depends on the states of the genital apparatus. That it is psychically influenced would have to be proven, but it has not been demonstrated because this, like any other pain, could be hallucinatorily produced in hypnosis, or because it can also be of psychic origin. Just like erythema or like one of the normal secretions it may originate through psychic or through purely somatic causes. Should we then call only the first kind hysterical? The one, whose psychic origin we know? Then, we would really have to eliminate the commonly observed ovaritis from the hysterical symptom complex, which is hardly possible.

If, following a slight trauma of a joint, there gradually develops a severe neurosis of this region, this process surely contains a psychic element. It is due to the concentration of attention on the injured region which enhances the sensibility of the nerve path in question; yet, one can hardly say that this hyperalgia was conditioned by ideas.

Nor is there anything different in the case of pathological diminution of feeling. It is altogether unproved and improbable that general analgesia, or analgesia of individual parts of the body without anesthesia is determined by ideas. And even if Binet's and Janet's discoveries should be fully confirmed, namely that hemianesthesia is conditioned by the special state of psychic splitting, it would indeed, be a psychogenetic, but not an ideogenic phenomenon, and hence, according to Moebius it could not be called hysterical.

Hence, if we cannot assume that a large number of characteristic hysterical phenomena are ideogenic, it seems only fair to reduce Moebius' statement. We do not say that, " Those morbid manifestations are hysterical, which are caused by ideas "; but we only mention that *a great many of the hysterical phenomena, probably more than we know today, are ideogenic*. But the common and fundamental morbid change, which makes it possible for the ideas as well as for the non-psychological stimuli to act pathogenically, is an anomalous irritation of the nervous system.[3] To what extent this is in itself of psychic origin is another question.

If, therefore, only one part of the hysterical phenomena should be considered ideogenic, it should be just these phenomena which can be designated as specifically hysterical, and hence, their investigation, the exposition of their psychic origin, constitutes the essential and new progress in the theory of the disease. The question that then arises is: How do they come about, and what is the " psychic mechanism " of these phenomena?

The two groups of ideogenic symptoms differentiated by Moebius assume essentially different attitudes to this question. Those, in which the morbid phenomenon corresponds to the exciting idea, are relatively comprehensible and transparent. If the idea of a voice heard does not simply quietly resound in the " inner hearing " as in a healthy person, but is perceived hallucinatorily as a real objective auditory sensation, it thus corresponds to a familiar phenomenon of normal life (dream), and is quite comprehensible under the assumption of abnormal irritability. We know that in every voluntary motion it is the idea of the result to be attained that releases the corresponding muscular contraction. It is also quite comprehensible that the idea, " this is impossible," will impede the movement (suggestion paralysis).

[3] Oppenheim's " Labilität der Molecüle." It may later perhaps be possible to substitute the above very vague expression by a more precise and contently richer formula.

The situation is different in those phenomena which have no logical connection to the causative idea. (For these, too, normal life offers analogies, as, *e.g.,* erythrophobia, etc.). How do these come about, why does an idea release in a sick person just this particular, quite irrational, and not its corresponding movement or hallucination?

We believed that we were able to present something in the " preliminary communication " concerning this causal connection, which was based on our observation. But in our exposition we have initiated and utilized, without anything further, the concept *" of the excitement which is discharged or must be abreacted."* Still, this concept of such fundamental importance for our theme and for the theory of the neuroses in general, seems to merit a more detailed examination. But before proceeding to it, I must ask forgiveness for returning here to the fundamental problem of the nervous system. Such " return to mother " has something oppressive about it, but an attempt to uncover the roots of a manifestation always leads unavoidably to the root of the problem, which cannot be avoided. I, therefore, hope that the obstruseness of the following considerations will be judged with consideration.

II. *The Intercerebral Tonic Excitements—The Affects*

A. We know two extreme states of the central nervous system, dreamless sleep and clear wakefulness. The transition between them is formed by all gradations of states of lesser clearness. We are not interested here in the question of the aim and the physical basis of sleep (chemical or vasomotor determinants), but in the essential differences between the two states.

We cannot say anything directly concerning the deepest dreamless sleep, because every observation and experience is excluded through that very state of perfect unconsciousness. But concerning the neighboring state of dream-sleep, we know that there is an effort of voluntary movements, such as speaking, walking, etc., but that unlike in the waking state, the corresponding muscular contractions are not actually released thereby. Sensible stimuli are perhaps perceived (for they frequently enter into the dream), but not apperceived, that is, they do not reach to conscious perception. Unlike the waking state, emerging ideas do not actuate all the existing ideas connected with them in potential consciousness, but large masses of them remain untouched (as, for example, speaking with a dead person without being reminded of death). Moreover, incompatible ideas can exist simultaneously without reciprocal impediment as in the waking state, and the associations flow scantily and incompletely. We can readily assume that in the most profound sleep this abolition of connection between the psychic elements is even more marked, it is complete.

In contrast to this, every voluntary act in clear wakefulness produces the corresponding movement, the sensible impressions become perceptions, and the ideas become associated with the whole possession of the potential consciousness. The brain is then a functioning entity with perfect inner association.

It is perhaps only a paraphrasing of this fact when we say that during sleep the association and conducting cerebral tracks, though not awake, are perfectly accessible to stimuli of the psychic elements (cortical cells?).

The existence of these two different states of the conducting paths becomes comprehensible only through the assumption that during wakefulness they are in a state of tonic excitement (Exner's intercellular tetanus); that this tonic *intracellular excitement* conditions the conducting capacity, and that its decrease and disappearance brings about the actual state of sleep.

We should not imagine that a cerebral (conducting) path is like a telephone wire which is only stimulated by electricity when it functions, that is, when it carries a signal; but rather as one of these telephone conduits through which there runs a constant galvanic stream and which becomes inactive when the latter stops.—Or perhaps better still, let us imagine an elaborate electrical system for transmission of light and motive power, which is to put into operation every light and motor by the simple production of a contact. In order to make this possible for the purpose of preparedness for work, it requires a certain sum of tension in the whole conduction net, even during the functional rest, which in turn necessitates an expenditure of a definite sum of energy by the dynamo.—Likewise, there exists a certain amount of excitability in the conducting paths of the resting, wakeful brain, which is always ready to function.[4]

[4] It is permitted here to allude briefly to the idea which lies at the basis of the above discussion. We usually think of the sensory nerve cells as a passive receptive apparatus, which is unjust. For the very existence of the system of association fiber shows that excitement flows from them into the nerve fibers. There must be a state of tension in a nerve fiber which connects two motor cells by continuity or contiguity if excitement flows into it from both cells. This state influences the discharging excitement, *e.g.*, in a peripheral motor fiber, as hydrostatic pressure to the force of the flowing water, or like electric

In favor of this view is the fact that the waking state itself, even without any functional activity, causes fatigue and a need for sleep; it conditions in itself an expenditure of energy.

Let us imagine a man in a state of expectant tension, which is not, however, confined to a sensory region. We are then confronted with a quiescent, but ready to function, brain. We may even assume that all the conducting paths are here adjusted to the maximum of their functional capacity; that is, they are in a state of tonic excitement. Language justly designates this state by the word "tension." Experience teaches how exerting and exhausting this state is, in which, however, no motor or psychic work has actually been performed.

This is an exceptional state, which just because of its large expenditure of energy cannot be long endured. But also the normal state of clear wakefulness produces intercerebral excitement, which shows moderate fluctuations corresponding in their diminution of the state of excitement to the various shades of consciousness from wakefulness to sleepiness and to actual sleep.

Real functional activity of the brain certainly requires a larger expenditure of energy than the mere readiness for work (as in the above given example of the electrical system, a larger amount of electrical energy must be passed through the conduits if many lights and machines are switched for action). In normal functioning no more energy is set free than is immediately consumed in the particular activity. But the brain behaves like such a system of restricted functional capacity, which cannot perhaps simultaneously produce large amounts of light and mechanical work. If the motive power transmission functions, there is little energy available for lighting, and *vice versa*. Thus, we see that in strong muscular exertion it is impossible to think continuously, that concentration of attention on one sensory sphere diminishes the functional capacity of other cerebral organs; in brief, that the brain works with an alternating, but restricted mass of energy.

The unequal distribution of energy is probably conditioned by

---

tension to the electric stream. If all the nerve cells are in a state of average excitement and stimulate their nervous appendages, the whole enormous network then forms a unified reservoir of "nerve-tension." Hence, besides the potential energy, which is in the chemical composition of the cell and that, to us, unknown form of kinetic energy which discharges in the state of excitement of the fiber, we must assume still another, as it were, resting state of nervous excitement, or the *tonic excitement of the nervous system.*

the " attentional paths " (Exner) in that the conductive capacity of the utilized paths is heightened and that of the others diminished, and so also is the " intercerebral tonic excitement " unequally distributed in the active brain.[5]

We awaken a sleeper; that is, we suddenly increase the quantum of his tonic intercerebral excitement by allowing a vivid sensory stimulus to influence him. Whether the changes caused thereby in the cerebral circulation are essential links in the causal chain, whether the blood vessels are primarily dilated through the stimulus, or whether this is the result of the excitement of the cerebral elements— all this is undecided. Certain it is, that the state of excitement forced in through a sensory gate afterwards spreads over the brain, becomes diffused, and puts all paths in a higher state of activity.

How spontaneous awakening occurs, whether one and the same cerebral region always first merges into the state of being awakened, and then functions as an awakener now on one, now on the other group of elements—all this is not perfectly clear.

Nevertheless, spontaneous awakening, which also occurs in perfect rest and darkness without outer stimuli, demonstrates that the development of energy in the life process of the cerebral elements is self-conditioned.

The muscle remains unstimulated and quiet no matter how long it has rested and accumulated in itself the maximum of tensions. But this is not so with the cerebral elements. We justly assume that in sleep they restore their stability and gather tension. If that continues up to a certain degree, if it reaches, so to say, a certain level, the excess flows off into paths, forms connections, and produces the intracerebral excitement of waking.

We can observe the same process in an instructive manner in the waking state. If the waking brain remains long in a state of rest, without changing tension into living energy through functioning, there appears the need and urge for action. Long motor rest produces the need for motion (aimless movements of animals in cages) if that need cannot be gratified. Lack of sensory impressions, such as darkness and soundless quietude become painful; mental rest, absence of perceptions, ideas and association activity, produce the

---

[5] The conception of the energy of the central nervous system as a quantity of fluctuating and alternating distribution over the brain is old. Cabanis states: " La sensibilité semble se comporter à la manière d'un fluide dont la quantité totale est déterminée et qui, toutes les fois qu'il se jette en plus grande abondance dans un de ses canaux, diminue proportionellement dans les autres." Cited from Janet, État mental II, p. 277.

torture of monotony. These painful feelings correspond to an "agitation," or to an enhancement of the normal intracerebral excitement.

The perfectly restored cerebral elements, therefore, set free a certain amount of energy even in a state of rest, which if not functionally utilized increases the intracerebral excitement. This produces a feeling of pain, which always originates when a need of the organism finds no gratification. But as those mentioned here vanish, when the free excessive quantity of excitement is functionally utilized, we conclude that this abrogation of excessive excitement is a need of the organism, and for the first time we encounter here the fact that in the organism *"there is a tendency to preserve at a constant level the intracerebral excitement"* (Freud).

An excess of it becomes burdensome and annoying, and there then arises an urge to consume it. If it cannot be consumed through sensory or ideational activity the excess flows off in aimless motor action, in up and down or similar motions, a behavior which we shall encounter later as the most frequent manner of discharging excessive tension.

How great the individual difference is in this respect is well known. Note, for example, the marked difference between vivacious and indolently torpid persons; those who cannot sit quietly, from those who show a congenital talent for warming the arm-chair; those who are mentally alert, from those who are so dull as to tolerate an immeasurable period of rest. These differences, which constitute the "emotional temperament" of people, surely depend upon profound differences of their nervous system; that is, on the amount of energy set free by the functionally resting cerebral elements.

We spoke of a tendency of the organism to preserve at a constant level the tonic cerebral excitement; but this can be understood only if we can see what need will, thereby, be fulfilled. We comprehend the tendency to preserve the average temperature at a constant level in the mammalia, because experience teaches us that this is the optimum of organic functioning. A similar constancy we also presupposed for the amount of water in the blood, etc. I believe that we can also assume a level of the intracerebral tonic excitement, namely, that it also has an optimum. On this level of tonic excitement, the brain is accessible to all external stimuli, the paths between the reflexes are open, but only to the extent of normal reflex activity. The sum of ideas is accessible to stimuli and associations in that reciprocal and relative relation of the single ideas, which corresponds to clear presence of mind. It is the state most suitable for action, But that uniform increase of the tonic excitement, which constitutes " expectation " already changes this relationship. It causes hyperesthesia of the sense organs, which soon becomes painful, and raises the reflex irritability beyond the useful need (frightfulness). This state is surely useful for some situations and purposes, but if it appears spontaneously without such preliminary condition it does not improve our functional capacity, on the contrary, it hurts it. In ordinary life we call this " to be nervous." By far in the greater number of forms of increased excitement we deal with disproportionate overexcitement which is directly damaging to the functional capacity. We designate this as " agitation." It is not inconceivable, but in analogy to other regulations of the organism, it strives to adhere to the optimum of excitement and to reattain it after it has exceeded its level.

We may here again be permitted to return to the comparison of the electric light system. The tension in the net of distribution has also such an optimum; if it is exceeded the function is easily damaged, as, for example, through the rapid burning out of the incandescent wires. Concerning the damage to the system itself through " short-circuiting," etc., we will speak later.

B. Our language, which is the resultant of the experience of many generations, distinguishes with admirable precision those forms and degrees of increase of excitement which are still useful to the psychic activity, because they equally raise the free energy of all cerebral functions, from those which damage the same, because disproportionately they partly enhance and partly inhibit the psychic functions.

It designates the first as *inciting* or *stimulating* and the second as *exciting*. An interesting conversation, tea, or coffee, incites or stimulates, while a quarrel, or a larger dose of alcohol excites. While incitement only awakens the impulse for functional utilization of enhanced irritability, excitement seeks disburdenment in a more or less violent manner; it either verges on or constitutes a real pathological process. It forms the psycho-physical foundation of the affects, of which we shall say more in the following chapter, but before this we must still rapidly touch on the physiological or endogenic causes of increased excitement.

These constitute, in the first place, the great physiological needs and impulses of the organism, such as hunger for oxygen and for nourishment, and thirst. As the excitement, which they produce, becomes connected with definite sensations and aims, it cannot be as well observed as the pure enhancement of excitement in those discussed above, which originate only through rest of the brain elements. It always has its special coloring, but it is unmistakable in the anxious excitement of dyspnoea, as well as in the restlessness of those who are starving.

The increased excitement, which is discharged from these sources, is conditioned by chemical changes of the brain elements themselves, which are short of oxygen, or by tension, or by water. It is discharged through preformed motor paths which lead to gratification of the generated need. The dyspnoea through the exertion of the breath, hunger and thirst, through seeking and obtaining nourishment and water. The principle of constancy of excitement hardly comes into play in this excitement, for the interests served by this increase of excitement are more important for the organism than for the restoration of the normal functional relations of the brain. To be sure, we see the animals in the menagerie running to and fro excitedly in their cages before the feeding hour, but this may well be a remnant of the preformed motor activity of searching for nourishment, which became aimless through captivity, and may, therefore, not be a means of freeing the nervous system from excitement.

If the chemical structure of the nervous system has become permanently changed through a continuous supply of foreign material, the lack of these excitable states, conditions the excitement of *abstinence* from *narcotics,* in the same way as the lack of normal nourishing material in a healthy person.

———————

The transition from these endogenic enhancements of excitement to the psychic affects in the narrower sense is formed by the sexual excitement and the sexual affect. Sexuality appears first as a vague, indefinite and aimless advancer of excitement during puberty. In the further course of its development there normally occurs a firm association between this endogenic increase of excitement, glands, and the perceptions or ideas of the opposite sex. This is glaringly observed in the wonderful phenomenon of being in love with a single person. This person becomes endowed with the whole quantity of excitement set free by the sexual instinct; she becomes, so to say, an " affective idea." That is, in assuming actuality in consciousness, she sets free the increased excitement which really originates in another source, namely, in the sexual glands.

The sexual instinct is certainly the mightiest source of long and continual increase of excitement, and as such, also of neuroses. This increase is most unequally distributed in the nervous system. In higher grades of intensity the flow of ideas is disturbed, the relative value of ideas is altered, and in the orgasm of the sexual act thought is almost entirely extinguished.

Also, perception, that is, the psychic elaboration of the sensory feeling, suffers. The animal, which is ordinarily shy and careful becomes blind and deaf to danger. On the other hand, at least in the male, there results an increase in the intensity of the aggressive impulse, the hitherto peaceful animal becomes dangerous, until the excitement is discharged in the motor functions of the sexual act.

C. A similar disturbance of the dynamic equilibrium in the nervous system, the disproportionate distribution of the increased excitement, constitutes the psychic side of the affect.

We shall not attempt to give here either a psychology or a physiology of the affects. Only one single point of pathological importance will be examined, namely, the one referring to the ideogenic affects, or to those which are produced by perceptions and ideas. Lange [6] has justly pointed out again that the affects can almost entirely be conditioned by toxic material, as demonstrated by psychiatry, primarily through pathological changes, as well as by ideas.

There is hardly any need for further confirmation of the fact that all these disturbances of the psychic equilibrium, which we call acute affects, appear with an increase of excitement. (In the chronic affects, such as grief and worry, i.e., in protracted anxiety, there is the complication of a deep state of exhaustion, which produces an unequal distribution of excitement and with it a disturbance of equilibrium, but it diminishes its height.) But this increased excitement cannot be utilized in psychic activity. All strong affects infringe upon the associations of the trend of ideas. In anger and fear one becomes " mad." Only that group of ideas which has stimu-

[6] Lange, Über Gemütsbewegungen, 1887.

lated the affect persists in consciousness with highest intensity, so
that a balancing of the excitement through associative activity is
impossible.

However, the " active," " sthenic " affects equalize the increased
excitement through motor discharge. The jubilance and leaping of
pleasure, the increased muscular tone in anger, the angry speech, and
the rewarded deed, all permit a discharge of excitement through
acts of motion. Psychic pain disburdens the same in respiratory
exertions and in a secretory act, such as sobbing, weeping. That
these reactions decrease the excitement and calm is a matter of
everyday experience. As already mentioned, language expresses this
in such terms as to " weep one's self out," " to spend one's rage,"
etc.; what is really given or spent thereby is the increased cerebral
excitement.

Only some of these reactions are purposeful, insofar as they
change something in the situation, as in the case of an angry actor's
speech. The others are entirely aimless, or better, they have no other
aim than to adjust the increased excitement and to establish the
psychic equilibrium. Insofar as they accomplish this, they serve the
" tendency to preserve a constant level of the cerebral excitement."

The " asthenic " affects of fright and anxiety lack this reactive
disburdening. Fright paralyzes quite directly the motility as well as
the associations, and likewise anxiety, if we exclude the one purposeful reaction of running away through the cause of the anxiety
affect and other circumstances. The excitement of fear disappears
only through gradual settlement.

Anger is discharged in adequate reactions, which correspond to
its causation. Should this become impossible through inhibition,
substitutes takes its place, the angry speech is a case in question.
But also other, quite aimless acts can take its place. If one has
to suppress his angry excitement before his superior, he may alleviate
his feeling by smashing a costly vase. This voluntary replacement
of a motor act by another, corresponds altogether to the substitution of the natural pain-reflex by another muscular contraction; the
preformed reflex at a tooth extraction is to push the doctor away
and cry. If instead we contract the arm muscles by pressing against
the chair, we thus transfer the sum of excitement of the released
pain from one group of muscles to another. In a spontaneous, severe
toothache, which has no preformed reflex besides groaning, the
excitement manifests itself in a to and fro aimless running. In the

same way we transport the excitement of anger from the adequate reaction to others, and feel relieved only if it is consumed through a strong motor innervation.

However, if the affect is altogether prevented from such a discharge of excitement, the state of affairs is the same in anger as it is in fear and anxiety, namely, the intracerebral excitement becomes enormously increased, but is neither utilized in associative or motor activity. In the normal person the disturbance gradually settles down, but in some it produces anomalous reactions, or Oppenheim's *"anomalous expression of the emotions."*

III. *The Hysterical Conversion*

It will hardly arouse the suspicion that I identify nervous excitement with electricity if I once more return to its comparison with an electrical system. If the tension in the latter becomes excessive, there is the danger that some weak spots in the insulation will break through. Electrical manifestations will then appear in abnormal places, or if two wires touch it may result in a short circuit. As a permanent change is produced in these places, the disturbance conditioned by it can always reappear if the tension is sufficiently increased, because an abnormal path has been established.

I can justly assert that the relationship of the nervous system is somewhat similar. It is a thoroughly connected entity, but in many places there are inserted large, yet not insuperable resistances, which prevent the general and equalized distribution of excitement. Thus, in the normal, conscious man the excitement from the ideation system does not pass over to the perceptual systems, we do not hallucinate. The nervous apparatus of the important organ-complexes, such as the circulation, and digestion, are separated by strong resistances from the organs of ideas, in the interest of security and functional capacity of the organism; their independence is guaranteed, they are not directly influenced by ideas. But only resistances of individually different forces impede the transition of the intracerebral excitement to the circulatory and digestive apparatus. Between the absolutely "non-nervous" person—a rare ideal today—whose heart action remains at a constant level in every state of life, and is only influenced by the work to be accomplished, who in every danger has a proportionably good appetite and digestion, and the nervous person, in whom every event produces palpitation and diarrhoea—between these two we find all gradations of affective excitability.

At all events, there are resistances in the normal man against the transition of cerebral excitement to the vegetative organs. They correspond to the insulation of electrical conduction. In those places where they are slightly anomalous, a very tense cerebral excitement causes a break-through, and these, the excitements of the affects, then pass over to the peripheral organ, and bring about the "anomalous expression of the emotions."

Of the two conditions just mentioned, one has already been exhaustively discussed. It represents a high degree of intracerebral excitement to which both adjustment through psychic, as well as through motor outlet is closed, or it is too high to be sufficiently discharged by the latter paths.

The second condition represents an abnormal weakness of the resistance in individual paths. This weakness may lie in the original make-up of the person (congenital disposition), or it can be conditioned by long continued states of excitement, which slacken, as it were, the structures of the nervous system and reduce all resistances (disposition of puberty), or it may be conditioned by debilitating influences, such as diseases, undernourishment, etc. (disposition of exhaustion). The resistance of an individual path can also become reduced through a previous disease of the concerned organ, whereby paths were formed to and from the brain. A weak heart succumbs more quickly to the influence of the affects than a healthy one. "I have a sounding board in my abdomen," said a woman suffering from a chronic parametritis, "whatever happens awakens the old pain"—(disposition through local disease).

The motor acts, through which the excitement of the affects is normally disburdened, are ordinated and coördinated, even if often aimlessly. But the excessive excitement can get around the coördinating centres, or break through them, and flow off in elementary movements. In the suckling, besides the respiratory act of crying, we see only such incoördinated muscular contractions as rearing and kicking, which are the effects, as well as the expressions, of the affect. With the advancement of development, the muscles become more subjected to the domination of coördination and will. But opisthotonus, which represents the maximum motor strain of the muscles of the whole body, and the clonic movements of fidgeting and kicking, remain throughout life as forms of reaction of the highest excitement of the brain, both for the purely physical expressions of the epileptic attacks, and for the discharge of the highest affects in the form of greater or lesser epileptoid convulsions. (The purely motor part of the hysterical attack.)

Such abnormal affective reactions certainly belong to hysteria, but they may also occur outside of this disease; they merely indicate a more or less high degree of nervousness and not necessarily hysteria. Such phenomena can be designated as hysterical only if they appear not as results of high graded, but objectively conditioned affects, but seemingly spontaneously, as morbid manifestations. Many observations, including our own, have demonstrated that they are based on memories which renew the original affect. Or better expressed, *they would renew, if those reactions would not have already originated before.*

Probably in all more active minded people, while psychically calm, there flows quietly through consciousness a stream of ideas and memories; most of the time the ideas are hardly vivid enough to leave any trace, so that one cannot tell how the associations have taken place. But if an idea comes to the surface which had originally been connected with a strong affect, it renews itself with greater or lesser intensity. This so "affectively accentuated" idea then comes into consciousness clearly and vividly. The force of the affect, which a memory can release, differs widely, depending on the time it was exposed to the diverse "usurping" influences. Above all, it depends on whether the original affect was "abreacted." In our "preliminary communication" we have called attention to the various degrees of affectivity, which are recalled to memory, let us say, in the case of anger over an insult, which was retaliated or silently endured. If the psychic reflex actually followed during the original causation, the memory releases a much smaller quantity of excitement.[7] If not, the memory continually forces on one's lips the scolding words which were suppressed at the time, and which would have been the psychic reflex of that stimulus.

[7] The impulse of revenge, which is so strong in primitive man and which in culture became more masked than suppressed, is really nothing but the excitement of an unreleased reflex. To defend an injury in a fight and thereby injure the adversary represents an adequately preformed psychic reflex. If this does not occur, or if it was insufficiently performed, it is then repeatedly released in memory, and gives origin to the "impulse for revenge," which like all other "impulses" is an irrational impulse of the will. The proof of this is its irrationality, its independence of all usefulness and of all expediency; indeed, its victory over all consideration of one's own security. But as soon as the reflex has been discharged, this irrationality can then come into consciousness.

If the original affect was discharged not in a normal, but in an "abnormal reflex," the latter, too, is again released by the memory, and the excitement emanating from the affective idea becomes *converted* into a physical phenomenon (Freud).

If this abnormal reflex has carved a perfect path for itself by means of frequent repetitions, the influence of the freed ideas can seemingly so fully exhaust itself thereby that the affect itself consists only of minimal strength, or is not at all generated, the "*hysterical conversion*" is then perfect. The idea, however, which now no longer exerts any psychic influence, can be overlooked by the individual, or its emergence is soon forgotten just as happens in other affectless ideas.

Such a substitution of cerebral excitement, which should have conditioned an idea, by an excitement of peripheral paths, becomes perhaps more acceptable through the memory of the opposite behavior at the emission of a preformed reflex. To illustrate this I choose a most trivial example, the sneezing reflex. If a stimulus of the mucous membrane of the nose does not for some reason release this preformed reflex, we know that it produces a feeling of excitement and tension. It is the excitement which could not flow off on the motor paths, which now inhibits every other activity and spreads itself over the brain. This most banal example offers, nevertheless, the scheme for the process which also takes place in the omission of the most complicated psychic reflexes. The above discussed excitement of the revenge impulse is essentially the same, and we can pursue this process into the highest spheres of human activity. *Goethe* was never through with an experience until he settled it in some poetic activity; to him this was the preformed reflex of an affect, and as long as it was not accomplished, he suffered from a painful enhancement of excitement.

The intracerebral excitement and the process of excitement in the peripheral paths are of reciprocal magnitude; the former grows if, and as long as, a reflex is not discharged, and sinks and vanishes if it has become transformed into peripheral nerve excitement. Thus, it also seems conceivable that no perceptible affect originates, if the idea which should have caused it has immediately released an abnormal reflex through which the generated excitement was at once discharged. The "hysterical conversion" is then complete, for the original intracerebral excitement of the affect was changed into the process of excitement of the peripheral paths, and the original affective idea no longer evokes the affect, but only the abnormal reflex.[8]

With this we have advanced one step further in the study of the "abnormal expression of the emotions." The hysterical phenomenon (abnormal reflex) does not seem ideogenic even to intelligent and observing patients, because the causative idea is no longer affectively accentuated and no longer distinguished from other ideas and memories. It appears as a purely somatic phenomenon, seemingly without psychological roots.

What now determines the discharge of the affective excitement to produce just the one abnormal reflex, and no other kind? Our observations answer this question for many cases by showing that this discharge, too, follows the "principle of least resistance," and occurs in those paths in which the resistance had become weakened through concurrent circumstances. We might mention the case already discussed above, namely, that some reflexes carve paths for themselves through somatic illness, e.g., if one frequently suffers from cardialgias, the latter will also be evoked by the affect.—Or a path is formed for a reflex through the fact that there was a wilful intention for the particular muscular innervation during the incipience of the affect. Thus, Anna O. (Obs. I) during the fear affect attempted to extend the right arm, which was motionless from the paralysis, and henceforth, the sight of all snake-like objects evoked a tetanus of the right arm. Or, she strongly converged her eyes while in the throes of the affect in order to see the watch hands, and this convergent strabismus then became one of the reflexes of this later affect, etc.

For this very effect of simultaneity dominates also our normal associations, every sensory perception calls back to consciousness another which originally appeared simultaneously with it.

Hence, if a vivid sensory impression existed simultaneously with

---

[8] I do not wish to work to death the comparison with an electrical system; considering the fundamental differences of the relations it can hardly illustrate the processes of the nervous system, and certainly cannot explain them. But we may here still recall the case that due to high tension the insulation of a light system had become damaged and in one place there was a "short circuit." If electrical phenomena like small sparks, etc., should appear in this place, the lamp, to which this conduction leads, will give no light, just as the affect does not come into being, if the excitement is discharged as an abnormal reflex and becomes converted into a somatic phenomena.

the original affect, it is again evoked by the renewed affect, especially because it dealt at the time with a discharge of an excess of
excitement, not as a memory, but as an hallucination. Almost all
our observations offer examples of this kind. Such an example
is also the case of a woman who went through a painful affect while
suffering from severe toothache as a result of periostitis, and thereafter every renewal of the affect, indeed every recollection of it,
provoked an infra-orbital neuralgia.

This represents the path of abnormal reflexes following the general laws of association. Sometimes, however (to be sure only in
the higher grades of hysteria), one finds a real series of associated
ideas between the affect and its reflex, which thus represents a *determination through a symbol.* Frequently these connections are in
the form of ridiculous play of words and clang associations, but this
only occurs in dream-like states with diminished criticism, and hence,
they do not belong to the group of phenomena considered here.

In a great many cases the determination remains incomprehensible because our insight into the psychic state and our knowledge
of the ideas which were actual at the origin of the hysterical phenomena, are often most incomplete. However, we may assume that
the process is not quite dissimilar from one which is clear to us in
more favorable cases.

The experience, which generated the original affect, the excitement of which was later converted into a somatic phenomenon, we
designate as a *psychic trauma,* and the morbid manifestations which
so originated as *hysterical symptoms of traumatic origin.* (The
designation, "traumatic hysteria," has already been given to that
phenomenon, which, as a result of physical injuries, in the narrowest
sense, traumas, constitute a part of the "traumatic neurosis.")

In perfect analogy with the origin of traumatically determined
hysterical phenomena is the hysterical conversion of that psychic
excitement, which originates not from external stimuli, not from
inhibition of normal psychic reflexes, but from inhibitions in the
stream of associations.

The elementary example and paradigm, which demonstrates this
is furnished by the excitement which is generated, because we cannot recall a name or solve a riddle, etc. As soon as the name is
uttered or the riddle solved, the excitement disappears because the
chain of association closes just as in the closure of a reflex chain.
The force of the excitement which emanates from such an impedi-

ment is proportionate to the interest which the situation has for us, that is, it depends on the force which stimulates the will. But as the search for the solution of the problem, etc., entails hard work, even if this work is unsuccessful, even strong excitement becomes consumed and does not press for discharge, and hence, never becomes pathogenic.

This actually happens if the stream of associations is so inhibited that equivalent ideas are *incompatible* with one another, as *e.g.,* when new thoughts get into a conflict with firmly rooted ideation complexes. The torment of religious doubt, to which so many people succumb and so many more have succumbed, is of this nature. It causes a rise in the excitement, which in turn enhances the psychic pain. This is particularly the case when a volitional interest of the individual is thereby brought into play, as when the doubter believes himself threatened in his happiness and welfare.

But this is always the case when there is a conflict between a complex of firmly instilled moral ideas and the memory of one's own acts, or even only of one's thoughts, which are incompatible with them, namely, the *pangs of conscience.* The volitional interest to find pleasure in one's own personality, to be satisfied with it, is thereby put into play, and thus increases to the highest degree the excitement of the inhibiting associations. That such a conflict of incompatible ideas becomes pathogenic is a matter of everyday experience. It is mostly a question of ideas and processes of the sexual life, such as masturbation in a morally sensitive adolescent, or the consciousness of a desire for a strange man in a strictly moral woman. Indeed, the first appearance of sexual feelings and ideas often enough suffices to produce a high degree of emotivity as a result of a conflict with firmly rooted ideas of moral purity.[9]

The consequences of such conflict are usually pathological depressions and attacks of anxiety (Freud). Concurrent circumstances frequently determine an anomalous somatic phenomenon in which the excitement disburdens itself in vomiting, if the feeling of moral soiling produces a physical disgust, or in a nervous cough, as in the case of Anna O., if the conscience anxiety evokes a spasm of the glottis, etc.[10]

[9] *Cf.* here some interesting reports and observations of Benedikt (1889) reprinted in the Journal, " Hypnotismus und Suggestion," p. 54, 1894.

[10] In Mach's *Bewegungsempfindungen* I find an observation which is pertinent here : " The reported (dizziness) experiments repeatedly showed that a feeling of disgust appeared mainly only when it was difficult to bring into harmony the feelings of motion with the optical impressions. It seemed as

The excitement which is produced by very vivid and irreconcilable ideas finds adequate reaction in verbal communications. The impulse for this we encounter with comic exaggeration in the story of the Barber of Midas, who cried out his secret to the ship. We also find it as one of the foundations of a great historical institution in the Catholic church, the auricular confession. Verbal communication eases and disburdens the tension even if it does not take place in the presence of a priest and is not followed by absolution. If this escape is closed to the excitement, it sometimes becomes converted into a somatic phenomenon just as in the excitement of traumatic affects, and we know a whole group of hysterical manifestations which have this origin and *which are designated by Freud as hysterical retention phenomena.*

The discussion hitherto given about the mechanics of the psychic origin of hysterical phenomena is open to the reproach that it schematizes and represents the process in a simpler way than it really is. In order that a real hysterical symptom should develop in a healthy, originally non-neuropathic person, with its apparent independence of the psyche and its self-dependent somatic existence, *there must always be a concurrence of many circumstances.*

The following case may serve as an example for the complicatedness of this process. A boy of twelve years, who formerly suffered from pavor nocturnus, the son of a very nervous father, returned home from school one day feeling ill. He complained of pain on swallowing, that is, he could only swallow with difficulty, and of headaches. The family physician thought that the cause of his condition was an angina, but even after many days the condition did not improve. The boy did not wish to eat, and vomited when he was urged to do so. He dragged himself around in a tired and dull manner, always wished to remain in bed, and was considerably reduced physically. When I saw him after five weeks he made the impression of a shy, shut-in child, and I became convinced that his illness was psychically conditioned. On urgent questioning he gave a banal reason, a strict rebuke from his father, which was apparently not the real reason for the disease. Nor was there anything to be

---

if a part of the stimulus emanating from the labyrinth would have been forced to leave the optic tract closed to it by another stimulus, and take an entirely new course. . . ." "I have also repeatedly observed a feeling of disgust in the experiment of combining stereoscopic views with strong differences." Here we have the exact physiological scheme for the origin of pathological, hysterical phenomena through the coexistence of vivid and incompatible ideas.

found from his school. I thought that I would have to obtain information in a state of hypnosis, but that became unnecessary. When his wise and energetic mother once persisted in questioning him, he tearfully told the following story. On the way home from school, he stopped in a urinal, and there a man held his penis before him with the request that he should take it in his mouth. He ran away full of fright, and nothing else happened to him. But from this moment on, he was sick. From the time he made the confession, he had remained in perfect health.—In order to produce the phenomena of anorexia, difficulty in swallowing and vomiting, the following elements were here necessary: A congenital neurotic disposition, fright, the incursion of sexuality in the most brutal form into the child's mind, and as a determining factor the disgusting idea. The persistence of the disease was due to his silence, which prevented the excitement from normal discharge.

As in this case, many factors must always coöperate in order that the hysterical symptom should be formed in one hitherto healthy. As Freud expresses it, " The symptom is always over-determined."

Such over-determination can also be produced when the same affect is evoked through many and repeated causes. The patient and the people of the environment attribute the hysterical symptom only to the last event, which in most cases has only brought to the surface that which had already been accomplished through other traumas.

A young girl had her first hysterical attack, which was later followed by a series of others, when a cat jumped on her shoulder in the dark. It seemed like a simple effect of fright, but more precise investigation showed that this strikingly beautiful and over-guarded 17-year-old girl was recently the object of many more or less brutal pursuits, and thus merged into sexual excitement (Disposition). On the same dark stairway she was attacked a few days before by a young man, from whose grasp she escaped with effort. This was the actual psychic trauma, the effect of which became manifest only through the cat. But in how many cases is such a cat responsible for a perfectly adequate *causa efficiens?*

For the production of the conversion through repetition of the affect it is not always necessary to have a number of external events. A renewal of the affect in the memory often suffices, if this follows in rapid and frequent repetitions soon after the trauma and before the affect had become blurred. That is sufficient, if the affect was very forceful, which is the case in traumatic hysterias in the narrow sense of the word.

Thus, during the days following a railroad accident, one relives the frightful scenes in sleep and in the waking state. The affect of fright is forever renewed until finally after this period of "psychic elaboration" (Charcot), or *incubation,* there occurs the conversion into a psychic phenomenon. (To be sure, there is also a coöperation of another factor, which will be discussed later.)

But usually the affective idea soon succumbs to the influences touched upon in the "preliminary communication" (p. 8) which gradually rob it of its affective value. A constantly decreasing amount of excitement conditions its return to the surface, and the memory thus loses the capacity to contribute to the formation of a somatic phenomenon. The path of the abnormal reflex then becomes lost and this restores the *status quo ante.*

However, the usurping influences are all functions of the associations, of thinking, and of correcting through other ideas. These become impossible if the affective idea is withdrawn from the "association tracks"; if that happens, the former retains all of its affective value. But as at every renewal it again sets free the whole sum of excitement of the original affect, the path of the abnormal reflex begun at that time is finally completed, or the one which then came into existence is retained and stabilized. The phenomena of hysterical conversion is then fully established and for a long time.

From our observations we know two forms of such exclusion of affective ideas from the associations.

The first is the "defense," or the voluntary suppression of painful ideas, through which man feels a threat to his joy of life or to his self-esteem. In his report on the "Defense-Neuro-Psychoses"[11] and in case histories given here, Freud spoke about this process, which surely is of high pathological importance.

It is not clearly conceivable how an idea can voluntarily be repressed from consciousness. But we know intimately the corresponding positive process, namely, the concentration of the attention on an idea, and can say just as little as to how we accomplish it.

We have, moreover, found that another class of ideas is kept away from the usurping influences by thought, not because one does not wish to remember, but because one cannot do so. This is due to the fact that these ideas originally came to the surface in certain

[11] Neurol. Central-Blatt, Nov. 10, 1894.

states, and were invested with an affect for which there is an amnesia in the waking consciousness, that is, they originated in hypnotic or hypnoid states. The latter seem to be of the highest importance for the theory of hysteria and, hence, merit a somewhat more exhaustive discussion.[12]

IV. *Hypnoid States*

When we expressed the view in the "preliminary communication" that the basis and condition of hysteria is the existence of hypnoid states, we overlooked the fact that Moebius had already said quite the same in 1890. To quote his words: "The assumption of the pathogenic action of ideas is congenital, *i.e.*, there is on the one hand the hysterical disposition, and on the other a special state of mind. Concerning this state of mind, one can have only a vague idea. It must be similar to the hypnotic state, it must correspond to a certain void of consciousness, in which the emerging idea is not confronted by any resistances from the others, in which the throne is, so to speak, free for anybody. We know that such a state can be produced through hypnosis as well as through mental shock (fright, anger, etc.), and through states of exhaustion (insomnia, hunger, etc.)."[13]

The question, the near solution of which Moebius herewith first attempts, refers to the origin of somatic phenomena through ideas. He calls to our attention the ease with which such an idea occurs in hypnosis, and he considers the efficacy of the affects as analogous to it. Our—in some respects—divergent view concerning this affective force was exhaustively discussed above. I do not, therefore, find it necessary to enter further into the difficulty which lies in the fact that Moebius assumes "a void of consciousness"[14] (which surely exists in fright and in the protracted anxiety), and into the question of how difficult it really is to form an analogy between the exciting state of the affect and the restfulness of the hypnosis. We

[12] If we speak here and thereafter about ideas which are actual, active, and still unconscious, it is only seldom a question of single ideas (like perhaps the hallucinated, large snake of Anna O., which produced the contracture) but almost always about a complex of ideas, associations, and memories of external processes and inner mental processes. The individual ideas contained in this complex are all occasionally consciously perceived, only the definite combination is banned from consciousness.

[13] Moebius: Ueber Astasie-Abasie, Neurol. Beiträge I, Heft. p. 17.

[14] Moebius perhaps means by this designation nothing more than the inhibition in the course of ideas, which surely exists in the affect, even if it originates altogether from other causes than in the hypnosis.

shall, however, later return to the statements of Moebius, which I believe contain an important truth.

For us, the importance of the hypnosis-like " hypnoid " states lies above all in the amnesia and in its capacity to condition that splitting of the psyche, to be discussed later, which is of fundamental importance for " major hysteria." This importance we admit even now, yet we must essentially restrict our statement. The conversion, or the ideogenic origin of somatic phenomena takes place also outside of the hypnoid states, and as for the formation of ideation complexes, which are excluded from the association paths, Freud found a second independent source in the voluntary amnesia of the ' defense.' But with this restriction, I still believe that the latter are the cause and condition of many, indeed of most, major and complicated hysterias.

To the hypnoid states we must naturally add first of all the real auto-hypnoses, which differ from the artificial ones only in their spontaneous origin. We find them in some fully developed hysterias with changing frequency and different duration, frequently in the most rapid alternation with the state of normal wakefulness.[15] Due to their dream-like ideational content they often deserve the name of *delirium hystericum*. In the waking state there is a more or less complete amnesia for the inner processes of this state, whereas in the artificial hypnosis they are perfectly recalled. The psychic results of these states, and the associations formed in them are kept away by the amnesia from all corrections of the waking state. And as criticism and control have been reduced in auto-hypnosis by other ideas, and mostly almost entirely vanish, it may give rise to the craziest delusions, which may maintain themselves for a long time. Thus, almost only such states give origin to a somewhat more complicated and irrational " symbolic relationship between the causative and the pathological phenomenon," which is quite frequently based on the most ridiculous sound similarities, and word associations. The indiscrimination of the same frequently permits the origin of auto-suggestions, as, *e.g.,* when an hysterical attack leaves behind a paralysis. Due perhaps to accident, we hardly ever came across in our analyses this origin of an hysterical phenomenon. We have always found it also in auto-hypnosis, where it was conditioned by the same process as outside of the same, namely by the conversion of an affective excitement.

[15] Observations I and II.

This " hysterical conversion " develops easier in auto-hypnosis than in the waking state, precisely as in artificial hypnosis, where suggestive ideas realize themselves much more easily physically, as hallucinations and motions. But the process of conversion excitement is essentially the same as it was described above. Once this comes into being the somatic phenomenon repeats itself, whenever affect and auto-hypnosis meet again. And it seems that the hypnotic state can later be provoked by the affect alone. As long as hypnosis alternates with full consciousness, the hysterical symptom remains above all restricted to the hypnotic state, and becomes reënforced by it through repetition. But the causative idea is protected against correction by the waking thought and its critique because it really never comes to the surface in clear wakefulness.

Thus, the contracture of the right arm in Anna O. (Observ. I), which associated itself in her auto-hypnosis with the anxiety affect and the snake idea, remained restricted for four months to the moments of the hypnotic state (or—if this name be considered inappropriate for *absences* of very short duration—the hypnoid), but repeated itself frequently. The same happened in other conversions which took place in the hypnoid state. Thus, there formed itself in complete latency that major complex of hysterical phenomena, which became manifest when the hypnoid state became continuous.

Phenomena of such origin only appeared in clear wakefulness after the occurrence of psychic splitting and after the alternations between waking and hypnoid states gave place to the co-existence of normal and hypnoid, ideational complexes.

Have such hypnoid states already existed before the illness, and how did they develop? I can say very little about it, because except in the case of Anna O., who could have informed us about it, we have no other observations at our disposal. It seems certain that in this patient the state of auto-hypnosis was prepared by the habitual day-dreaming, and that it was then fully established through a protracted affect of anxiety, which in itself conditioned a hypnoid state. It does not seem improbable that this process is quite general.

Very diverse states produce " absent-mindedness," but only some of them form a disposition for auto-hypnosis or directly pass over into such state. The investigator who is absorbed in a problem is to a certain extent probably also anesthetic, and forms no conscious perceptions out of large groups of sensory impressions, he is just like one versifying with phantastic vividness (Anna O.'s " private theater "). Nevertheless, energetic psychic work is accomplished in these states, which thus consume the excitement set free in the nervous system. On the other hand, in states of distraction or in crepuscular states, the intracerebral excitement sinks below the level of clear wakefulness. These states border on sleepiness and pass over into sleep. But if a group of affectively accentuated ideas come to life in such states of engrossment and in inhibited streams of ideas, it then creates a high level of the intracerebral excitement, which is not consumed by psychic work, and therefore, becomes available for anomalous functions, for conversion.

Thus, neither " absent mindedness " during energetic work, nor the unemotional dawny state is pathogenic, but the affectful reveries as well as the exhaustion from protracted affect are really so. The brooding of the worrier, the anxiety of those who watch at the sick bed of a beloved person, and the reveries of lovers represent such states. The " absence " is conditioned in the first place by the concentration on an affective idea. The ideation stream slows up gradually, finally almost to the point of stagnation, but the affective idea with its affect remains vivid and with it also the large quantity of excitement, which was not functionally used up. The similarity of the relations to those which condition hypnosis is unmistakable. Moreover, the person to be hypnotized need not really fall alseep, that is, his intracerebral excitement need not sink to the level of sleep, but the stream of ideas must be inhibited. The whole mass of excitement is then at the disposal of the suggested idea.

Pathogenic auto-hypnosis may originate in some persons through the entrance of the affect into the habitual reveries. This is perhaps one of the reasons for the fact that in hysterical amnesia we frequently encounter the two major pathogenic factors, namely, being in love, and nursing the sick. With the longing desires for the absent lover, the first creates a " displacement " or a dimming of the environmental reality and then an affectful stoppage of thought. In nursing, the outer calm, the concentration on an object, the listening to the patient's breathing, produce exactly the same conditions which are employed in inducing hypnotism. The twilight state thus produced is then filled with the affect of anxiety. It is possible that these states differ only in quantity from real auto-hypnosis and can change into it.

Once this has been established, the hypnosis-like state repeats itself again and again under the same circumstances, so that instead of the two normal psychic states the individual then has three, namely wakefulness, sleep, and hypnoid state, precisely as we observe it in frequent repetitions of deep artificial hypnosis.

I do not know whether spontaneous hypnotic states can develop also without such influences of the affect, as a result of an original predisposition, but I think that this is quite probable. When we see how the capacity for artificial hypnosis differs in the normal and in the sick, and how easily it manifests itself in some, the presumption is justified, that in the latter they might also occur spontaneously. And, in order to change the reveries into auto-hypnosis, a special predisposition may perhaps be required. I am, therefore, far from assuming that the mechanisms of origin, which we learned from Anna O., exist in all hysterias.

I speak of hypnoid states instead of hypnosis itself because the former are very poorly demarcated in the development of these very important states of hysteria. We do not know whether revery, which was designated above as the prodromal stage of auto-hypnosis, cannot itself already produce the same pathogenic effects, and whether they could not also be produced by the protracted affect of anxiety. They can surely be produced by fright. Insofar as fright inhibits the ideation stream while an affective idea (danger) is still very active, it is perfectly parallel to the affectful revery, and, as the continually renewed memory always reproduces this psychic state, there develops a "fright-hypnoidal state," in which the conversion is either formed or stabilized, that is, the incubation period of "traumatic hysteria," in the strict sense of the term.

As so many different states conjoin in auto-hypnosis, of which all, however, agree in the most important point, the term, "hypnoid," recommends itself because it emphasizes this inner similarity. It sums up that view, which Moebius had maintained in the above cited statements.

But above all it designates the auto-hypnosis itself, the importance of which for the origin of hysterical phenomena is based on the facilitation of the conversion, on the protection of the converted phenomena from usurpation (through amnesia) and from the psychic splitting, which ultimately results from it.

Now, if a physical symptom is caused by an idea and is always released again by it, one would expect that intelligent patients capable of self-observation would become aware of this connection, that they would learn from experience that somatic phenomena can come simultaneously with the recollection of a definite idea. To be sure, the inner causal connection is unknown to them, but we all always know what ideas can make us cry, laugh, or blush, even if the nervous mechanism of these ideogenic phenomena are far from clear.— Sometimes, the patients really observe the connection and are conscious of it. Thus, a woman said that her mild hysterical attack in the form of trembling and palpitation came from a severe mental excitement and repeated itself only at every process which recalled it to her. But that is not true of many, probably not of the majority of hysterical symptoms. Even intelligent patients do not know that they appear in consequence of an idea, but they consider them as independent physical phenomena. If that were different, the psychic theory of hysteria must have had a hoary age.

We obviously can believe that the morbid manifestations in question may have actually originated ideogenically, but to borrow an expression from Romberg, the repetitions have been " impressed " on the body, and now they no longer depend on a psychic process, but on the changes in the nervous system, which have meanwhile developed. They, as it were, became independent, or real somatic symptoms.

This view is from the beginning, neither impossible nor improbable. But I believe that the new views, which our observations bring to the theory of hysteria, definitely show that the older theories are wide of the mark, at least in a great many cases. We saw that the " individual hysterical symptoms immediately disappeared without returning if we succeeded in thoroughly awakening the memories of the causal process with its accompanying affect, and if the patient circumstantially discussed the process in the most detailed manner and gave verbal expression to the affect." The case histories here reported furnish some illustrations for this assertion. " In reversing the sentence: *cessante causa cessat effectus,* we may surely conclude from this observation that the causative process (*i.e.,* the memory of it) continues to act even after years not indirectly through the agency of causal links, but directly as a releasing cause, somewhat the same as a recollected psychic pain in waking consciousness will evoke the secretion of tears in later times. The hysteric suffers mostly from reminiscences."

However, if this is the case, if the memory of the psychic trauma behaves in the manner of a foreign body for a long time after its intrusion, acting as an active agent of the present, and yet the patient has no knowledge of this memory and its emergence—if that is so, we must admit that *unconscious ideas* exist and are active.

Such ideas we find in the analysis of hysterical phenomena, not isolated ones, but as has actually been shown, large complexes of ideas and complicated and consequential psychic processes, which in some patients remain altogether unconscious, and exist hand in hand with the conscious psychic life. We also find that splitting of the psychic activity occurs, and is of fundamental importance for the understanding of complicated hysterias.

May we now be permitted to enter slightly into this difficult and dark region? The need for establishing the meaning of the expressions which we have used may perhaps excuse the theoretical explanation.

V. *Unconscious and Ideas Incapable of Consciousness. Splitting of the Psyche*

That idea which we know we call conscious. In the human being there exists the wonderful fact of self-consciousness, we are able to follow successively ideas which emerge in us and consider them and observe them like objects. This does not always happen, as there are only rare occasions of self-observation. But it is a capability which is common to all human beings, for everybody says: " I have thought of this and that." Those ideas which we observe in us as active or would observe, if we paid attention to them, we call conscious. There are very few of these at all periods of time; and if besides these still others should be present, we would have to call them *unconscious* ideas.

To speak for the existence of actual, but unconscious or subconscious ideas now hardly seems necessary. These are facts of everyday life. If I have forgotten to make a professional visit, I experience vivid restlessness. From experience I know what this feeling signifies: forgetting. It is futile to test my memory, I cannot find the cause, until it suddenly flashes into consciousness, often after hours. But throughout the whole time I am restless. Well, is the idea of this visit always active, that is always existing, but not in consciousness?—A busy man has had an annoyance in the morning. He is thoroughly engrossed in his work, and during his activity his conscious thinking is fully occupied and he does not think of his annoyance. But his decisions are influenced thereby, and he actually says " No " when he would otherwise say " Yes." Despite this the memory is active, hence, the idea exists. A large part of what we call "moods" come from such sources, that is, from ideas which exist and act under the threshold of consciousness.—Indeed, our whole conduct of life is continually influenced by unconscious ideas. We see daily, as for example, in psychic deterioration of incipient paresis, how the inhibitions, which otherwise impede some acts, become weaker and vanish. But the paretic who tells smutty jokes to ladies was not detained from it in his healthy days by conscious memories or reflections. He avoided it ' instinctively ' and ' automatically,' that is to say, he was detained from it by ideas which the impulse for such an act awakened. The ideas, however, remained under the threshold of consciousness and still impeded the impulse.—All intuitive action is guided by ideas which are for the most part unconscious. Only the clearest and most intensive ideas of self-consciousness are perceived, while the large mass of actual but weaker ideas remains unconscious.

The arguments against the existence and activity of "unconscious ideas" mostly amount to verbal chicanery. Of course, the word, "idea," belongs to the terminology of conscious thinking, and hence, the term, "unconscious idea," is a contradictory expression. But the physical process which lies at the basis of the idea is contently and formally (even if not quantitatively) the same, whether the idea appears above the threshold of consciousness or remains below. It would suffice to coin a term like "idea—substratum," to contravene the contradiction and escape the reproach.

It seems, therefore, that in principle there is no hindrance against the recognition of unconscious ideas also as causes of pathogenic phenomena. However, on closer examination of this matter other difficulties present themselves. If the intensity of unconscious ideas increases, they *eo ipso* appear in consciousness. They remain unconscious only when the intensity is low. But it is difficult to understand how an idea could at the same time be sufficiently intensive to evoke, for example, lively motor action, and still not active enough to become conscious.

I have already expressed a view before, which should not perhaps be lightly dismissed. The clearness of our ideas and with it their capacity to be observed by the self-consciousness, that is, to be conscious, depends also on the feeling of pleasure-pain which they arouse, or on their affective value. If an idea immediately releases an active somatic result, the excitement emanating from it, which would have been disseminated in the brain, flows off into the particular path. And precisely because this has physical results, because its psychic sum of excitement has become converted into the somatic, it loses that clearness which would have otherwise characterized it in the stream of ideas; it, as it were, loses itself among the others.

For example, while partaking of a meal, someone experienced a violent affect, which was *not abreacted*. In consequence, the patient later experienced choking and vomiting while eating, which he interpreted as purely physical symptoms. The hysterical vomiting existed for a long time, but it disappeared after it was revived in hypnosis, related and reacted to. There is no doubt that the attempt to eat has each time revived that memory, and thus released the act of vomiting. Nevertheless, it did not appear clearly in consciousness, because it was now affectless, whereas the entire attention was absorbed by the vomiting.

For this reason it is conceivable that some ideas, which release hysterical phenomena, are not recognized as the cause of the same. But it is impossible that such neglect of ideas, which became affectless, because of conversion, should be the cause of it when in other cases, complexes of ideas, which are no less affectless, do not enter into consciousness. Our case histories offer many examples of this sort.

In such patients it is the rule that moodiness, anxiety, angry irritation, and grief precede the somatic symptom, or soon follow it, and increase until the solution is either attained through expression, or the affect and the somatic phenomena gradually disappear again. If the former happened, the quality of the affect then became quite evident, even though its intensity must have seemed out of proportion to the normal person, and after the solution, also to the patient. These are, therefore, ideas, which are intensive enough, to produce not only strong physical phenomena, but to awaken also their appropriate affect, and to influence the associations by giving preference to related ideas,—and yet, they, themselves, remain outside of consciousness. To bring them to consciousness it requires hypnosis (as shown in Observations I and II), or intensive subsequent help from the physician through most painstaking searching (as in Observations IV and V).

Such ideas, which are (actual but) unconscious, we may call

incapable of consciousness, not on account of their relatively weak activity, but despite their great intensity.

The existence of such ideas, which are incapable of consciousness, is pathological. In healthy persons all ideas which can at all become actual, enter consciousness if they possess sufficient intensity. In our patients we found next to each other a large complex of ideas capable of consciousness and a smaller one which was incapable of consciousness. The realm of ideational psychic activity does not, therefore, coincide in them with the potential consciousness, but the latter is more limited than the former. The psychic ideational activity is here divided into conscious and unconscious parts, while the ideas are divided into those capable of consciousness and those not capable of consciousness. Hence we cannot speak of a splitting of consciousness, but rather of a *splitting of the psyche*.

Conversely, these subconscious ideas cannot even be influenced or corrected by conscious thought. In many cases, it is a question of experiences, which have since become devoid of meaning, as fear of events which did not come to pass, or fright which has changed to laughter or joy, because the individual was saved. These after-effects take away all affectivity from the memory for conscious thought, while the unconscious idea which produces somatic phenomena remains entirely unaffected by them.

Let me cite still another case: For some time a young woman lived in deep apprehension concerning the fate of her younger sister. This situation prolonged her otherwise regular menstrual period by two weeks, she also felt pain in the left hypogastric region, and on two occasions she found herself lying rigidly on the floor, coming out of a "fainting spell." These spells were followed by a left-sided ovaritis with signs of a severe peritonitis. A contracture of the left leg (and the back) characterized the disease as a pseudo-peritonitis, but when the patient died a few years later, the autopsy showed only "a slight cystic degeneration" of both ovaries without any remnant of a former peritonitis. The severe symptoms gradually subsided leaving the ovaritis and contraction of the muscles of the back, so that the trunk was as rigid as a beam, and the contraction of the left leg. This last symptom was removed in hypnosis through direct suggestion. The contraction of the back remained uninfluenced. Meanwhile, her sister's affair was perfectly settled, so that all fear from this direction vanished. But the hysterical phenomena which must have resulted from it continued unchanged. It was an obvious presumption that we dealt with changes in the innervation which became independent and no longer associated with the causative ideas. But, when the patient was forced to relate in hypnosis the whole history until the appearance of " peritonitis " (which she did reluctantly), she sat up freely in bed immediately thereafter, and the contractures disappeared forever. (The ovaritis, the first origin of which was surely much older, remained uninfluenced.) The pathogenic idea of anxiety, nevertheless, continued very vividly throughout months, and she remained absolutely impervious to all corrections.

If we are then forced to recognize the existence of complexes of ideas which never appear in waking consciousness and are never influenced by conscious thinking, we thus already admit that in the just discovered simple hysterias there is a splitting of the psyche into two relatively independent parts. I do not maintain that everything called hysteria has such splitting as a basis and determinant, but I feel that " that splitting of the psychic activity, which is so striking in the familiar cases of *double consciousness,* exists in rudimentary form in every " major " hysteria, and that the capacity and tendency for this dissociation forms the basic phenomenon of this neurosis."

Before I enter, however, into the discussion of these phenomena I must add still another observation in regard to unconscious ideas, which cause somatic manifestations. As in the above reported case of contracture, many of the hysterical phenomena are really of long and continual duration. Shall we, and can we assume, that throughout this whole time the causative idea was always active and was actually existing? I believe, yes. In the normal we certainly see the psychic activity carried into effect with rapid changes of ideas. But the severe melancholiac is for a long time continually sunk in the same painful idea, which is always active and actual. Indeed, we may well believe that the normal, too, may be harassed by a profound worry, judging by the dominating effect of his facial expression, even though his consciousness is filled with other thoughts. But that dissociated part of the psychic activity, which we imagine in the hysterical individual to be filled with the unconscious ideas, is mostly so poorly cathected by it, so inaccessible to the change of outer impressions, that we can believe it possible that we have here an idea of continuous activity.

If we believe with Binet and Janet that the splitting of a part of the psychic activity seems to form the central point of hysteria, we, therefore, feel obliged to search for possible clearness concerning this phenomenon. One falls only too easily into the mental habit of assuming substance behind a substantive, or of gradually conceiving an object by the term, consciousness. And if one has formed the habit of using such local relationships as "unconscious" metaphorically, he will in time actually build up an idea, in which the metaphor will be forgotten, and which he will manipulate as if it were real. Thus, mythology came into being.

Spatial relationships obtrude themselves as companions and helpers of all our thoughts, and we speak in spatial metaphors. Thus, there almost forcibly appear the images of the trunk of the tree which stands in the light, and its roots which are in the dark, or of the building and its dark basement, when we speak of the ideas which exist in clear consciousness and in the unconscious which never appear in the clearness of self-consciousness. But if we always bear in mind that everything spatial is here metaphorical, and are not perhaps misled to localize it in the brain, we may at any rate, speak of a conscious and an unconscious. But only with this reservation.

We are surely in danger of being duped by our own figures of speech, if we always bear in mind that it is really the same brain, and most probably the same cerebral cortex in which the conscious and unconscious ideas originate. But we really know so little of the psychic activity of the cortex, that a puzzling complication will hardly magnify still more our infinite ignorance. We must acknowledge the fact that in hysterics a part of the psychic activity is inaccessible to perception through the self-consciousness of the wakeful person, and in this way the psyche is split.

A well known case of such division of the psychic activity is the hysterical attack in many of its forms and stages. In its beginning conscious thinking is frequently quite blurred, but it then gradually awakens. One hears from many intelligent patients that their conscious ego was quite clear during the attack and that they could have inhibited the attack with their firm will, and they are inclined to blame themselves for it. They say that they did not have to do it. (The self-reproach of simulation is based in a large measure on this feeling.) But at the next attack the conscious ego can do as little to master the processes as in the former one.—Here we have the thinking and ideas of the conscious wakeful ego side by side with the ideas which are ordinarily in the depth of the unconscious, but which have now won control over the musculature and speech; indeed, even over a large part of the ideational activity, thus the splitting of the psyche is manifest.

The name of splitting not only of the psychic activity but also of consciousness is well deserved according to the findings of Binet and Janet. As is known, these observers succeeded in putting themselves in touch with the " subconscious " of their patients, or with every part of the psychic activity of which the conscious wakeful ego knows nothing. In some cases they have thereby demonstrated all psychic functions, including self-consciousness. For one finds therein the memory of former psychic processes. This half psyche is, therefore, totally complete and conscious in itself. The split-off part of the psyche in our cases is " brought into darkness "; like the Titans banned in the chasm of Etna, they may shake the earth, but can never come to light. In Janet's cases a complete division of the realms took place. There was still a differentiation of rank, but this, too, disappeared if the two halves of consciousness alternated as in the familiar cases of *double* conscience, and did not differentiate themselves in their functioning capacity.

Let us, however, return to those ideas which we have demonstrated in our patients as causes of their hysterical phenomena. We lack much to enable us to call them all precisely unconscious and " incapable of consciousness." From the perfectly conscious idea which releases an unusual reflex to those which never enter into consciousness in the waking state, except in hypnosis, there is a hardly interrupted step-ladder, which runs through all grades of shadows and unclearness. Nevertheless, we maintain that we have demonstrated that a splitting of psychic activity exists in the higher degrees of hysteria, and that alone seems to make it possible to give a psychic theory of the disease.

What can one now say or conjecture with probability concerning the cause and origin of this phenomenon?

P. Janet, to whom we are extremely indebted for a very large part of the theory of hysteria and with whom we agree in most points, has developed a new view about it, which we cannot adopt as our own.

Janet maintains that the " splitting of personality " is based on an original psychic weakness *(insufficiance psychologique)*. All normal psychic activity presumes a certain capacity of synthesis, or the possibility of connecting many ideas into one complex. Such synthetic activity no doubt represents a fusion of the various sense perceptions into an image of the environment. This capacity of the psyche is found to be below normal in hysterics. If attention is highly concentrated on one point, *e.g.,* on the perception of one of the senses, a normal person will probably lose for the moment the capacity to apperceive the other senses, *i.e.,* to absorb them into his conscious thinking, but in hysterics this may occur without any special concentration of attention. If they perceive anything, they are at the time inaccessible to other sense perceptions. Indeed, they are not even capable of perceiving altogether the impressions of only one sense. They are able, for example, to apperceive the tactile perceptions of only one half of the body; those of the other side reach the center and are used up for coördinating movements, but they are not apperceived. Such a person is hemianesthetic.

In the normal person one idea associatively evokes other ideas into consciousness, which form for example a friendly or antagonistic relationship with the first, and only ideas of the highest activity are really so excessively strong as to keep the associations below the threshold of consciousness. In hysterics this is always the case. Every idea entirely absorbs the whole lighter psychic activity. This accounts for the patient's enormous affectivity.

This peculiarity of their psyche Janet designates by the name of " narrowing of the field of consciousness " of hysterics, in analogy to the " narrowing of the field of vision." The sensory impressions which are not apperceived and those ideas which were aroused, but did not enter consciousness, are mostly wiped out without any further consequences. Sometimes, however, they collect together and form complexes: the sub-conscious, or the psychic stratum withdrawn from consciousness.

Hysteria, which is based essentially on this splitting of the psyche, is *" une malade de faiblesse "* (a disease of feebleness) and hence, it develops best if other enfeebling influences act on the original weak psyche, or if they put high demands upon it in contrast to which the psychic force seems still more inferior.

In this exposition of his views, Janet has also already answered the important question of the disposition to hysteria. He assumes a *typus hystericus* in the same sense as the *typus phtisicus,* by which we understand the long, narrow thorax, the small heart, etc. Janet assumes a definite form of congenital psychic weakness for the disposition for hysteria. In contrast to this, we would like to formulate briefly our own view as follows: The splitting of consciousness does not occur because the patients are weak-minded, but the patients seem weak-minded because their psychic activity is divided, and only a part of the functional capacity is at the disposal of conscious thought. We cannot consider psychic weakness as the *typus hystericus,* or as the essence of the disposition for hysteria.

What is meant by the first sentence may be elucidated by an example. On many occasions we could observe the following course in one of our patients (Mrs. Cecilia M.): During relative well being, there appeared an hysterical symptom, a tormenting and obsessing hallucination, a neuralgia, or something similar, which increased in intensity for some time. Simultaneously with it the psychic activity became continually reduced, and after a few days even an uninitiated observer was forced to call the patient weak-minded. She was then disburdened of the unconscious idea (the memory of a long past psychic trauma), either through the physician in hypnosis or through the fact that she suddenly merged into an excited state and recited the situation with lively affectivity. Thereafter, she not only became calm and cheerful as if freed from the tormenting symptoms, but we were again and again astonished at the rich and clear intellect and the keenness of her intelligence and judgment. She was fond of playing (excellent) chess and liked to play two games at the same time, which is hardly a sign of a lack of psychic synthesis. The impression was indisputable, that during such attacks the unconscious idea drew to itself a continually increasing part of her psychic activity. The longer this continued, the smaller became the share of her psychic activity, until it became reduced to almost complete imbecility, but later she was herself again, to use a popular expression, and she possessed an excellent psychic functional capacity.

As a comparison from normal states we would prefer to use *preoccupation* instead of concentration of attention. If a person is "preoccupied" by, let us say, worry, his psychic functional capacity will be reduced in a similar manner.

Every observer is preponderately under the influence of the objects of his observation, and we would like to believe that Janet's conception was formed from his comprehensive study of those weak-minded hysterics who are usually in hospitals or sanatoria, because as a result of their illness and the psychic weakness conditioned by it, they could not maintain themselves at large. Our observations of educated hysterics force us to an essentially different opinion of their psyche. We believe " that among hysterics one can find persons who are most clear mentally, who have the strongest will power, the best character, and the clearest judgment." Hysteria does not exclude any amount of real and genuine psychic endowment, even though the disease makes real accomplishment impossible. Was not the patron saint of hysteria, St. Theresa, a genial woman of the greatest practical thoroughness?

But it is also true, that no amount of stupidity, uselessness, and weak-mindedness guarantees against hysteria. But even if one disregards all that which is only the result of the disease, one must admit that the type of the weak-minded hysteric *exists in large numbers*. But here, too, it is not a question of torpid and phlegmatic stupidity, but rather of an excessively high degree of psychic mobility, which causes unfitness. We shall later discuss the question of the original disposition. Here, we only wish to repeat that Janet's opinion that psychic weakness is generally at the bottom of hysteria and of psychic splitting is unacceptable to us.

In absolute opposition to Janet's view, I believe that in a great many cases the disaggregation depends on the psychic over-functioning or on the habitual co-existence of two heterogenous series of ideas. It was pointed out that frequently we are not merely " mechanically " active, while a series of ideas, which have nothing in common with our activities flow through our conscious thinking, but that we are also undoubtedly capable of mental functioning while our thoughts are " wandering elsewhere," as *e.g.,* when we read aloud with the proper intonation and later know nothing of what we have read.

There is undoubtedly a large number of activities running from the mechanical, like knitting, scale-playing, to such as are still conditioned by some psychic functioning, which are performed by many people with only half of their presence of mind. This is especially true of temperamental people who, irritated by monotonous, simple, and unstimulating occupations, have in the first place deliberately created for themselves the diversion of thinking of something else. A good example of this kind is the " private theater of Anna O.," mentioned above. Another, but similar case, is found in the intrusion of an interesting group of ideas from reading or plays. This intrusion becomes more energetic if the foreign ideas are of strong " emotional accentuations," as in worry and amorous longing. This furnishes the above-mentioned state of preoccupation which does not, however, prevent many people from performing moderately complicated acts. Social relations often force such doubling of very intensive thinking, as in the case of a woman tormented by worry or passionate excitement, who, nevertheless, fulfills her social duties and functions as an amiable hostess. Lighter activities of this sort we all accomplish in our vocations. But self-observation seems to prove to everyone that the affective group of ideas is not associatively awakened now and then, but that it continually exists actually in the psyche, and appears in consciousness if the latter is not held by a vivid external impression or by an act of will.

Even in people in whom no habitual daydreaming runs side by side with their everyday activities, some situations may for a long time condition such continuity of alternating impressions and reactions of the outer life, as well as an emotionally accentuated group of ideas. *Post equitem sedet atra cura.* Such situations are above all common in the nursing of those dear to us, and in love affairs. According to our experience, nursing of the sick and love affects also played the principal part in most of the case histories of hysterics, who were more thoroughly analyzed.

I believe that the habitual or the conditioned doubling of psychic activity through affectful situations would essentially *predispose* to a real pathological psychic splitting. If the two co-existing groups of ideas no longer have the same kind of content, if one of them contains ideas which are incapable of consciousness, that is, ideas which are rejected, or came about in hypnoid states, a psychic splitting may then develop. The confluence of the two temporarily separated groups, which always takes place in the normal, then becomes impossible, and a split-off region of unconscious psychic activity establishes itself here permanently. This hysterical splitting behaves towards the " double-ego " of the normal like the hypnoid state to the normal day-dreaming. The pathological quality is here determined by the amnesia, and there, by the incapacity to become conscious of the ideas.

The observation of Anna O., to whom I must always return, offers us clear insight into this process. The girl was in perfect health, but had the habit of letting phantastic ideas flow next to her usual activities. In one situation favorable for auto-hypnosis, an anxiety affect entered into the day-dreaming and created a hypnoid state for which she had an amnesia. This repeated itself on various occasions, and its ideational content gradually became richer, but it still alternated with the state of perfectly normal and conscious thinking.

After four months, the hypnoid state entirely dominated the patient, and as the individual attacks coalesced, there developed an *état de mal,* a most severe acute hysteria. After many months' duration in different forms (somnambulic period) this state was violently interrupted, and now alternated again with the normal psychic behavior. But even in this state there was a persistence of the somatic and psychic phenomena, concerning which *we now know* that they were based on the hypnoid state (contractures, hemianesthesia, and change of speech). This proves that even during the normal behavior of the ideational complex of the hypnoid state, the " unconscious " is actual, and that the splitting of the psyche continues.

I cannot give here a second example of such development, but I believe that this throws some light on the development of the traumatic neuroses. In the latter, the memory of this fright-hypnoidal state repeats itself a few days after the accident. But while this occurs more and more frequently, its intensity, nevertheless, diminishes to such an extent that it no longer alternates with wakeful thinking, but exists next to it. However, I can only conjecture that it proceeds in this manner, as I have not analyzed such a case.

Freud's observations and analyses demonstrate that the splitting of the psyche can also be conditioned by a " defense," or by an intentional turning away of consciousness from the painful ideas. This is true only in some people to whom we must, therefore, attribute a special psychic peculiarity. In the normal person the suppression of such ideas is successful, and then they disappear in consciousness. In what this peculiarity consists, I am not able to state. I only venture the assumption that if the defense does not merely make single, converted ideas unconscious, but brings about a real splitting of the psyche it requires help from the hypnoidal state. The auto-hypnosis produces, so to say, the space, the region of unconscious psychic activity, into which the rejected ideas are pushed. Be that as it may, we must recognize the fact of the pathogenic significance of the " defense " mechanism.

I do not believe, however, that with the discussion of half-way understandable processes we have even nearly exhausted the genesis of psychic splitting. Thus, incipient hysterias of a higher grade present a syndrome mostly lasting some time, which can justly be designated as acute hysteria. In the anamnesis of male hysterics we encounter this form of illness, frequently under the name of inflammation of the brain; in women, the ovaritis that sometimes accompanies it, leads to the diagnosis of peritonitis.

Psychotic features are very distinct in this acute state of hysteria. Thus, we encounter manic and irascible states of excitement, rapid alteration of hysterical phenomena, hallucinations, etc. In such states the splitting of the psyche may perhaps proceed in a different manner than the one we attempted to describe above.

This whole stage may perhaps be looked upon as a long hypnoidal state, the residuum of which furnishes the nucleus of the unconscious complex of ideas, while the wakeful thoughts show an amnesia for it. As the conditions for the origin of such acute hysteria are mostly unknown (I do not dare to consider the origin of the case of Anna O. as general), this would be another, and in contrast to the one discussed above, it might be designated as an irrational form of psychic splitting.[16] And there probably exist still other forms of this process which have still escaped the new psychological cognition. For we have surely taken only the first steps in this realm, and further experiences will essentially transform the present views.

Let us ask what the knowledge of the psychic splitting gained during the last years has done for the understanding of hysteria. It seems to be much and of great importance.

This cognition makes it possible to trace seemingly pure somatic symptoms to ideas. It would be superfluous to discuss this again.

It has at least partially taught us that the attack is an accomplishment of an unconscious complex of ideas (Charcot).

But it also explains some of the psychic peculiarities of hysteria, and this point merits perhaps a more detailed discussion.

The "unconscious ideas" certainly never, or only seldom and

[16] I must state, however, that precisely in the most familiar and transparent cases of major hysteria, with a manifest double consciousness (I am referring to the case of Anna O.) no remnant from the acute stage was carried over into the chronic stage, and all the phenomena of the latter have already been produced in the "period of incubation," in the hypnoid, and affective states.

with difficulty, appear in wakeful thinking, but they influence it through their efforts, as when the patient is tormented by a perfectly incomprehensible and senseless hallucination whose meaning and motivation becomes clear in the hypnosis.

Moreover, they influence the associations by permitting some ideas to become more active than they would have been without the reënforcement emanating from the unconscious. Thus, the same definite groups of ideas then obtrude themselves on the patient with such force that he is compelled to think of them.[17] Furthermore, they dominate the emotional situation, the feelings. At the unwinding of her recollections, whenever Anna O. was approaching a process which had originally been connected with a vivid affect, the corresponding emotional feelings became evident days before the memory seemed clear, even in the hypnotic consciousness.

This also explains the "moods," or those incomprehensible, unfounded and unconscious unmotivated depressions of the patient. For the impressionability of hysterics is for the most part actually conditioned by their original irritability, but the lively affects into which they merge for relatively slight reasons, become comprehensible only when we bear in mind that the "split-off" psyche acts like a sounding board for the tone of the tuning fork. Every occurrence, which stimulates "unconscious" memories, sets free the whole affective force of these unusurped ideas, and the evoked affect is then quite disproportionate to the one which would have originated solely in the conscious psyche.

We have reported above (p. 172) the case of a patient, whose mental activity always stood in reversed relation to the vividness of her unconscious ideas. The reduction of her conscious thinking was based partially, but only partially, on a peculiar kind of distractibility. After each momentary "absence," which appeared continually, she did not know what she had thought of during this time. She oscillated between the "condition prime" and "seconde," between the conscious and the unconscious ideational complex. But it was not solely through this that her mental activity diminished, not also through the affect which dominated her from her unconscious. Her conscious thinking in such state lacked energy, her judgment was infantile she seemed to say, quite imbecilic. I believe that this was

---

[17] This resembles Janet's hemianaesthetic patients, who though failing to feel the repeated touching of their anaesthetic hands, nevertheless when requested to mention any number, always selected the number which corresponded to the touches.

determined by the fact, that her conscious thinking had a smaller amount of energy at its disposal, because a large mass of the psychic excitement was usurped by the unconscious.

If such a case is not merely temporary, if the split-off psyche is in continuous excitement as in Janet's hemianesthetics in whom all sensations from one side of the body could only be perceived by the unconscious, there remains so little of the cerebral function for conscious thinking that the psychic weakness, described by Janet and considered by him as original, can be fully explained by it. Of only very few people can one say, as of Uhland's " Bertrand de Born," that " they never need more than half of their mind." The majority of people show just such a weakmindedness whenever there is reduction of their psychic energy.

The very consequential peculiarity of *some* hysterics, their suggestibility, can seemingly also be explained by the mental weakness conditioned by the psychic splitting. I said " some hysterics " because it is certain that among patients of this sort one also finds people who are most sure of their judgment and criticism.

By suggestibility we understand in the first place only that lack of criticism of ideas and ideational complexes (judgments) which appear in one's own consciousness, or are inducted into it from without, through outside talk or reading. All criticism of such ideas which have just appeared in consciousness is based upon the fact that associatively they arouse other thoughts and among them some which are incompatible with them. The resistance against them, therefore, depends on the possession of a potential consciousness of such resistive ideas, and its force corresponds to the relationship between the vividness of the new ideas and those aroused from memory. This relationship varies markedly even in normal intellects. What we call an intellectual temperament mostly depends on this. The sanguine nature who is always enthused by new people and things behaves in this manner, because the intensity of his memory pictures, in comparison to those of the new impressions, is less than in the more calm " phlegmatic " individual. In pathological states, the preponderance of fresh ideas and the lack of resistance against them depends on the memory pictures; the less the latter are aroused, the weaker and poorer are the associations. This can be readily seen in sleep, in dreaming, in hypnosis, and wherever there is a reduction of psychic energy, as long as it does not injure also the activity of the fresh ideas.

The unconscious split psyche of hysteria is eminently suggestible due to the poverty and deficiency of its ideational content. But the suggestibility also of the conscious psyche of some hysterics seems to be based on this. According to their original predisposition, they are irritable, and fresh ideas assume in them great vivacity. In contrast to this, the actual intellectual activity, the associations, are reduced, because due to a split-off "unconscious," the wakeful thought has only a part of the psychic energy at its disposal.

It is for this reason that their resistance capacity to auto-suggestion and to outside suggestions is reduced and sometimes destroyed. The suggestibility of their will, too, probably arises solely from that. On the other hand, the hallucinatory suggestibility, which immediately transforms every idea of a sense perception into the perception itself, requires, as does every hallucination, an abnormal degree of excitability of the organ of perception, and cannot have its origin in the psychic splitting only.

VI. *Original Disposition; the Development of Hysteria*

Almost at every stage of this explanation I have had to admit that most of the manifestations which we strove to understand can also be based on a congenital peculiarity. This withdraws itself from every explanation, which should lead to the confirmation of the facts. But as the *capacity to acquire hysteria* must surely also be connected with something peculiar to man, the attempt, therefore, to define it more precisely may not perhaps entirely be without value.

I have explained above why Janet's view, that the disposition to hysteria is based on psychic weakness, is untenable. The practitioner, who as family physician, observes the members of an hysterical family in all stages of existence, will surely be inclined to seek this disposition in a surplus rather than in a defect. The adolescents who later become hysterical are before their illness mostly vivacious, talented, and full of mental interests; their will power is often remarkable. Among them one sees those girls who get up at night to study something which the parents prohibit, lest they should overwork. The capacity of thoughtful judgment is surely not more granted to them than to other people. But one rarely finds among them simple-mindedness, dullness, mental laziness, and stupidity. The ebullient productivity of their psyche brought one of my friends to the assertion that hysterics are the bloom of mankind, to be sure, as sterile, but also as beautiful as blooming flowers.

Their vivacity and restlessness, their craving for sensations and mental activity, their inability to endure monotony and tediousness, may be formulated by saying, that they belong to those people whose nervous system sets free an excessive quantity of free nervous excitement, which craves utilization (see p. 143). During the development of puberty, and as a result of it, the original surplus becomes enriched with an enormous increase of excitement, which emanates from the awakened sexuality, or from the sexual glands. In this manner there results an excessive quantity of free nervous excitement which becomes available for pathological phenomena. But in order that these should take the form of hysterical manifestations, there is an apparent need of still another specific peculiarity of the individual. For the great majority of vivacious and excitable people do not necessarily become hysterical.

This peculiarity I could only designate above in the vague and empty words: " abnormal irritability of the nervous system." Still, one can perhaps go still further and say that this abnormality lies in the very fact that in such people the excitement can flow into the sensory nervous apparatus which is normally accessible only to peripheral stimuli, and into those of the vegetative organs, which are isolated by strong resistances from the central nervous system. This concept of the constantly existing surplus of excitement, to which the sensible vasomotor and visceral apparatus are accessible, can perhaps already account for some pathological phenomena.

As the attention is forcibly concentrated on one part of the body in people so constituted, the " attentional connection " (Exner) of the concerned sensible path exceeds the normal measure. The free floating excitement then settles, so to say, on this path, and there develops a local hyperalgesia, which produces a maximum intensity of all pains which are in any way conditioned, so that they are all felt as " frightful " and " intolerable." But when the quantity of excitement once occupies a path, it never leaves it again as in the case of a normal person; it does not just remain there, but it increases through a flowing in of new excitement. Thus, after a slight trauma to a joint, there develops a neurosis of the joint, and the painful feeling of an ovarian enlargement frequently becomes a permanent *ovaritis*.

The nervous apparatus of the circulation is more accessible to cerebral influence than in the normal, and hence, we find nervous palpitation, tendency to syncope, excessive blushing and paling, etc.

But to be sure, the peripheral nervous apparatus is not only more amenable to excitement through central influences, but it also reacts to the adequate, functional stimuli in excessive and perverse manner. Palpitation follows moderate exertion like emotional excitement, and the vasomotors produce a contraction of the arteries ("dying fingers") without any psychic influence. And just as a slight trauma may be followed by a neurosis of the joint, a mild bronchitis may be followed by nervous asthma, and indigestion frequently by cardialgias. We must thus recognize that the accessibility of sums of excitement of central origin is nothing but a special form of the general abnormal excitability,[18] even though it is most important for our theme.

Hence, I also do not believe that the old "reflex theory" of these symptoms, which might perhaps better be called simple "nervousness," which, however, belongs to the empirical morbid picture of hysteria, should be entirely rejected. The vomiting which really accompanies the distention of the gravid uterus may in abnormal irritability well be the result of a reflex from slight uterine stimuli; indeed, perhaps also from the fluctuating enlargement of the ovaries. We know so many distant effects of organic changes, so many strange "conjugated points" that we cannot dismiss the fact that a large number of nervous symptoms which are sometimes psychically conditioned might in other cases be the effects reflected from a distance. Indeed, I venture into the highest unmodern heresy, when I say that even the motor weakness of a leg could sometimes be determined not psychically, but by a direct reflex from a genital disease. I believe, however, that it is well not to concede too much exclusiveness to our theories and not to generalize about all cases.

Other forms of abnormal sensible excitement, such as general analgesia, anesthetic plaques, etc., are still beyond our understanding. It is possible and perhaps probable that further observations will demonstrate the psychic origin of the one or the other stigmata and thus explain the symptom; until now this has not happened (I do not dare generalize the points of support obtained from our first observation), and I do not consider it justified to presume it before we have succeeded in demonstrating such a derivation.

On the other hand, the described peculiarity of the nervous system and the psyche seems to explain some, only too familiar, qualities of many hysterics. The excess of excitement, which their nervous system sets free while at rest, conditions their incapacity to endure

[18] Oppenheim's "Labilität der Molecüle."

a monotonous and irksome existence. Their hankering for sensation impels them, after the outbreak of the disease to interrupt the monotony of their sick existence through all sorts of happenings among which pathological phenomena naturally play a part. In this way they are supported by their auto-suggestion. They are led into it more and more by their need for sickness, that remarkable trait which is as pathognomonic for hysteria as is the fear of disease for hypochondria. I know an hysterical woman whose self-injuries, which were frequently quite serious, were meant for her own use, and neither those about her nor her physician discovered anything of them. If she had nothing to do, she performed all sorts of mischief in her room, if only to prove to herself that she was not normal. She really had a distinct feeling of her morbidity, she fulfilled her duties incompletely and through such acts she sought to justify herself. Another patient, a very sick woman of a morbid conscientiousness, and full of distrust of herself, conceived every hysterical symptom as guilt: "because she wouldn't have had this if she had been decent." When the paralysis of her legs was mistakenly diagnosed as a spinal disease, she felt pleased, and the explanation that it was "just nervousness" and would soon disappear sufficed to produce in her deep pangs of conscience. The need for the disease originated through the patient's longing to convince herself and others of the reality of her illness. If it then associated itself with the torment, which was conditioned by the monotony of the sick room, there developed the strongest desire to get more new symptoms.

But if this develops into lying and leads to real simulation—and I believe that we now reject the idea of simulation as much as we formerly accepted it—then it is not based on the hysterical disposition, but as Moebius so excellently expressed it, on a complication of the same with other degenerations, or with an original moral deficiency. In the same way the "irascible hysterica" develops through the fact that an original irritable and unsocial personality becomes additionally afflicted with an egotistically spoiled character, which is easily imposed by chronic suffering. Moreover, the irascible hysterica hardly exists more frequently than the irascible tabetic in the later stages of the disease.

The excess of irritability produces pathological phenomena also in the motor spheres. Thus, some children easily develop tic-like movements, which were at first stimulated by some sensation in the eyes or in the face or through an article of dress, which become persistent if not immediately treated. The reflex paths are easily and quickly formed.

Nor can it be denied, that there is a purely motor convulsive attack, independent of all psychic factors which discharges a mass of excitement accumulated only by a summation, just like the mass of excitement of the epileptic attack, which is conditioned by automatic changes. That would represent the non-ideogenic, hysterical attack.

We so frequently see adolescents, who though excitable have remained healthy until the development of puberty when they became ill with hysteria, that we must ask ourselves whether this process does not create a disposition where it had not originally existed. And we certainly must attribute more to puberty than the simple increase in the quantity of excitement. For sexual maturity affects the whole nervous system, it produces a general enhancement of the excitement and a diminution of the resistances. Observation of non-hysterical adolescents teaches this, and we therefore are justified in believing that it also produces the hysterical disposition, insofar as the latter consists of this quality of the nervous system. With this, we already recognize sexuality as one of the great components of hysteria, and we shall see later that its rôle in hysteria is still greater, that it participates in many ways in the construction of the disease.

If the stigmata originate directly from the original native soil of hysteria and are not ideogenic, then it is also impossible to place ideogeny as the central point of hysteria, as is sometimes done today. For what can be more genuinely hysterical than the stigmata or those pathognomonic findings which confirm the diagnosis, and yet they do not seem to be ideogenic. But if the basis of hysteria is a peculiarity of the whole nervous system, the complex of ideogenic and psychically determined symptoms rises on it like a building on its foundation. And it is a *building of many floors*. But just as such a structure can only be understood by distinguishing the ground plans of the various floors, so I believe that the understanding of hysteria is conditioned by the observations of the different etiological complication of the symptoms. If one disregards this and attempts to explain hysteria by the application of one causal connection, there always remains a very large remnant of unexplained phenomena; it is, as if one wished to put the various rooms of the many floored house into the sketch of one floor.

Like the stigmata there is a group of other nervous symptoms, as we saw above, which are not caused by ideas, but are direct results of the fundamental anomaly of the nervous system, such as some algias, vasomotor phenomena, and perhaps also the purely motor convulsive attack.

Next to them we have the ideogenic phenomena, which are simple conversions of affective excitement (p. 148). They originate as results of affects in persons of hysterical disposition, and represent, to begin with, only the anomalous expression of the emotions (Oppenheim).[19] Through repetition the latter develops into a real, seemingly pure somatic hysterical symptom, while the causative ideas remain imperceptible (p. 151), or repressed from consciousness as a result of a defense reaction. Most of the rejected and converted ideas, or the most important of them, have a sexual content. They are at the basis of a large part of hysteria of puberty. The maturing girls, whom we have mostly in mind, behave in different ways towards the sexual ideas and feelings which obtrude themselves on them; sometimes, with complete ingenuousness, whereby some ignore and overlook the whole situation. Others look upon sex in the same way as boys, and this is especially the rule in peasant and working girls. Still others seize, with more or less perverse curiosity, everything containing anything sexual in speech or writing. And finally, we have the delicately organized natures of marked sexual excitability, but of equally great moral purity, who conceive everything sexual as incompatible with their moral content, as something that soils and pollutes.[20] They repress the sexuality from their consciousness, and the affective ideas of such content which have caused somatic phenomena become unconscious through the " reaction of defense."

The tendency to defend herself against the sexual become reënforced through the fact that the sensuous excitement in a virgin contains a mixture of anxiety, the fear of the unknown, and the presentiment of what is to happen, whereas in the natural and healthy young man it is simply a pure aggressive impulse. The young girl senses in Eros the frightful force which dominates and decides her fate, and is frightened by it. The greater, therefore, is

[19] That disposition is precisely that, which Strümpell designates as " the disturbance in the psycho-physical," which is at the basis of hysteria.

[20] Some observations lead us to believe that the fear of touching, or really the fear of dirt, which compels women to wash their hands every moment, has this origin. The washing is aroused by the same psychic process as in Lady Macbeth.

the inclination to look away and to repress from consciousness that which causes anxiety.

Marriage brings new sexual traumas. One wonders that the wedding night does not more frequently act pathogenically, for unfortunately it is more often rape than an erotic seduction. To be sure, hysterias of young women, traceable to this experience, are not rare, and they disappear when, in the course of time, sexual pleasure appears and the trauma is wiped out. But also in the further course of many marriages sexual traumas occur. Those case histories which we could not publish contain a large number of perverse demands by husbands, unnatural practices, etc. I do not think that I exaggerate when I assert that the *great majority of severe neuroses in women originate in the marriage bed.*[21]

According to Freud's discovery, a part of the sexual injuries, which mainly consist in insufficient gratification (coitus interruptus, ejaculatio praecox, etc.), leads not to hysteria, but to anxiety neurosis.[22] But in my opinion even in such cases the excitement of the sexual affect is frequently converted into hysterical somatic phenomena.[23]

It is quite evident, and has also been sufficiently shown in our observations, that the non-sexual affects of fright, anxiety, and anger, lead to the origin of hysterical phenomena. But it is perhaps not too superfluous to emphasize again that the sexual factor is by far the most important and pathologically the most fertile etiological factor. The naïve observations of our predecessors, the residuum of which we retained in the word, "hysteria," came nearer to the truth than the modern views which put sexuality almost in the last line, in order to guard the patients against moral reproaches. Of course, the sexual needs of hysterics show as many individual variations as in normal persons, and are not stronger than in the latter. But the hysterics become sick from it, and what is more, mostly through the struggle of defending themselves against sexuality.

[21] It is certainly sad that one of the most important pathogenic factors is ignored in the clinic, or only delicately touched upon by allusions. This is really a subject where the experience of the experienced should be imparted to the young physician, who quite usually blindly passes over sexuality, at least insofar as concerns his patients.

[22] Freud: On the Right to Separate from Neurasthenia a Definite Symptom-Complex, as Anxiety Neurosis. Chapter V in Selected Papers on Hysteria, translated by Brill, Monograph Series.

[23] This has later been verified by Freud and his pupils. There is really no pure anxiety neurosis. *Cf.* Freud's Introduction to Stekel's " Nervöse Angstzustände," Urban and Schwarzenberg, Wien, 1908.

Next to the sexual we must here also mention the *fright-hysteria,* the actual traumatic hysteria. It forms one of the most familiar and most recognized types of hysteria.

In the same stratum, so to say, with the phenomena which originated through conversion of emotional excitement, there are those which owe their origin to suggestion (mostly auto-suggestion) in originally suggestible individuals. High graded suggestibility, *i.e.,* an uninhibited preponderance of freshly excited ideas, does not belong to the nature of hysteria, but it may be found as a complication in those hysterically predisposed, in whom this very peculiarity of the nervous system makes possible the physical realization of the overvalued idea. For the rest, they are mostly only affective ideas which become realized suggestively in somatic phenomena, and hence, we can often also conceive the process as a conversion of the accompanying fright or anxiety affect.

These processes of *affect conversion and of suggestibility* remain identical also in the complicated forms of hysteria which are now to be considered. There they find only more favorable conditions, but psychically determined hysterical phenomena always originate through one of these two processes.

––––––––––

The *hypnoid* state, or the tendency to auto-hypnosis (p. 158), forms the third constituent of the hysterical disposition which joined some of the cases discussed above. This state favors and alleviates conversion as well as suggestion to the highest extent, and thereby, so to speak, constructs over the petty hysteria, which presents only a single hysterical phenomenon, the upper floors of the major hysteria. It constitutes a state which is at first only transient, and alternating with the normal. We may ascribe to it the same increase of psychic influence on the body, which we have observed in the artificial hypnosis. But here this influence is all the more intensive and further reaching because it concerns a nervous system which has an anomalous irritability even without the hypnosis.[24] To what extent, and in which cases, the tendency to auto-hypnosis is an

[24] It would be in order to identify the disposition for hypnosis with the original abnormal excitement, because even the artificial hypnosis shows ideogenic changes of the secretion, of local hyperaemia, formation of blisters, etc. This seems to be the view of Moebius. But I believe that this makes one move about in a vicious circle. This thaumaturgy of hypnosis we observe, as far as I see, only in hysterics. We would, therefore, attribute to hypnosis the functions of hysteria, and then trace this back again to hysteria.

original peculiarity of the organism we do not know. I have expressed above (p. 161) the view that this state develops from affectful reveries. But it is certain that an original disposition also belongs to it. If that view is correct, it becomes quite clear here, how great an influence must be attributed to sexuality in the development of hysteria. For besides nursing, there is no psychic factor which is as apt to produce reveries as amorous longing. And besides, the sexual organism by virtue of its superfluous affects and narrowing of consciousness is closely related to the hypnoid states.

The hypnoid state manifests itself most distinctly in the hysterical attack, in that state which can be designated as acute hysteria, and which it seems plays so significant a part in the development of major hysteria (p. 176). These states last long, sometimes many months, and are distinctly of a psychotic nature, so that one must frequently designate them as hallucinatory confusions. But even if the disturbance does reach so far in such states, there appear manifold hysterical phenomena, some of which continue persistently. The psychic content of these states consists in part of those very ideas which were rejected in the waking state and repressed into the unconscious ("hysterical deliria of saints and nuns, of abstinent women, and of well bred children").

As these states are so often real psychoses and, nevertheless, originate directly and exclusively from hysteria, I cannot accept Moebius' opinion that "disregarding those whose attacks are associated with deliria, one cannot speak of an actual hysterical insanity." [25] These states are of such a nature in many cases, and in the further course of the hysteria such psychoses also repeat themselves. In their nature they are, of course, nothing but the psychotic stage of the attack, but as they continue for months they cannot really be designated as attacks.

How do these acute hysterias originate? In the most familiar cases (Observation I), it developed from a summation of hypnoid attacks. In another case (of an already existing, complicated hysteria), it appeared as an appendage to a withdrawal of morphine. For the most part, the process is quite obscure and awaits elucidation through further observations.

The cases of hysteria discussed here fit into the following statement of Moebius: "The essential change of hysteria consists in the

[25] Moebius: Gegenwärtige Auffassung der Hysterie. Monatsschrift für Geburtshilfe und Gynakologie, 1895, I Bd., p. 18.

fact that whether transient or persistent, the psychic state of the hysteric resembles the state of those hypnotized. " [26]

The continuation of the hysterical symptoms which originated in the hypnoid state, during the normal state, agrees perfectly with our experiences concerning post-hypnotic suggestions. But this also implies that complexes of ideas incapable of consciousness co-exist with groups of ideas which function consciously; that is to say, there is a *splitting of the psyche* (p. 170). It seems certain that this, too, can originate without hypnoidism from an abundance of rejected ideas which were repressed, but not suppressed from consciousness. In this or that way there develops a sphere of psychic existence, which is now ideationally impoverished and rudimentary, and now more or less equal to the waking thoughts, for the cognition of which we are indebted above all to Binet and Janet. The splitting of the psyche is the consummation of hysteria, and it was demonstrated above how it explained the fundamental character traits of the disease. Permanent, but with vivid fluctuations of its ideas, a part of the patient's psyche is in a hypnoid state and is always prepared to gain control of the whole person whenever conscious thought becomes reduced (attack, delirium). This occurs as soon as a strong affect disturbs the normal flow of ideas as in twilight, or exhaustive states. From this persistent hypnoidism there obtrude themselves into consciousness unmotivated ideas, which are foreign to the normal associations, hallucinations which are thrust into the perceptions, and motor acts independent of the conscious will become innervated. This hypnoid psyche is capable to the highest degree of producing conversions of affects and suggestions, thus giving rise with ease to new hysterical phenomena, which without the psychic splitting could have come into existence only with difficulty and under the pressure of repetitive affects. The split-off psyche is that demon of whom the patients were believed possessed by the naïvely observing age of superstitious times. That a ghost who is a stranger to the wakeful consciousness of the patient holds sway in him, is true, only he is *no real stranger*, but a part of himself.

––––––––––––

The attempt ventured here to reconstruct hysteria synthetically from our present knowledge is open to the reproach of eclecticism, if this is at all justified. So many formulations of hysteria from the

[26] See p. 15.

old " reflex theory " to the " dissociation of the personality " had to find a place here. But it could hardly be otherwise. So many excellent observers and ingenious heads have interested themselves in hysteria. It is improbable that each of their formulations does not contain a part of the truth. The future presentation of the real state of affairs will surely contain them all, and will only combine all the one-sided views of the subject into a material reality. Eclecticism, therefore, seems to me no reproach.

But how far are we today from the possibility of such complete understanding of hysteria! With what uncertain features have the contours been outlined, with what clumsy new ideas have the gaping chasms been covered rather than filled. The only consideration that is somewhat mitigating lies in the fact that this evil sticks, and must stick to all physiological explanations of complicated psychic processes. What Thesseus said of the tragedy in " Midsummer Night's Dream " is also true of them: " The best of this kind are but shadows " (Act V, Scene 1). And even the feeblest is not worthless, if it seeks faithfully and humbly to hold firmly to the silhouettes which were thrown on the wall by the unknown real objects. Moreover, the hope is always justified that some measure of agreement and similarity will endure between the real processes and our conception.

CHAPTER IV

THE PSYCHOTHERAPY OF HYSTERIA

By Dr. Sigmund Freud

In our "Preliminary Communication" we have stated that while investigating the etiology of hysterical symptoms, we have also discovered a therapeutic method which we consider of practical significance. *"We found, at first to our greatest surprise, that the individual hysterical symptoms immediately disappeared without returning if we succeeded in thoroughly awakening the memories of the causal process with its accompanying affect, and if the patient circumstantially discussed the process in the most detailed manner and gave verbal expression to the affect"* (p. 3).

We furthermore attempted to explain how our psychotherapeutic method acts: *"It abrogates the efficacy of the original non-abreacted ideas by affording an outlet to their strangulated affects through speech. It brings them to associative correction by drawing them into normal consciousness (in mild hypnosis) or by eliminating them through medical suggestion in the same way as in somnambulism with amnesia"* (p. 12).

Although the essential features of this method have been enumerated in the preceding pages, a repetition is unavoidable, and I shall now attempt to show connectedly how far-reaching this method is, its superiority over others, its technique, and its difficulties.

I

I, for my part, may state that I can firmly adhere to the "Preliminary Communication," but I must confess that in the years that have elapsed since then, and after continuous occupation with the problems touched on there, new viewpoints obtruded themselves on me, as a result of which the former material underwent at least a partial change in grouping and conception. It would be unjust to impute too much of the responsibility for this development to my honored friend, J. Breuer. The responsibility for the following elucidations, therefore, rests preponderately upon me.

In attempting to use Breuer's method for treating hysterical

190

symptoms in a great number of patients by investigation and abreaction in hypnosis, I encountered two obstacles, the pursuit of which led me to change the technique, as well as the conception. (1) Not all persons were hypnotizable who undoubtedly showed hysterical symptoms, and in whom there most probably existed the same psychic mechanism. (2) I had to take an attitude towards the question of what essentially characterizes hysteria, and in what it differs from other neuroses.

How I overcame the first difficulty, and what it taught me, I will show later. I will first state what position I have taken in my daily practice towards the second problem. It is very difficult to examine a case of neurosis before it has been subjected to a thorough analysis, such as would result only through the application of Breuer's method. But before we have such a thorough knowledge we are obliged to decide upon the diagnosis and kind of treatment. Hence, the only thing left to me was to select such cases for the cathartic method which could, for the time being, be diagnosed as hysteria, and which showed some or many stigmata, or the characteristic symptoms of hysteria. Yet, it sometimes happened that in spite of the diagnosis of hysteria, the therapeutic results were very poor, and even the analysis revealed nothing of importance. At other times I attempted to treat cases by Breuer's method, which no one took for hysteria, and I found that I could influence them, and even cure them. Such, for example, was my experience with obsessions, the real obsessions of Westphal's type, in cases which did not show a single feature of hysteria. Thus, the psychic mechanism revealed in the " Preliminary Communication " could not, therefore, be pathognomonic of hysteria. Nor could I, for the sake of this mechanism, throw so many neuroses into the same pot with hysteria. Out of all the instigated doubts I finally seized upon a plan to treat all the other neuroses in question just like hysteria, to investigate the etiology and the form of psychic mechanisms, and to leave the decision for the justification of the diagnosis of hysteria to the outcome of this investigation.

It thus happened, that proceeding from Breuer's methods I occupied myself mostly with the etiology and the mechanism of the neuroses. After a relatively brief period I was fortunate in obtaining useful results. First, I became impressed with the cognition that if one may speak of a causation through which neuroses would be acquired, that the etiology must be sought in sexual factors. This agrees with the findings that, generally speaking, various sexual factors may also produce various pictures of neurotic diseases. And depending on the amount of confirmation of the latter relation, one could now also venture to utilize the etiology for the characteristics of the neuroses, and build up a sharp line of demarcation between the morbid pictures of the neuroses. If the etiological characters constantly agreed with the clinical, then this was really justified.

In this way it was found that *neurasthenia* really corresponds to a monotonous morbid picture in which, as shown by analysis, " psychic mechanisms " play no part. From neurasthenia we sharply distinguished the compulsion neurosis (obsessions, doubts, impulses), the neurosis of genuine obsessions, in which we can recognize a complicated psychic mechanism, an etiology resembling the one of hysteria, and a far-reaching possibility of its reduction by psychotherapy. On the other hand, it seemed to me absolutely imperative to separate from neurasthenia a neurotic symptom complex which depends on a totally divergent, indeed, strictly speaking, on a contrary etiology, the partial symptoms of this complex have already been recognized by E. Hecker [1] as having a common character. They are either symptoms, or equivalents, or rudiments of *anxiety manifestations,* and it is for that reason that in order to distinguish this complex from neurasthenia, that I have called it *anxiety neurosis.* I maintained that it originates from an accumulation of physical tension, which is in turn of sexual origin. This neurosis, too, has no psychic mechanism, but regularly influences the psychic life, so that among its regular manifestations we have " anxious expectation," phobias, hyperesthesias to pain, and other symptoms. This anxiety neurosis, as I take it, certainly corresponds in part to the neurosis called "hypochondria," which in some features resembles hysteria and neurasthenia. Yet, I cannot consider the demarcation of this neurosis in the existing works as correct, and moreover, I find that the usefulness of the name hypochondria is impaired by its close relation to the symptom of " nosophobia."

After I had thus constructed for myself the simple picture of neurasthenia, anxiety neuroses, and obsessions, I turned my attention to the commonly occurring cases of neuroses which enter into consideration in the diagnosis of hysteria. I now had to say to myself that it would not do to mark a neurosis as a whole hysterical, merely because its symptom complex evinced some hysterical features. I could readily explain this practice by the fact that hysteria is the

[1] E. Hecker: Centralblatt für Nervenheilkunde, December, 1893.

oldest, the most familiar, and the most striking neurosis under consideration, but it was an abuse none-the-less to put so many characteristics of perversion and degeneration under the caption of hysteria. Whenever an hysterical symptom, such as anesthesia or a characteristic attack, could be discovered in a complicated case of psychic degeneration, the whole thing was called " hysteria," and hence, one could naturally find united under this same trade mark the worst and most contradictory features. As certain as this diagnosis was incorrect, it is also certain that our classification must be made on neurotic lines, and as we knew neurasthenia, anxiety neurosis, and similar conditions in the pure state, there was no need of overlooking them in combination.

It seemed, therefore, that the following conception was more warrantable: The neuroses usually occurring, are generally to be designated as " mixed." Neurasthenia and anxiety neurosis can be found without effort in pure forms, and most frequently in young persons. Pure cases of hysteria and compulsion neurosis are rare, they are usually combined with an anxiety neurosis. This frequent occurrence of mixed neuroses is due to the fact that their etiological factors are frequently mixed, now only accidentally, and now in consequence of a causal relation between the processes which give rise to the etiological factors of the neuroses. This can be sustained and proven in the individual cases without any difficulty. But it follows from this that for the purpose of examination it is hardly possible to take hysteria out of its association with the sexual neuroses, that hysteria, as a rule, presents only one side, one aspect of the complicated neurotic case, and that only, as it were, in the borderline case can it be found and treated as an isolated neurosis. In a series of cases we can perhaps say *a potiori fit denominatio.*

I shall now examine the cases reported to see whether they speak in favor of my view of the clinical dependence of hysteria. Breuer's patient, Anna O., seems to contradict this and exemplifies a pure hysterical disease. Yet, this case, which became so fruitful for the knowledge of hysteria, was never considered by its observer under the guise of a sexual neurosis and hence, cannot at present be utilized as such. When I began to analyze the second patient, Mrs. Emmy v. N., the idea of a sexual neurosis on an hysterical basis was far from my mind. I had just returned from the Charcot school, and considered the connection of hysteria with the sexual theme as a sort of insult—just as my patients were wont to do. But when I now review my notes on this case, there is absolutely no doubt that I have to consider it as a severe case of anxiety neurosis with anxious expectations and phobias, due to sexual abstinence, which was combined with hysteria.

The third case, Miss Lucy R., could perhaps more than any other be called a borderline case of pure hysteria. It is a short episodic hysteria based on an unmistakably sexual etiology, which would correspond to an anxiety neurosis in an over-ripe, amorous girl, whose love was too rapidly awakened through a misunderstanding. Yet, the anxiety neurosis could either not be demonstrated or had escaped me. Case IV, Katharina, is really a model of what I have called virginal anxiety; it is a combination of an anxiety neurosis and hysteria, the former creates the symptoms, while the latter repeats them and works with them. At all events, it is a typical case of many juvenile neuroses called "hysteria." Case V, Miss Elisabeth v. R., was again not investigated as a sexual neurosis. I could only suspect that there was a spinal neurasthenia at its basis, but I could not confirm it. I must, however, add that since then pure hysterias have become still rarer in my experience. That in grouping together these four cases of hysteria I could disregard in the discussion the decisive factors of sexual neuroses, was due to the fact that they were older cases in which I had not as yet carried out the intentional and urgent investigation for the neurotic sexual subsoil. Moreover, the reason for my reporting four instead of twelve cases of hysteria, the analyses of which would confirm our claims of the psychic mechanism of hysterical phenomena, is due to one circumstance, namely, that the analysis reveals these cases simultaneously as sexual neuroses, though there is no doubt that any diagnostician would have denied them the name "hysteria." However, the discussion of such sexual neuroses would have overstepped the limits of our joint publication.

I do not wish to be misunderstood and give the impression that I refuse to accept hysteria as an independent neurotic affection, that I conceive it only as a psychic manifestation of the anxiety neurosis, that I ascribe it to only "ideogenous" symptoms, and that I attribute the somatic symptoms, like hysterogenic points and anesthesias to the anxiety neurosis. None of these statements are true. I believe that hysteria, purified of all admixtures, can be treated independently in every respect except in therapy. For in the treatment we deal with a practical purpose, namely, we have to do away with the whole diseased state, and if hysteria occurs in most cases as a component of a mixed neurosis, the case merely resembles a mixed infection, where the task is to preserve life and not merely to combat the effect of one inciting cause of the disease.

I, therefore, find it important to separate the hysterical part in the pictures of the mixed neuroses from neurasthenia, anxiety neurosis, etc., for after this separation I can express concisely the therapeutic value of the cathartic method. Similarly I would venture to assert that—principally—it can readily dispose of any hysterical symptom, whereas, as can be easily understood, it is perfectly powerless in the presence of neurasthenic phenomena, and can only seldom and only through detours, influence the psychic results of the anxiety neurosis. Its therapeutic efficacy in the individual case will depend on whether or not the hysterical components of the morbid picture can claim a practical and significant position in comparison to the other neurotic components.

Still another limitation is placed on the efficacy of the cathartic method, which we have already mentioned in our " Preliminary Communication." It does not influence the causal determinations of hysteria, and hence, it cannot prevent the origin of new symptoms in the place of those removed. Hence, on the whole, I must claim a prominent place for our therapeutic method in the realm of a therapy of neuroses, but I would caution against attaching any importance to it, or putting it into practice outside of this connection. As I am unable to give here a " Therapy of Neuroses " as would be required by the practicing physician, the proceding statements are put on a level with a deferred reference to some later communication; still, for purposes of discussion and elucidation, I can add the following remarks:

1. I do not claim that I have actually removed all the hysterical symptoms which I have undertaken to influence by the cathartic method, but I believe that the obstacles were due to the personal circumstances of the cases, and not to the general principles. In passing sentence, these cases of failure may be left out of consideration, just as the surgeon puts aside all cases who die as a result of narcosis, hemorrhage, accidental sepsis, etc., when deciding upon a new technique. Later when I will again consider the difficulties and drawbacks of this method, I will again discuss the failures of such origin.

2. The cathartic method does not become valueless simply because

it is a *symptomatic* and not a *causal* therapy. For a causal therapy is really in most cases only prophylactic; it stops the further progress of the injury, but it does not necessarily remove the products which have already resulted from it. It requires, as a rule, a second agent to solve the latter task, and in cases of hysteria the cathartic method is really unsurpassable for this purpose.

3. Where a period of hysterical production, or an acute hysterical paroxysm, has been overcome, and the only remnant manifestations left are hysterical symptoms, the cathartic method fulfills all indications, and achieves a full and lasting success. Such a favorable constellation for the therapy rarely results in the realm of the sexual life, in consequence of the marked fluctuations in the intensity of the sexual need and the complications of the required determination for a sexual trauma. Here the cathartic method accomplishes all that is required of it, for the physician cannot possibly change an hysterical constitution. He must rest content if he can remove the disease for which such a constitution shows a tendency, and which can arise through the assistance of external determinants. He must be satisfied if the patient will again be able to function. Moreover, he needs not despair of the future, even if he considers the possibility of a relapse, for he knows the main character of the etiology of the neuroses, namely that their origin is mostly *overdetermined,* and that many factors must coöperate to produce this result. He can hope that this coöperation will not take place very soon, even if some of the etiological factors remained in force.

It may be argued that in such subsided cases of hysteria the remaining symptoms would spontaneously disappear without anything else, but this can be answered by stating that such spontaneous cures very often terminate neither rapidly nor fully, and that the cure will be extraordinarily advanced by the treatment. Whether the cathartic treatment cures only that which is capable of spontaneous recovery, or incidentally also, that which would not cease spontaneously, that question may surely be left open for the present.

4. Wherever we encounter an acute hysteria during the most acute production of hysterical symptoms, and the consecutive overwhelming of the ego by the morbid products (hysterical psychosis), even the cathartic method will change little in the expression and course of the disease. One finds himself in the same position to the neurosis as the doctor to an acute infectious disease. The etiological factors have exerted a sufficient amount of affect for some time past,

which is now beyond the reach of influence, and now that it has overcome the interval of incubation, it comes to the surface. The affection cannot be warded off, it has to run its course, but meanwhile one must bring about the most favorable conditions for the patient. If during such an acute period one can remove the morbid products, the newly formed hysterical symptoms, it may be expected that their places will be taken by new ones. The physician will not be spared the depressing impression of fruitless effort, the enormous expenditure of exertion, and the disappointment of the relatives to whom the idea of the necessary duration of time of an acute neurosis is hardly as familiar as in the analogous case of an acute infectious disease; these, and many other things, will probably largely impede the consequent application of the cathartic method in the assumed case. Nevertheless, it still remains to be considered whether, even in an acute hysteria, the frequent removal of the morbid products does not exercise a curative influence by supporting the normal ego, which is occupied with the defense, and thus preventing it from merging into a psychosis or into ultimate confusion.

That the cathartic method can accomplish something, even in an acute hysteria, and that it can even reduce the new productions of the morbid symptoms quite practically and noticeably, is undoubtedly evident from the case of Anna O., in which Breuer first learned to use this psychotherapeutic method.

5. Where we deal with chronic, progressive hysterias with moderate or continued productions of hysterical symptoms, we feel most the lack of a causally effective therapy, but we also learn to value the importance of the cathartic method as a symptomatic remedy. We then have to deal with an injury produced by a chronically acting etiology. We have to strengthen the capacity of resistance of the nervous system of our patient, and we must bear in mind that the existence of an hysterical symptom signifies a weakening of resistance of the nervous system, and represents a predisposing factor. From the mechanism of monosymptomatic hysteria we know that a new hysterical symptom generally originates as an addition to, and as an analogy of, one already in existence. The location once penetrated [2] represents the weak spot which can be penetrated again. The already split-off psychic group plays the part of the provoking crystal from which a formerly omitted crystallization emanates with great facility. To remove the already existing symptoms, to do away

with the psychic alterations lying at their bases, is to return to the patients the full measure of their resistance capacity, with which they are successfully able to resist the noxious influences. One can do a great deal for the patient by such long continued watchfulness and occasional " chimney-sweeping." [3]

6. I still have to mention the apparent contradiction between the admission that not all hysterical symptoms are psychogenic, and the assertion that they can all be removed by psychotherapeutic procedures. The solution lies in the fact that some of these non-psychogenic symptoms, though they represent morbid symptoms, as for instance, the stigmata, need, nevertheless, not be designated as affections. It is, therefore, practically unimportant if they outlast the successful treatment. Other symptoms of a similar nature seem to be pulled along indirectly by some psychogenic symptoms, for indirectly they really depend on some psychic causation.

I shall now speak of those difficulties and inconveniences of our therapeutic method which are not evident from the preceding case histories, or from the following remarks concerning the technique of the method.—I will rather enumerate and indicate them than go into details. The process is toilsome and wearisome for the physician, it presupposes in him a profound interest for psychological occurrences, and yet also a personal sympathy for the patient. I could not imagine myself entering deeply into the psychic mechanism of an hysteria in a person who would impress me as common and disagreeable, and who would not, on closer acquaintanceship, be able to awaken in me human sympathy; whereas I can treat a tabetic or a rheumatic patient regardless of such personal interest. No less demanding are the requisites on the patient's side. The method is especially inapplicable in a person below a certain level of intelligence, and it becomes extremely difficult wherever there is any tinge of mental deficiency. It requires the full consent, the full attention of the patients, but, above all, their confidence, for the analysis regularly leads to the inmost and most secretly guarded psychic processes. A large proportion of the patients suitable for such treatment withdraw from the physician as soon as they get an inkling whither this investigation tends. The physician remains a stranger to them. In others who have determined to give themselves up to the physician and

[3] See p. 20.

bestow their confidence upon him, something only voluntarily given, but never demanded; in all those I say it is hardly avoidable that the personal relation to the physician should not become unduly prominent, at least for some time. Indeed, it seems as if such an influence exerted by the physician is a condition under which alone a solution of the problem is possible. I do not believe that it makes any essential difference in this state of affairs whether one resorts to hypnosis or has to avoid or substitute it. Yet, fairness demands that we emphasize the fact that although these inconveniences are inseparable from our method, they, nevertheless, cannot be charged to it. On the contrary, it is very obvious that they are conditioned in the presuppositions of the neuroses destined to be cured, and that they are interwoven in every medical activity which intensively concerns itself with the patient, and produce in him a psychic change. I could see no harm or danger in the application of hypnosis, even in these cases where it was used excessively. The causes for the harm produced lay elsewhere and deeper. When I review the therapeutic efforts of those years since the communications of my honored teacher and friend, J. Breuer, gave me the cathartic method, I believe that I have more often produced good than harm, and brought about some things which could not have been produced by any other therapeutic means. On the whole it was, as expressed in the " Preliminary Communication," a " distinct therapeutic gain."

I must mention still another advantage from the application of this method. No severe case of complicated neurosis, with either an excessive or slight tinge of hysteria, can better be explained than by subjecting it to an analysis by Breuer's method. In making this analysis, I find that whatever shows the hysterical mechanism, disappears first, while the rest of the manifestations I, meanwhile, learn to interpret and trace back to their etiology. I thus gain the essential factors indicated by the instrument of the therapy of the neurosis in question. When I think of the ordinary differences between my opinion of a case of neurosis *before* and *after* such an analysis, I am almost tempted to maintain that the analysis is indispensable for the knowledge of a neurotic disease. Moreover, I have made it a practice of applying the cathartic psychotherapy in acute cases in conjunction with a Weir-Mitchell rest cure. This advantage lies in the fact that, on the one side I avoid the very disturbing intrusion of new psychic impressions which may be produced during psychotherapy; on the other hand, I exclude the monotony of the Weir-Mitchell treatment, during which the patient frequently merges into harmful reveries.

II

I will now add to my former observations that in attempting to use Breuer's method in greater latitude I encountered the difficulty, that although I made the diagnosis of hysteria, and the probabilities spoke in favor of the prevalence of the psychic mechanism described by us, yet a number of the patients could not be hypnotized. But as hypnosis was necessary to broaden consciousness in order to find the pathogenic reminiscences which do not exist in the ordinary consciousness, I was, therefore, forced to either give up such patients or bring about this broadening by other means.

The reason why one person is hypnotizable and another not, I could no more explain than others, and hence, I could not start on a causal way towards the removal of the difficulties. I also observed that in some patients the obstacle was still more marked, they even refused to submit to hypnosis. The idea then occurred to me that both cases might be identical, and that in both it might merely signify an unwillingness. Those who entertain psychic doubts against hypnotism are not hypnotizable, it makes no difference whether they express their unwillingness or not. It is not fully clear to me whether I can firmly adhere to this view or not.

I was, therefore, forced to dispense with hypnotism and yet obtain the pathogenic reminiscences. I attained this in the following manner:

On asking my patients during our first interview whether they remembered the first motive for the symptom in question, some said that they knew nothing, while others thought of something which they designated as an indistinct recollection, yet were unable to pursue it. I then followed *Bernheim's* example of forcibly awakening apparently forgotten impressions from somnambulism.[4] I assured them that they did know it, and that they would recall it, etc., and in this way some thought of something, while in others the recollections went even further. I urged still more, I ordered the patient to lie down and voluntarily shut his eyes so as to " concentrate " his mind, and I then discovered that without any hypnosis there emerged new and retrospective reminiscences which probably belonged to our theme. Through such experiences I gained the

[4] *Cf.* p. 78, the case of Miss Lucy.

impression that through urging alone it would really be possible to bring to light the definitely existing pathogenic series of ideas; and as this urging necessitated much exertion on my part, and showed me that I had to overcome a resistance, I, therefore, formulated this whole state of affairs into the following theory: *Through my psychic work I had to overcome a psychic force in the patient which opposed the pathogenic idea from becoming conscious* (remembered). A new insight seemed to have revealed itself to me when it occurred to me, that this must really be the same psychic force which assisted in the origin of the hysterical symptom, and which at that time prevented the pathogenic idea from becoming conscious. What kind of force could here be assumed as effective; and what motive could have brought it into activity? I could easily formulate an opinion, for I already had some complete analyses at my disposal, in which I found examples of pathogenic, forgotten, and repressed ideas. From these I could judge the general character of such ideas. They were altogether of a painful nature adapted to provoke the affects of shame, of reproach, of psychic pain, or the feeling of injury; they were altogether of that kind which one would not have liked to expereince and preferred to forget. From all these there resulted the thought of defense, as if spontaneously. Indeed, it is generally admitted by all psychologists that the acceptance of a new idea (acceptance in the sense of belief, admission of reality) depends on the mode and drift of the ideas already united in the ego, and for the process of censorship, to which the newly arrived idea is subjected, special technical names have been created. An idea entered into the patient's ego, which proved to be unbearable and evoked a force of repulsion on the part of the ego, the object of which was a *defense* against this unbearable idea. This defense actually succeeded, and the idea concerned was crowded out of consciousness and out of memory, so that its psychic trace could not apparently be found; yet, this trace must have existed. When I made the effort to direct the attention to it, I felt the same force as a *resistance* which showed itself as a *repulsion* in the genesis of the symptom. If I could now make it probable that the idea became pathogenic in consequence of the exclusion and repression, the chain would seem complete. In many epicrises of our histories, and in a small work concerning the defense neuropsychoses (1894), I have attempted to indicate the psychological hypotheses with the help of which this connection, as well as the fact of conversion, could be made clear.

Hence, a psychic force, the repugnance of the ego, has originally crowded the pathogenic idea from the association, and now opposed its return into the memory. The not knownig of the hysterics was really a—more or less conscious—not willing to know, and the task of the therapist was to overpower this association resistance by psychic labor. Such accomplishment is, above all, brought about by " urging "; that is, by applying a psychic force in order to direct the patient's attention to the ideas that one wishes to trace. It does not, however, stop here, but as I will show, it assumes new forms in the course of the analysis, and calls to aid more psychic forces.

I shall above all still linger at " the urging." One cannot go very far with such simple assurances as, " You do know it, just say it," or, " It will soon come to your mind." After a few sentences the thread breaks, even in the patient who is in a state of concentration. We must not, however, forget that we deal everywhere here with a quantitative comparison, with the struggle between motives of diverse force and intensity. The urging by a strange and inexperienced physician does not suffice to overcome " association resistance " in a grave hysteria. One must think of more forceful means.

Here, I utilize in the first place a small technical artifice. I inform the patient that in the next moment I will exert pressure on his forehead, I assure him that during this pressure he will see some reminiscence in the form of a picture, or some thought will occur to him, and I obligate him to communicate to me this picture or this thought, no matter what it may be. He must not keep it to himself because he may think that it is not the desired or the right thing, or because it is too disagreeable to say. There should be neither criticism nor reservation because of affect or underestimation. Only thus could we find the things desired, and only thus have we unfailingly found them. I then exerted pressure for a few seconds on the forehead of the patient lying in front of me, and after ceasing it, I asked in a calm tone, as if any disappointment was out of the question, " What have you seen ? " or " What occurred to your mind ? "

This method [5] taught me a great deal and led me to the goal every time. Of course, I know that I can substitute this pressure on the forehead by any other sign, or any other physical influence, but as the patient lies before me, the pressure on the forehead, or the grasping of his head between my two hands, is the most suggestive and

[5] As mentioned in the preface, the author has long since discarded this pressure procedure. [Translator's note.]

most convenient thing that I could undertake for this end. To explain the efficacy of this artifice I may perhaps say that it corresponds to a " momentary reënforced hypnosis "; but the mechanism of hypnosis is so enigmatical to me that I would not like to refer to it as an explanation.[6] I rather think that the advantage of the process lies in the fact that through it I dissociated the attention of the patient from his conscious quest and reflection, in brief, from everything upon which his will could manifest itself. The fact that under the pressure of my hand there always appeared that which I was looking for taught me that the supposedly forgotten pathogenic ideas always lie ready, " close by," and are attainable through easily approachable associations, all that is necessary is to clear away some obstacle. This obstacle again seems to be the person's will, and different persons learn in different ways how to discard their wilfulness and to assume a perfectly objective attitude towards the psychic processes within them.

It is not always a " forgotten " reminiscence which comes to the surface under the pressure of the hand; in the rarest cases the real pathogenic reminiscences can be superficially discovered. More frequently an idea comes to the surface which is a link between the first idea and the desired pathogenic idea of the association chain, or it is an idea forming the starting point of a new series of thoughts and reminiscences, at the end of which is the pathogenic idea. The pressure, therefore, has really not revealed the pathogenic idea, which, if torn from its connection without any preparation, would be incomprehensible; but it has shown the way to it, and indicated the direction towards which the investigation must proceed. The idea which is at first awakened through the pressure may correspond to a familiar reminiscence which was never repressed. If the connection becomes torn on the road to the pathogenic idea, all that is necessary for the reproduction of a new orientation and connection is a repetition of the procedure, that is of the pressure.

In still other cases the pressure of the hand awakens a reminiscence well known to the patient, which appearance, however, causes him surprise because he has forgotten its relation to the original idea. In the further course of the analysis this relation becomes clear. From all these results of the pressure one receives a delusive

[6] The solution of this problem was later found by the author and his pupils. *Cf.* here " Group Psychology and the Analysis of the Ego," p. 98, Int. Psycho. Press, and Ferenczi's " Contributions to Psychoanalysis," Chapter II, Badger, Boston, 1916. [Translator's note.]

impression of a superior intelligence outside of the patient's consciousness, which systematically holds a large psychic material for definite purposes, and has provided an ingenious arrangement for its return into consciousness. I presume, however, that this unconscious second intelligence is really only apparent.

In every complicated analysis one works repeatedly, nay continuously, with the help of this procedure (pressure on the forehead), which leads us from the place where the patient's wakeful reconductions became interrupted, it shows us the way to reminiscences which remained known, and calls our attention to connections which have sunk into forgetfulness. It also evokes and connects memories which have for years been withdrawn from association, though they can still be recognized as memories; and finally, as the highest performance of reproduction, it causes the appearance of thoughts which the patient never wishes to recognize as his own, which he does not remember, although he admits that they are inexorably required by the connection, and is convinced that precisely these ideas will cause the termination of the analysis and the cessation of the symptoms.

I will now attempt to give a series of examples which will show the excellent achievements of this procedure. I treated a young lady who suffered for six years from an intolerable and protracted nervous cough, which apparently was nurtured by every common catarrh, but must have had its strong psychic motives. Every other remedy had long since shown itself powerless, and I, therefore, attempted to remove the symptom by psychic analysis. All that she could remember was that the nervous cough began at the age of fourteen while she boarded with her aunt. She remembered absolutely no psychic excitement during that time, and did not believe that there was a motive for her suffering. Under the pressure of my hand, she at first recalled a large dog. She then recognized the memory picture; it was her aunt's dog which was attached to her, and used to accompany her everywhere, and without any further aid it occurred to her that this dog died and that the children buried it solemnly; and on the return from this funeral her cough appeared. I asked her why she began to cough, and the following thought occurred to her: " Now I am all alone in this world; no one loves me here; this animal was my only friend, and now I have lost it." She then continued her story. " The cough disappeared when I left my aunt, but reappeared a year and a half later."—" What was the reason for it? "—" I do not know."—I again exerted some pressure on the forehead and she recalled the news of her uncle's death during which the cough again manifested itself, and also recalled a train of thought similar to the former. The uncle was apparently the only one in the family who sympathized with her and loved her. That was, therefore, the pathogenic idea: People do not love her, everybody else is preferred; she really does not deserve to be loved, etc. To the idea of love there clung something which caused a marked resistance to the communication. The analysis was interrupted before this explanation was obtained.

Some time ago I attempted to relieve an elderly lady of her anxiety attacks, which, considering their characteristic qualities, were hardly suitable for such treatment. Since her menopause she had become extremely religious, and always received me as if I were the Devil, she was always armed with a small ivory crucifix which she hid in her hand. Her attacks of anxiety, which bore a hysterical character, could be traced to her early girlhood, and were supposed to have originated from the application of an iodine preparation to reduce a moderate swelling of the thyroid. I naturally repudiated this origin, and sought to substitute it by another which was in better harmony with my views concerning the etiology of neurotic symptoms. To the first question for an impression of her youth, which would stand in causal connection to the attacks of anxiety, there appeared the reminiscences of reading a so-called devotional book wherein piously enough there was some mention of the sexual processes. The passage in question made an impression on this girl, which was contrary to the intention of the author. She burst into tears and flung the book away. That was before the first attack of anxiety. The next reminiscence referred to her brother's teacher, who showed her great respect and for whom she entertained a warmer feeling. This reminiscence culminated in the reproduction of an evening in her parents' home during which they all sat around the table with the young man, and delightfully enjoyed themselves in a lively conversation. During the night following this evening, she was awakened by the first attack of anxiety which surely had more to do with some resistance against a sensual feeling than perhaps with the coincidental use of iodine. In what other way could I have succeeded in revealing in this obstinate patient, prejudiced against me and every worldly remedy, such a connection contrary to her own opinion and assertion?

On another occasion I had to deal with a young happily married woman, who as early as in the first years of her girlhood, was found every morning for some time in a state of lethargy, with rigid limbs, opened mouth, and protruding tongue. Similar attacks, though not so marked, recurred at the present time on awakening. A deep hypnosis could not be produced, so that I began my investigation in a state of concentration, and assured her during the first pressure that she would see something that would be directly connected with the cause of her condition during her childhood. She acted calmly and willingly, she again saw the residence in which she had passed her early girlhood, her room, the position of the bed, the grandmother who lived with them at the time, and one of her governesses whom she dearly loved. Then there was a succession of small scenes in these rooms and among these quite indifferent persons, the conclusion of which was the leavetaking of the governess who married from the home. I did not know what to start with these reminiscences; I could not bring about any connection between them and the etiology of the attacks. To be sure, the various circumstances were recognized as having occurred at the same time as the attacks first appeared.

Before I could continue the analysis, I had occasion to talk to a colleague, who, in former years, was my patient's family physician. From him I obtained the following explanation: At the time that he treated the mature and physically well developed girl for these first attacks, he was struck by the excessive affection in the relations between her and the governess. He became suspicious and caused the grandmother to watch these relations. After a short while the old lady informed him that the governess was wont to pay nightly visits to the child's bed, and that quite regularly after such visits the child was found in the morning in an attack. She did not hesitate to bring about the quiet removal of this corruptress of youth. The children, as well as the mother, were made to believe that the governess left the house in order to get married.

The treatment, which was above all successful, consisted in informing the young woman of the explanations given to me.

Occasionally the explanations, which one obtains by the pressure procedure, follow in very remarkable form, and under circumstances which make the assumption of an unconscious intelligence appear even more alluring. Thus, I recall a lady who suffered for years from obsessions and phobias, and who referred the origin of her trouble to her childhood, but could mention nothing to which it could have been attributed. She was frank and intelligent, and evinced only a very slight conscious resistance. I will add here that the psychic mechanism of obsessions is very closely related to that of hysterical symptoms, and that the technique of the analysis in both is the same.

On asking the lady whether she had seen or recalled anything under the pressure of my hand, she answered, " Neither, but a word suddenly occurred to me."—"A single word?"—" Yes, but it is too foolish."—" Just tell it."—" Teacher."—" Nothing more?"—" No." I exerted pressure a second time, and again a single word flashed through her mind: " Shirt."—I now observed that we dealt with a new mode of replying, and by repeated pressure I evoked the following apparently senseless series of words: Teacher—shirt—bed—city—wagon. I asked, " What does all that mean?" She reflected for a moment, and it then occurred to her that " it can only refer to this one incident which now comes to my mind. When I was ten years old, my older sister of twelve had a violent emotional attack one night and had to be bound, put in a wagon and taken to the city. I remember distinctly that it was the teacher who overpowered her and accompanied her to the asylum."—We then continued this manner of investigation, and received from our oracle another series of words which, though we could not altogether interpret them, could nevertheless be used as a continuation of the story, and as an appendix to a second. The significance of this reminiscence was soon clear. The reason why her sister's illness made such an impression on her was because they both shared a common secret. They slept in the same room, and one night they both submitted to a sexual assault by a certain man. In discovering this sexual trauma of early youth, we revealed not only the origin of the first obsession, but also the trauma which later acted pathogenically.—The peculiarity of this case lies only in the appearance of single catch-words, which we had to elaborate into sentences, for the seeming irrelevance and incoherence in these oracle-like words generally occur in all ideas and scenes as a result of pressure. On further investigation it is regularly found that the seemingly disconnected reminiscences are connected by intimate streams of thought, and that they lead quite directly to the desired pathogenic factor.

I, therefore, recall with pleasure a case of analysis in which my confidence in the results of this method was very splendidly justified. A very intelligent, and apparently very happy, young woman consulted me for persistent pain in her abdomen, which yielded to no treatment. I found that the pain was located in the abdominal wall and was due to palpable muscular hardening, and I, therefore, ordered local treatment.

After months I again saw the patient who said that "the pain had disappeared after taking the treatment and remained away a long time, but it has now reappeared as a nervous pain. I recognize it by the fact that I do not perceive it now on motion as before, but only during certain hours, as for example, in the morning on awakening, and during certain excitements." The patient's diagnosis was quite correct. It was now important to discover the cause of this pain, but in this she could not assist me in her uninfluenced state. When I asked her in a state of concentration and under the pressure of my hand whether anything occurred to her, or whether she saw anything, she began to describe her visual pictures. She saw something like a sun with rays, which I naturally had to assume to be a phosphene produced by pressure on the eyes. I expected that the needful pictures would follow, but she continued to see stars of a peculiar pale blue light, like moonlight, etc., and I believed that she merely saw glittering, shining, and twinkling spots before the eyes. I was already prepared to add this attempt to the failures, and I was thinking how I could quietly withdraw from this affair, when my attention was called to one of the manifestations which she described. She saw a big, black, inclined cross, the edges of which were surrounded with a subdued moon-like light, in which all the pictures thus far seen were shining, and upon the cross beam there flickered a little flame that was apparently no longer a phosphene. I continued to listen. She saw numerous pictures in the same light, peculiar signs resembling somewhat Sanscrit. She also saw figures like triangles, among which there was one big triangle, and again the cross. I now thought of an allegorical interpretation, and asked, "What does this cross mean?"—"It is probably meant to interpret pain," she answered. I argued, saying that, "By cross one usually understands a moral burden," and asked her what was hidden behind that pain. She could not explain that and continued looking. She saw a sun with golden rays which she interpreted as God, the primitive force; she then saw a gigantic lizard which she examined quizzically, but without fear; then a heap of snakes, then another sun, but with mild silvery rays, and in front of it, between her own person and this source of light, there was a barrier which concealed from her the center of the sun.

I knew for some time that we dealt here with allegories, and I immediately asked for an explanation of the last picture. Without reflecting she answered: " The sun is perfection, the ideal, and the barrier represents my weakness and failings which stand between me and the ideal."—" Indeed, do you reproach yourself? " Are you dissatisfied with yourself? "—" Yes."—" Since when? "—" Since I became a member of the Theosophical Society and read the writings edited by it. I have always had a poor opinion of myself."—" What was it that made the last strongest impression upon you? "—"A translation from the Sanscrit, which now appears in serial numbers." A minute later I was initiated into her mental conflicts, and into her self-reproaches. She related a slight incident which gave occasion for a reproach, and in which, as a result of an inciting conversion, the former organic pain at first appeared. The pictures, which I had at first taken for phosphenes, were symbols of occultistic streams of thought, perhaps plain emblems from the title pages of occultistic books.

———————

Thus far, I have warmly praised the achievements of the pressure procedure, and have entirely neglected the aspect of the defense or the resistance, so that I certainly must have given the impression that by means of this small artifice one is placed in a position to become master of the psychic resistances to the cathartic method. But to believe this would be a gross mistake. Such advantages do not exist in the treatment so far as I can see; here, as everywhere else, a great change requires much effort. The pressure procedure is nothing but a trick serving to surprise for awhile the defensive ego; in all graver cases it soon recalls its intentions and continues its resistance.

I need only recall the various forms in which this resistance manifested itself. At first, the pressure experiment usually fails the first or second time. The patient then expresses himself disappointedly, saying, " I believed that some idea would occur to me, but I only thought how anxious I was for it, but nothing came." Such attitudes assumed by the patient are not yet to be counted as a resistance; we usually answer to that, " You were really too anxious, the second time things will come." And they really come. It is remarkable how completely the patients—even the most tractable and the most intelligent—can forget the agreement into which they have previously entered. They have promised to tell everything that occurs to them, be it intimately related to them or not, be it agreeable to say or not; that is, they are to tell everything without any choice, or influence of criticism or affect. Yet, they do not keep their promise, it is apparently beyond their powers. The work repeatedly stops, they continue to assert that this time nothing came to their mind. One need not believe them, and one must always assume, and also say, that they hold back something because they believe it to be unimportant, or perceive it as painful. One must insist, and assume an assured attitude until one really hears something. The patient then usually adds, " I could have told you that the first time."— " Why did you not say it ? "—" I could not believe that that could be it. Only after it returned repeatedly have I decided to tell it," or, " I had hoped that it would not be just that, that I could save myself saying it, but only after it could not be repressed have I noticed that I could not avoid it."—Thus, the patient subsequently betrays the motives of a resistance which he did not at first wish to admit. He apparently could do nothing but offer resistances.

It is remarkable under what subterfuges these resistances are frequently hidden. " I am distracted today ; the clock or the piano playing in the next room disturbs me," they say. I become accustomed to answer to that, " Not at all, you simply struck something that you are not willing to say. That does not help you at all. Just stick to it."—The longer the pause between the pressure of my hand and the utterance of the patient, the more suspicious I become, and the more it is to be feared that the patient arranges what comes to his mind, and distorts it in the reproduction. The most important explanations are frequently ushered in as superfluous accessories, just as the princes of the opera who are dressed as beggars. " Something now occurred to me, but it has nothing to do with it. I only tell it to you because you wish to know everything." With this introduction we usually obtain the long desired solution. I always listen when I hear a patient talk so lightly of an idea. That the pathogenic idea should appear of so little importance on its reappearance is a sign of the successful defense. One can infer from this, of what the process of defense consisted. Its object was to make a weak out of a strong idea, that is, to rob it of its affect.

Among other signs, the pathogenic memories can also be recog-

nized by the fact that they are designated by the patient as unessen-
tial, despite the fact that they are uttered with resistance. There are
also cases where the patient seeks to disavow the recollections, even
while they are being reproduced, with such remarks as these: " Now
something occurred to me, but apparently you talked it into me ";
or " I know what you expect to this question, you surely think that
I thought of this and that." An especially clever way of shifting
responsibility is found in the following expression: " Now something
really occurred to me, but it seems to me as if I added it, and that it
is not a reproduced thought."—In all these cases I remain inflexibly
firm, I admit none of these distinctions, but I explain to the patient
that these are only forms and subterfuges of the resistance against
the reproduction of a recollection, which in spite of all we are forced
to recognize.

One generally experiences less trouble in the reproduction of
pictures than thoughts. Hysterical patients who are usually visual
are easier to manage than patients suffering from obsessions. Once
the picture emerges from the memory we can hear the patient state
that as he proceeds to describe it, it proportionately fades away and
becomes indistinct; the patient wears it out, so to speak, by transforming it into words. We then orient ourselves through the
memory picture itself in order to find the direction towards which
the work should be continued. We say to the patient, " Just look
again at the picture, has it disappeared? "—"As a whole, yes, but I
still see this detail."—" Then this must have some meaning, you will
either see something new, or this remnant will remind you of something." When the work is finished, the visual field becomes free
again, and a new picture can be called forth; but at other times such
a picture, in spite of its having been described, remains persistently
before the inner eye of the patient, and I take this as a sign that he
still has something important to tell me concerning its theme. As
soon as this has been accomplished, the picture disappears like a
wandering spirit returning to rest.

It is naturally of great value for the progress of the analysis to
carry our point with the patient, otherwise we have to depend on
what he thinks it proper to impart. It, therefore, will be pleasant
to hear that the pressure procedure never failed except in a single
case which I shall discuss later, but which I can now characterize by
the fact that there was a special motive for the resistance. To be
sure, it may happen under certain conditions that the procedure may

be applied without bringing anything to light; as, for example, we may ask for the further etiology of a symptom when the same has already been exhausted; or we may investigate for the psychic genealogy of a symptom, perhaps a pain, which really is of somatic origin. In these cases the patient equally insists that nothing occurred to him, and he is right. We should strive to avoid doing an injustice to the patient by making it a general rule not to lose sight of his features while he calmly lies before us during the analysis. One can then learn to distinguish, without any difficulty, the psychic calm in the real non-appearance of a reminiscence from the tension and emotional signs under which the patient labors in trying to disavow the emerging reminiscences with the object of defense. The differential diagnostic application of the pressure procedure is really based on such experiences.

We can thus see that even with the help of pressure procedure the task is not an easy one. The only advantage gained is the fact that we have learned from the results of this method in which direction to investigate, and what things we have to force upon the patient. For some cases this suffices, for it is essentially a question of finding the secret, and telling it to the patient, so that he is then usually forced to relinquish his resistance. In other cases more is necessary; here the surviving resistance of the patient manifests itself by the fact that the connections become torn, the solutions do not appear, and the recalled pictures come indistinctly and incompletely. On reviewing, at a later period, the earlier results of an analysis, we are often surprised at the distorted aspects of all the occurrences and scenes which we have snatched from the patient. It usually lacks the essential part, the relations to the person or to the theme, and for that reason the picture remained incomprehensible. I will now give one or two examples showing the effects of such a censoring during the first appearance of the pathogenic memories. The patient sees the upper part of a female body on which a loose covering fits carelessly, only much later he adds to this torso the head, and thereby betrays a person and a relationship. Or, he relates a reminiscence of his childhood about two boys whose forms are very indistinct, and to whom a certain mischievousness was attributed. It required many months and considerable progress in the course of the analysis before he again saw this reminiscence and recognized one of the children as himself and the other as his brother. What means have we now at our disposal to overcome this continued resistance?

We have but few, yet we have almost all those by which one otherwise exerts a psychic influence on the other. In the first place, we must remember that psychic resistance, especially of long continuance, can only be broken slowly, gradually, and with much patience. We can also count on the intellectual interest which manifests itself in the patient after a brief period of the analysis. On explaining and imparting to him the knowledge of the marvelous world of psychic processes, which we have gained only through such analysis, we obtain his collaboration and cause him to view himself with the objective interest of the investigator, and we thus drive back the resistance which rests on an affective basis. But finally—and this remains the strongest motive force—after the motives for the defense have been discovered, we must make the attempt to reduce them or even substitute them by stronger ones. Here, the possibility of expressing the therapeutic activity in formulæ ceases. One does as well as he can as an explainer where ignorance has produced shyness, as a teacher, as a representative of a freer and more superior philosophy of life, and as a confessor, who through the continuance of his sympathy and his respect imparts, so to say, absolution after the confession. One endeavors to do something humane for the patient as far as the range of one's own personality and the measure of sympathy which one can set apart for the case allows. It is an indispensable prerequisite for such psychic activities to have approximately discovered the nature of the case and the motives of the defense that are here effective. Fortunately the technique of urging and the pressure procedure take us just so far. The more we have solved such enigmas the easier will we discover new ones, and the earlier will we be able to manage the actual curative psychic work. For it is well to bear in mind that although the patient can rid himself of an hysterical symptom only after reproducing and uttering under emotion its causal pathogenic impressions, yet the therapeutic task merely consists in inducing him to do it, and once the task has been accomplished, there remains nothing for the doctor to correct or abolish. All the contrary suggestions necessary have already been employed during the struggle carried on against the resistance. The case may be compared to the unlocking of a closed door, where as soon as the door knob has been pressed downward, no other difficulties are encountered in opening the door.

Among the intellectual motives employed for the overcoming of the resistance one can hardly dispense with one affective factor, that is, the personal equation of the doctor, and in a number of cases this alone is enough to break the resistance. The conditions here do not differ from those found in any other branch of medicine, and one should not expect any therapeutic method to fully disclaim the coöperation of this personal factor.

III

In view of the discussions in the preceding section concerning the difficulty of my technique, which I have unreservedly exposed—I have really collected them from my most difficult cases, though it will often be easier work—in view then of this state of affairs, everybody will wish to ask whether it would not be more suitable, instead of all these tortures, to apply one's self more energetically to hypnosis, or to limit the application of the cathartic method to only such cases as can be put into deep hypnosis. To the latter proposition I should have to answer that the number of patients available for my skill would shrink considerably, but to the former advice I will advance the supposition that even where hypnosis could be produced the resistance would not be very much lessened. My experiences in this respect are not particularly extensive, so that I am unable to go beyond this supposition, but wherever I achieved a cathartic cure in the hypnotic state, I found that the work devolved upon me was not less than in the state of mere concentration. I have only recently finished such a treatment during which course I caused the disappearance of an hysterical paralysis of the legs. The patient merged into a state, psychically very different from the conscious, and somatically distinguished by the fact that she was unable to open her eyes or rise without my ordering her to do so; and still I never had a case showing greater resistance than this one. I placed no value on these physical signs, and towards the end of the ten months' treatment, they really became imperceptible. The state of the patient on which we worked has, therefore, lost nothing of its psychic peculiarities, such as the ability to recall the unconscious, and its very peculiar relation to the person of the physician. To be sure, in the history of Mrs. Emmy v. N. I have described an example of a cathartic cure accomplished in a profound somnambulism in which the resistance played almost no part. But nothing that I obtained from this woman would have required any special effort; I obtained nothing that she could not have told me in her waking state after a longer acquaintanceship and some personal regard. The real causes of her disease, which were surely identical with the causes of her relapses after my treatment, I have never found—it was my first attempt in this therapy—and when I once asked her accidentally for a reminiscence which contained a fragment of the erotic, I found her just as resistive and unreliable in her statements as any one of my later non-somnambulic patients. This patient's resistance, even in the somnambulic state, against other requirements and exactions I have already discussed in her history. Since I have witnessed cases which, even in deep somnambulism were absolutely refractory therapeutically despite their obedience in everything else, I really have become skeptical as to the value of hypnosis for the facilitation of the cathartic treatment. A case of this kind I have in brief reported (p. 72) and could still add others. Besides, I admit that even this experience fell badly short of my need for a quantitative relation between cause and effect in the psychic spheres.

In our discussion thus far the idea of resistance has thrust itself to the foreground. I have shown how, in the therapeutic work, one is led to the conception that hysteria originates through the repression of an unbearable idea as a motive of defense, that the repressed idea remains as a weak (mildly intensive) reminiscence, and that the affect snatched from it is used for a somatic innervation, that is, for conversion of the excitement. By virtue of its repression the idea becomes the cause of morbid symptoms, that is, pathogenic. A hysteria showing this psychic mechanism may be designated by the name of "defense hysteria," but both Breuer and myself have repeatedly spoken of two other kinds of hysterias which we have named "hypnoid- and retention-hysteria." The first to reveal itself to us was really the hypnoid-hysteria, for which I can mention no better example than Breuer's case of Miss Anna O. For this form of hysteria Breuer gives an essentially different psychic mechanism than for the form which is characterized by conversion. Here the idea becomes pathogenic through the fact that it is conceived in a peculiar psychic state, having remained from the very beginning external to the ego. It, therefore, needs no psychic force to keep it away from the ego, and it need not awaken any resistance when, with the help of the somnambulic psychic authority, it is initiated into the ego. The history of Anna O. really shows nothing of such a resistance.

I hold this distinction as so essential that it has readily induced me to adhere to the formation of the hypnoid-hysteria. It is, however, remarkable that in my own experience I encountered no genuine hypnoid-hysteria, whatever I treated changed itself into a defense hysteria. Not that I have never dealt with symptoms which manifestly originated in separated conscious states, and, therefore, were excluded from being accepted into the ego. I encountered this also in my own cases, but I could show that the so-called hypnoid state owed its separation to the fact that a split-off psychic group originated before through defense. In brief, I cannot suppress the suspicion that hypnoid and defense hysteria meet somewhere at their roots, and that the defense is the primary thing, but I know nothing about it.

Equally uncertain is at present my opinion concerning the retention hysteria in which the therapeutic work is also supposed to follow without any resistance. I had a case which I took for a typical retention hysteria, and I was pleased with the anticipation of an easy and certain success, but this success failed to come, easy as the work really was. I, therefore, presume, and again with all caution appropriate to ignorance, that in retention hysteria, too, we can find at its basis a fragment of defense, which has thrust the whole process into hysteria. Let us hope that new experiences will soon decide whether I am running into the danger, of one-sidedness and error, in my tendency to spread the conception of defense for the whole of hysteria.

Thus far I have dealt with the difficulties and technique of the cathartic method. I would now like to add a few indications to show how one does an analysis with this technique. For me this is a very interesting theme, but I do not expect that it will excite similar interest in others who have not practiced such analyses. Properly speaking, we shall again deal with technique, but this time with those difficulties concerning which the patient cannot be held responsible, and which must in part be the same in a hypnoid and a retention hysteria as in the defense hysteria which I have in mind as a model. I start with this last fragment of discussion with the hope, that the psychic peculiarities to be revealed here might sometimes attain a certain value as raw material for ideational dynamics.

The first and strongest impression which one gains from such an analysis is surely the fact that the pathogenic psychic material, apparently forgotten and not at the disposal of the ego, which plays no rôle in the association and in memory, still lies ready in some manner and, what is more, in proper and good order. All that is necessary is to remove the resistances blocking the way. Barring that, everything is known as well as we know anything at all. The proper connections of the individual ideas among themselves and with the non-pathogenic, which are frequently remembered, are present; they have been produced in their time and retained in memory. The pathogenic psychic material appears as the property of an intelligence which is not necessarily inferior to the normal ego. The semblance of a second personality is often most delusively produced.

Whether this impression is justified, whether the arrangement of the psychic material resulting after the adjustment is not transferred back into the period of the disease—these are questions, which I do not like to consider in this place. One cannot certainly describe the experiences gained from such analyses more easily and more clearly than by placing one's self in the position which one may take for a survey after the whole thing has been completed.

The situation is usually not so simple as one represents it in special cases, as, for example, in a single case in which a symptom originates through a large trauma. We frequently deal not with a single hysterical symptom, but with a number of such, which are partially independent of one another and partially connected. We must not expect a single traumatic reminiscence, and as its nucleus one single pathogenic idea, but we must be ready to assume a series of partial traumas and concatenations of pathogenic mental streams. The monosymptomatic traumatic hysteria is, as it were, an elementary organism, a single being in comparison to the complicated structure of a grave hysterical neurosis, as we generally encounter it.

The psychic material of such hysteria presents itself as a multi-dimensional formation of at least *triple stratification*. I hope to be able to justify soon this figurative expression. First of all there is a nucleus of such reminiscences (either experiences or mental streams) in which the traumatic moment culminated, or in which the pathogenic idea has found its purest formation. Around this *nucleus* we often find an incredibly rich mass of other memory material which we have to elaborate in the analysis in the triple arrangement mentioned before. In the first place, there is an unmistakable *linear chronological* arrangement, which takes place within every individual theme. As an example of this, I can only cite the arrangement in Breuer's analysis of Anna O. The theme is that of becoming deaf, of not hearing,[7] which then becomes differentiated according to seven determinants, and under each heading there were from ten to one hundred single reminiscences in chronological order. It read like an abstract from an orderly kept archive. The analysis of my patient Emmy v. N. contained similar memory fascicles though not so fully described, but they formed part of every analysis. They always appeared in chronological order which were as definitely reliable as the serial sequences of the days of the week or the names of the months in psychically normal individuals. They increased the work of the analysis through the peculiarity of reversing the series of their origin in the reproduction; the freshest and the most recent occurrence of the accumulation occurred first, so to speak, as a "wrapper," and the one with which the series really began gave the impression of the conclusion.

The grouping of similar reminiscences in a multiplicity of linear stratifications, as represented in a bundle of documents, in a package, etc., I have designated as the formation of a *theme*. These themes now show a second form of arrangement. I cannot express it differently than by saying that they are *concentrically stratified around the pathogenic nucleus*. It is not difficult to say what determines these strata, and according to what decreasing or increasing magnitude this arrangement follows. They are *layers* of *equal resistance* tending towards the nucleus, *accompanied by zones of similar alteration of consciousness* into which the individual themes extend. The most peripheral layers contain those reminiscences (or fascicles) of the different themes, which can readily be recalled and which were always perfectly conscious. The deeper one penetrates the more difficult it becomes to recognize the emerging reminiscences, until one strikes those near the nucleus which the patient disavows, even at the reproduction.

As we shall hear later, it is the peculiarity of the concentric stratification of the pathogenic psychic material which gives to the course of such an analysis its characteristic features. We must now mention the third and most essential arrangement concerning which a general statement can hardly be made. It is the arrangement according to the content of thought, the connection which reaches the nucleus through the logical threads, which might in each case correspond to a special, irregular, and manifoldly devious road. This

[7] *Cf.* p. 24.

arrangement has a dynamic character in contradistinction to both morphological stratifications mentioned before. Whereas, in a specially formed scheme, the latter would be represented by rigid, arched, and straight lines, the course of the logical concatenation would have to be followed with a wand, over the most tortuous route, from the superficial into the deep layers and back, generally, however, progressing from the peripheral to the central nucleus, and touching thereby all stations; that is, its movement is similar to the zigzag movement of the knight in the solution of a chess problem.

I shall still adhere for a moment to the last comparison in order to call attention to a point in which it does not do justice to the qualities of the thing compared. The logical connection corresponds not only to a zigzag-like devious line, but rather to a ramifying and especially to a converging system of lines. It has a junction in which two or more threads meet, only to proceed thence united, and, as a rule, many threads running independently, or here and there connected by by-paths, open into the nucleus. To put it in different words, it is very remarkable how frequently *a symptom is manifoldly determined, that is overdetermined.*

I will introduce one more complication, and then my effort to illustrate the organization of the pathogenic psychic material will be achieved. It can happen that we may deal with more than one single nucleus in the pathogenic material, as, for example, when we have to analyze a second hysterical outbreak having its own etiology, but which is still connected with the first outbreak of an acute hysteria, which has been overcome years before. It can readily be imagined what strata and streams of thought must be added in order to produce a connection between the two pathogenic nuclei.

I will still add a few observations to the given picture of the organization of the pathogenic material. We have said of this material that it behaves like a foreign body, and that the therapy also acts like the removal of a foreign body from the living tissues. We are now in position to consider the shortcomings of this comparison. A foreign body does not enter into any connection with the layers of tissue surrounding it, although it changes them and produces in them a reactive inflammation. On the other hand, our pathogenic psychic group does not allow itself to be cleanly shelled out from the ego, its outer layers radiate in all directions into the parts of the normal ego, and really belong to the latter as much as to the pathogenic organization. The boundaries between both become purely conventional in the analysis, being placed now here, now there, and in certain locations no demarcation is possible. The inner layers become more and more estranged from the ego without showing a visible beginning of the pathogenic boundaries. The pathogenic organization really does not behave like a foreign body, but rather like an infiltration. The infiltrate must, in this comparison, be assumed to be the resistance. Indeed, the therapy does not consist in extirpating something—psychotherapy cannot do that at present— but it causes a melting of the resistance, and thus opens the way for the circulation into a hitherto closed territory.

(I make use here of a series of comparisons all of which have only a very limited resemblance to my theme, and do not even agree among themselves. I am aware of that, and I am not in danger of over-estimating their value; but, as it is my intention to illustrate the many sides of a most complicated and not as yet depicted idea, I, therefore, take the liberty of dealing also in the following pages with comparisons which are not altogether free from objections.)

If, after a thorough adjustment, one could show to a third party the pathogenic material in its present recognized, complicated and multidimensional organization, he would justly propound the question, " How could such a camel go through the needle's eye?" Indeed, one does not speak unjustly of a " narrowing of consciousness." The term gains in sense and freshness for the physician who accomplishes such an analysis. Only one single reminiscence can enter into the ego-consciousness; the patient, occupied in working his way through this one, sees nothing of that which follows, and forgets everything that has already wedged its way through. If the conquest of this one pathogenic reminiscence strikes against impediments, as, for example, if the patient does not let up the resistance against it, but wishes to repress or distort it, the strait is, so to speak, blocked; the work comes to a standstill, it cannot advance, and the one reminiscence in the breach confronts the patient until he takes it up into the breadth of his ego. The whole spatially extended mass of the pathogenic material is thus drawn through a narrow fissure and reaches consciousness as if disjointed into fragments or strips. It is the task of the psychotherapist to put it together again into the conjectured organization. He who desires still more comparisons may think here of a Chinese puzzle.

If one is about to begin an analysis in which one may expect such an organization of the pathogenic material, the following results of experience may be useful: *It is perfectly hopeless to attempt to make any direct headway towards the nucleus of the pathogenic organization.* Even if it could be guessed, the patient would still not know what to start with the explanation given to him, nor would it change him psychically.

There is nothing left to do but follow up the periphery of the pathogenic psychic formation. One begins by allowing the patient to relate and recall what he knows, during which one can already direct his attention, and may even overcome slight resistances. Whenever a new way is opened, it can be expected that the patient will follow it for some distance without any new resistance.

After having worked for a while in such manner, a cooperating activity is usually manifested in the patient. A number of reminiscences now occur to him without any need of questioning or setting him a task. A way has thus been opened into an inner stratum, within which the patient now spontaneously disposes of the material of equal resistance. It is well to allow him to reproduce for a while without influencing him; of course, he is unable to reveal important connections, but he may be allowed to clear things within the same stratum. The things which he thus reproduces often seem disconnected, but they give up the material which is later revived by the recognized connections.

One has to guard here in general against two things. If the patient is checked in the reproduction of the inflowing ideas, something is apt to be " buried " which must be uncovered later with great effort. On the other hand, one must not overestimate his " unconscious intelligence," and one must not allow it to direct the whole work. If I should wish to schematize the mode of labor, I could perhaps say that one should himself undertake the opening of the inner strata and the advancement in the radial direction, while the patient should take care of the peripheral extension.

The advancement is brought about by the fact that the resistance is overcome in the manner indicated above. As a rule, however, one must at first solve another problem. One must obtain a piece of a logical thread by which direction alone one can hope to penetrate into the interior. One should not expect that the voluntary information of the patient, the material which is mostly in the superficial strata, will make it easy for the analyst to recognize its deep seated locations, and to which points the desired connections of thought are attached. On the contrary, just this is cautiously concealed, the patient's assertion sounds as if perfect and firm in itself. One is at first confronted, as it were, by a wall which shuts off every view, and gives no suggestion of anything hidden behind it.

If, however, one views with a critical eye the assertion obtained from the patient without much effort and resistance, one will unmistakably discover in it gaps and damages. Here the connection is visibly interrupted and scantily supplemented by the patient through phrases which convey only insufficient information. There one strikes against a motive which in a normal person would be designated as flimsy. The patient refuses to recognize these gaps when his attention is called to them. The physician, however, does well to seek under these weak points access to the material of the deeper layers and hope to discover just here the threads of the connection, which he traces by the pressure procedure. One, therefore, tells the patient, " You are mistaken, what you assert can have nothing to do with the thing in question ; here we will have to strike against something which will occur to you under the pressure of my hand."

The hysterical stream of thought, even if it reaches into the unconscious, may be expected to show the same logical connections and sufficient motivations as those that would be expected in a normal individual. A looseness of these relationships does not lie within the sphere of the neurosis. If the association of ideas of neurotics, and especially of hysterics, makes a different impression, if the relation of the intensities of different ideas does not seem to be explainable here on psychological determinants alone, we know that such manifestations are due to the existence of *concealed unconscious motives*. Such secret motives may be expected, wherever such a deviation in the connection, or a transgression from the normally justified motivations can be demonstrated.

One must naturally free himself from the theoretical prejudice that one has to deal with abnormal brains of *dégénerés* and *déséquilibrés,* in whom the freedom of overthrowing the common psychological laws of the association of ideas is a stigma, or in whom a preferred idea without any motive may grow intensively excessive, and another without psychological motives may remain indestructible. Experience shows the contrary in hysteria ; as soon as the hidden—often unconsciously remaining—motives have been revealed and brought to account, there remains nothing in the hysterical mental stream that is enigmatical and anomalous.

Thus, by tracing the breaches of the patient's first statements, which are often hidden by " false connections," one gets hold of a part of the logical thread at the periphery, and thereafter continues the route by the pressure procedure.

Very seldom do we succeed in working our way into the inner strata by the same thread, usually it breaks on the way and yields either no experience, or one which cannot be explained or be continued despite all efforts. In such a case we soon learn how to protect ourselves from the obvious confusion. The expression of the patient must decide whether one really reached an end or encountered a case needing no psychic explanation, or whether it is the enormous resistance that halts the work. If the latter cannot be overcome soon, it may be assumed that the thread has been followed into a stratum which is, as yet, impenetrable. One lets it fall in order to grasp another thread, which may, perhaps, be followed up just as far. If one had followed all the threads into this stratum, if the nodes have been reached through which no single isolated thread can be followed, it is well to think of seizing anew the resistances on hand.

One can readily imagine how complicated such a work may become. By constantly overcoming the resistance, one pushes his way into the inner strata, gaining knowledge concerning the accumulative themes and passing threads found in this layer; one examines as far as he can advance with the means at hand, and thus gains first information concerning the content of the next stratum, the threads are dropped, taken upon again, and followed until they reach the juncture; they are always retrieved, and by following a memory fascicle one reaches some by-way which finally opens again. In this manner it is finally possible to leave the stratifications, and advance directly on the main road to the nucleus of the pathogenic organization. With this the fight is won, but not finished. One has to follow up the other threads and exhaust the material; but now the patient again helps energetically, for his resistance has mostly been broken.

In these later stages of the work it is of advantage if one can surmise the connection and tell it to the patient before it has been revealed to him. If the conjecture is correct, the course of the analysis is accelerated, but even an incorrect hypothesis helps, for it urges the patient to participate and elicits from him energetic refutation, thus revealing that he surely knows better.

One, thereby, becomes astonishingly convinced *that it is not possible to press upon the patient things which he apparently does not know, or to influence the results of the analysis by exciting his expectations.* I have not succeeded a single time in altering or falsifying the reproductions of memory or the connections of events by my predictions; had I succeeded it surely would have been revealed in the end by a contradiction in the construction. If anything occurred as I predicted, the correctness of my conjecture was always attested to by numerous trustworthy reminiscences. Hence, one must not fear to express his opinion to the patient concerning the connections which are to follow; it does no harm.

Another observation which I had occasion to see again and again refers to the patient's independent reproductions. It can be asserted that not a single reminiscence comes to the surface during such an analysis which has no significance. An interposition of irrelevant memory pictures which has no connection with the important associations, does not really occur. An exception not contrary to the rule may be postulated for those reminiscences which, though in themselves unimportant, are indispensable as intercalations, since the associations between two closely related reminiscences pass over them. As mentioned above, the period during which a reminiscence abides in the narrow pass of the patient's consciousness is directly proportionate to its significance. A picture which does not disappear requires further consideration; a thought which cannot be abolished must be followed further. A reminiscence never recurs if it has been adjusted, a picture spoken away cannot be seen again. However, if that does happen, it can be definitely expected that the second time the picture will be joined by a new content of thought, that the idea will contain a new inference which will show that no perfect adjustment has taken place. On the other hand, a recurrence of different intensities, at first vaguely, then quite plainly, often occurs, but it does not, however, contradict the assertion just advanced.

If one of the tasks of the analysis is to remove a symptom (pains, symptoms like vomiting, sensations and contractures), which is capable of aggravation or recurrence, the symptom shows during the work the interesting and not undesirable phenomenon of "*joining in the discussion.*" The symptom in question reappears, or appears with greater intensity, as soon as one penetrates into the region of the pathogenic organization containing the etiology of this symptom, and it continues to accompany the work with characteristic and instructive fluctuations. The intensity of the same (let us say of a nausea) increases the deeper one penetrates into its pathogenic reminiscences; it reaches its height shortly before the latter has been expressed, and suddenly subsides or disappears completely for a while after it has been fully expressed. If through resistance the patient delays the expression, the tension of the sensation of nausea becomes unbearable, and if the expression cannot be forced, vomiting actually sets in. One, thus, gains a plastic impression of the fact that the vomiting takes the place of a psychic action (here, that of speaking) just as was asserted in the conversion theory of hysteria.

These fluctuations of intensity on the part of the hysterical symptom recur as often as one of its new and pathogenic reminiscences is attacked; the symptom remains, as it were, all the time on *the order of the day*. If it is necessary to drop for a while the thread upon which this symptom hangs, the symptom, too, merges into obscurity in order to emerge again at a later period of the analysis. This play continues until, through the completion of the pathogenic material, there occurs a definite adjustment of this symptom.

Strictly speaking, the hysterical symptom does not behave here differently than a memory picture or a reproduced thought which is evoked by the pressure of the hand. Here, as there, the adjustment necessitates the same obsessing obstinacy of recurrence in the memory of the patient. The difference lies only in the apparent spontaneous appearance of the hysterical symptom, whereas one readily recalls having himself provoked the scenes and ideas. But in reality the *memory symbols* run in an uninterrupted series from the unchanged *memory remnants* of affectful experiences and thinking-acts to the hysterical symptoms.

The phenomenon of " joining in the discussion " of the hysterical symptom during the analysis carries with it a practical inconvenience to which the patient should be reconciled. It is quite impossible to undertake the analysis of a symptom in one stretch or to divide the pauses in the work in such a manner as to precisely coincide with the resting points in the adjustment. Furthermore, the interruption which is categorically dictated by the accessory circumstances of the treatment, like the late hour, etc., often occurs in the most awkward locations, just when some critical point could be approached or when a new theme comes to light. These are the same inconveniences which every newspaper reader experiences in reading the daily fragments of his newspaper romance, when, immediately after the decisive speech of the heroine, or after the report of a shot, etc., he reads, " To be continued." In our case, the raked-up, but unabolished theme, the symptom at first strengthened but not yet explained, remains in the patient's psyche, and troubles him perhaps more than before. But the patient must understand this, as it cannot be differently arranged. Indeed, there are patients who during such an analysis are unable to get rid of the theme once touched; they are obsessed by it even during the interval between two treatments, and as they are unable to advance alone with the adjustment, they suffer more than before. Such patients, too, finally learn to wait for the doctor, postponing all interest which they have in the adjustment of the pathogenic material for the hours of the treatment, and they then begin to feel freer during the intervals.

The general condition of the patient during such an analysis seems also worthy of consideration. For a while it remains uninfluenced by the treatment, expressing the former effective factors, but then a moment comes in which the patient is " seized," and his interest becomes chained, and from that time his general condition becomes more and more dependent on the condition of the work. Whenever a new explanation is gained and an important contribution in the chain of the analysis is reached, the patient feels relieved and experiences a presentiment of the approaching deliverance, but at each standstill of the work, at each threatening entanglement, the psychic burden, which oppresses him, grows, and the unhappy sensation of his incapacity increases. To be sure, both conditions are only temporary, for the analysis continues, disdaining to boast of a moment of well being, and continues regardlessly over the period of gloominess. One is generally pleased if it is possible to substitute the spontaneous fluctuations in the patient's condition by such as one himself provokes and understands, just as one prefers to see in place of the spontaneous discharge of the symptoms that order of the day which corresponds to the state of the analysis.

Usually the deeper one penetrates into the above described layers of the psychic structure, the more obscure and difficult the work will at first become. But once the nucleus is reached, light ensues and there is no more fear that a strong gloom will overcast the condition of the patient. However, the reward of the labor, the cessation of symptoms of the disease can be expected only when the full analysis of every individual symptom has been accomplished; indeed, where the individual symptoms are connected through many junctures, one is not even encouraged by partial successes during the work. By virtue of the great number of existing causal connections every unadjusted pathogenic idea acts as a motive for the complete creation of the neurosis, and only with the last word of the analysis does the whole picture of the disease disappear, very similarly to the behavior of the individually reproduced reminiscence.

If a pathogenic reminiscence or a pathogenic connection which was previously withdrawn from the ego-consciousness is revealed by the work of the analysis and inserted into the ego, one can observe in the psychic personality which was thus enriched, the many ways in which it gave utterance to its gain. Especially does it frequently happen that after the patients have been painstakingly forced to a certain knowledge, they say: " Why I have known that all the time, I could have told you that before." Those who have more insight recognize this afterwards as a self-deception and accuse themselves of ingratitude. In general the position that the ego takes towards the new acquisition depends upon the stratum of the analysis from which the latter originates. Whatever belongs to the outermost layers is recognized without any difficulty, for it always remained in the possession of the ego, and the only thing that was new to the ego was its connection with the deeper layers of the pathogenic material. Whatever is brought to light from these deeper layers also finds appreciation and recognition, but frequently only after long hesitation and reflection. Of course, visual memory pictures are here more difficult to deny than reminiscences of mere streams of thought. Not very seldom the patient will at first say, " It is possible that I thought of that, but I cannot recall it," and only after a longer familiarity with this assumption recognition will appear. He then recalls and even verifies by side associations that he once really had this thought. During the analysis I make it a point of considering the value of an emerging reminiscence independently of the patient's recognition. I am not tired of repeating that we were obliged to accept everything that we bring to light with our means. Should there be anything unreal or incorrect in the material thus revealed, the connection will later teach us to separate it. I may add that I rarely ever have occasion to subsequently withdraw the recognition from a reminiscence which I had preliminarily admitted. In spite of the deceptive appearance of an urgent contradiction, whatever came to the surface finally proved itself correct.

Those ideas which originate in the deepest layer, and from the nucleus of the pathogenic organization, are recognized by the patient as reminiscences only with the greatest difficulty. Even after everything is accomplished, when the patients are overcome by the logical force and are convinced of the curative effect accompanying the emergence of this idea—I say even if the patients themselves assume that they have thought " so and so," they often add, " but to *recall, that I have thought so, I cannot.*" One readily comes to an understanding with them by saying that these were *unconscious* thoughts. But how should we note this state of affairs in our own psychological views? Should we pay no heed to the patient's demurring recognition, which has no motive after the work has been completed; should we assume that it is really a question of thoughts which never occurred, and for which there was only a possibility of existence, so that the therapy consisted in the consummation of a psychic act, which at that time was omitted? It is obviously impossible to state anything about it, that is, to state anything concerning the condition of the pathogenic material previous to the analysis, before one has thoroughly explained his psychological views, especially concerning the essence of consciousness. It is, however, a fact worthy of reflection that in such analyses one can follow a stream of thought from the conscious into the unconscious (that is, absolutely not recognized as a reminiscence), thence draw it for some distance through consciousness, and again see it end in the unconscious; and yet this alteration of the " psychic elucidation " would change nothing in it, in its logic, and in the connection of its single parts. Should I then have this stream of thought freely before me, I could not conjecture what part was, and what part was not, recognized by the patient as a reminiscence. In a measure I see only the points of the stream of thought that merge into the unconscious, just the reverse of that which has been claimed concerning our normal psychic processes.

I have still another theme to treat which plays an undesirably great part in the work of such a cathartic analysis. I have already admitted the possibility that the pressure procedure may fail, and despite all assurance and urging it may evoke no reminiscences. I also stated that two possibilities are to be considered, there is really nothing to evoke, in the place where we investigate,—that can be recognized by the perfectly calm expression of the patient—or, we have struck against a resistance to be overcome only at some future time. We are confronted with a new layer into which we cannot as yet penetrate, and this can again be read from the drawn and psychic exertion of the patient's expression. A third cause may be possible which also indicates an obstacle, not from within, but externally. This cause occurs when the relation of the patient to the physician is disturbed, and signifies the worst obstacle that can be encountered. One can expect this in every more serious analysis.

I have already alluded to the important rôle falling to the personality of the physician in the creation of motives which are to overcome the psychic force of the resistance. In not a few cases, especially in women and where we deal with explanations of erotic streams of thoughts, the coöperation of the patients becomes a personal sacrifice which must be recompensed by some kind of a substitute for love. The great effort and the patient friendliness of the physician must suffice for such substitutes. If this relation of the patient to the physician is disturbed, the readiness of the patient's collaboration fails; if the physician desires information concerning the next pathogenic idea, the patient is confronted by the consciousness of the unpleasantness which has accumulated in her against the physician. As far as I have discovered, this obstacle occurs in three principal cases:

1. In personal estrangement, if the patient believes herself slighted, disparaged and insulted, or if she hears unfavorable accounts concerning the physician and his methods of treatment. This is the least serious case. This obstacle can readily be overcome by discussion and explanation, although the sensitiveness and the suspicion of hysterics can occasionally manifest itself in unimaginable dimensions.

2. If the patient is seized with the fear that she is becoming too dependent on her physician, that in his presence she loses her independence and could even become sexually dependent upon him; this case is more significant because it is less determined individually. The occasion for this obstacle lies in the nature of the therapeutic distress. The patient has now a new motive for resistance which manifests itself not only in a certain reminiscence, but at each attempt of the treatment. Whenever the pressure procedure is started, the

patient usually complains of headache. Her new motive for the resistance remains for the most part unconscious, and she manifests it by a newly created hysterical symptom. The headache signifies the aversion towards being influenced.

3. If the patient fears lest the painful ideas emerging from the content of the analysis would be transferred to the physician. This happens frequently, and, indeed, in many analyses it is a regular occurrence. The transference to the physician occurs through false connections. I must here give an example. The origin of a certain hysterical symptom in one of my hysterical patients was the wish she entertained years ago which was immediately banished into the unconscious, that the man with whom she at that time conversed would heartily grasp her and force a kiss on her. After the ending of a session such a wish occurred to the patient in reference to me. She was horrified and spent a sleepless night, and at the next session, although she did not refuse the treatment she was totally unfit for the work. After I had discovered the obstacle and removed it, the work continued. The wish that so frightened the patient appeared as the next pathogenic reminiscence, that is, as the one now required by the logical connection. It came about in the following manner: The content of the wish at first appeared in the patient's consciousness which would have transferred this wish into the past. Through the associative force prevailing in her consciousness the existing wish became connected with my own person, with which the patient could naturally occupy herself, and in this mesalliance—which I call a false connection—the same affect awakened which originally urged the patient to banish this clandestine wish. Now that I have discovered this, I can presuppose in every similar claim on my personality that this is another transference and false connection. It is remarkable how the patient falls a victim to deception on every new occasion.

No analysis can be brought to an end if one does not know how to meet the resistances resulting from the causes mentioned. The way can be found if one bears in mind that the new symptom produced after the old model should be treated like the old symptoms. In the first place it is necessary to make the patient conscious of the obstacle. In one of my patients, in whom I had cause to assume an unconscious idea like the one mentioned above in 2, I met it for the first time with an unexpected attack. I told her that there must have originated some obstacle, and then pressed her head. She then said, surprisingly, " I see you sitting here on the chair, but that is nonsense, what can that mean? "—But now I could explain it.

In another patient the obstacle did not usually show itself directly on pressure, but I could always demonstrate it by taking the patient back to the moment in which it originated. The pressure procedure never failed to bring back this moment. By discovering and demonstrating the obstacle, the first difficulty was removed, but a greater one still remained. The difficulty lay in inducing the patient to give information where there was an obvious personal relation and where the third person coincided with the physician. At first I was very much annoyed about the increase of this psychic work until I had learned to see the lawful part of this whole process, and I then also noticed that such a transference does not cause any considerable increase in the work. The work of the patient remained the same, she perhaps had to overcome the painful affect of having entertained such a wish, and it seemed to be the same for the success whether she took this psychic repulsion as a theme of the work in the historical case or in the recent case with me. The patients also gradually learned to see that in such transferences to the person of the physician they generally dealt with a force or a deception which disappeared when the analysis was accomplished. I believe, however, that if I should have delayed in making clear to them the nature of the obstacle, I would have given them a new, though a milder, hysterical symptom for another spontaneously developed.

I now believe that I have sufficiently indicated how such analyses should be executed, and the experiences gained from them. They perhaps make some things appear more complicated than they are, for many things really result by themselves during such work. I have not enumerated the difficulties of the work in order to give the impression that in view of such requirements it does not pay the physician or patient to undertake a cathartic analysis except in the rarest cases. However, in my medical activities I am influenced by contrary suppositions.—To be sure, I am unable to formulate the most definite indications for the application of the therapeutic method discussed here without entering into the valuation of the more significant and more comprehensive theme of the therapy of the neuroses in general. I have often compared the cathartic psychotherapy to surgical measures, and designated my cures as psychotherapeutic operations; the analogies follow the opening of a pus pocket, the curetting of a carious location, etc. Such an analogy finds its justification, not so much in the removal of the morbid material as in the production of better curative conditions for the issue of the process.

When I promised my patients help and relief through the cathartic method, I was often obliged to hear the following objections, "You say, yourself, that my suffering has probably much to do with my own relation and destinies. You cannot change any of that. In what manner, then, can you help me?" To this I could always answer: "I do not doubt at all that it would be easier for fate than for me to remove your sufferings, but you will be convinced that much will be gained if we succeed in transforming your hysterical misery into everyday unhappiness, against which you will be better able to defend yourself with a restored nervous system."

INDEX

233